LIFELINES

INTERMEDIATE

WORKBOOK

TOM HUTCHINSON

OXFORD UNIVERSITY PRESS

1997

Oxford University Press
Great Clarendon Street
Oxford OX2 6DP

Oxford   New York
Athens   Auckland   Bangkok   Bogota   Bombay
Buenos Aires   Calcutta   Cape Town   Dar es Salaam
Delhi   Florence   Hong Kong   Istanbul   Karachi
Kuala Lumpur   Madras   Madrid   Melbourne
Mexico City   Nairobi   Paris   Singapore
Taipei   Tokyo   Toronto   Warsaw

and associated companies in
Berlin   Ibadan

OXFORD and OXFORD ENGLISH
are trade marks of Oxford University Press

ISBN 0 19 433810 X with key
ISBN 0 19 433811 8 without key

Designed by Keith Shaw
              Threefold Design
              Oxford
Printed in Italy

ACKNOWLEDGEMENTS

Illustrations by:
Katherine Baxter
Gay Galsworthy
Ian Jackson
Technical Graphics Dept, OUP
Harry Venning
Margaret Wellbank

Commissioned photography by:
Emily Andersen

**The author and publishers would like to thank the
following for permission to reproduce their
photographs:**
Ardea (London) Ltd, Comstock, Robert Harding, David
Hoffman, Images Colour Library, Impact: *Chris Moyse, Petteri
Kokkonen*, Jerry Lambert, Pictor International, Popperfoto, Rex
Features, Splash, Tony Stone: *Lori Adamski Peek, David Stewart*,
Topham.

Contents

Starting out

Introductions; revision

1 **Jack Roberts is talking to the people going on the *Thrillseekers* trip.**

a Complete the text with the verbs in the box.

> will bring   told   met   're going to have
> came   decided   survive   put   would love
> had ... wanted   has been stolen   looked for
> said   led   're leaving   know   've made
> won't ... be   were caught   don't worry

My name's Jack Roberts and I'm from South Africa.
I ....*came*........ to Britain about eight years ago and
.... a job. I was working in a
supermarket for a while, then one day I
.... Marie at a party. She ....
me that she .... always .... to
travel and I .... that I .... to
travel, too, and, well one thing .... to
another and we .... to set up
Thrillseekers. We .... about forty trips
now, but we .... that each trip
.... new experiences. Mind you, they
.... all .... pleasant
experiences. Our vehicle .... three times
and we .... in a war last year. But we
always ...., so ....! You
.... a great time. So, ... all
your bags in the van. We .... in half an
hour.

b Find examples of the following verb forms in the text.

a regular verb in the past simple	*..decided...*
an irregular verb in the past simple	....
3 ways of expressing the future	....
	....
	....
a phrasal verb	....
a verb in the present simple	....
a verb in the present continuous	....
a verb in the passive	....
a conditional form	....
a positive imperative	....
a negative imperative	....
a verb in the present perfect	....
a verb in the past perfect	....
a verb in the past continuous	....

Questions

2 **Make questions.**

a Match the items from columns **A** and **B**.

A	B
1 Have you ever	would you most like to live?
2 Do you	type?
3 How long	food do you like best?
4 Who	are you doing this evening?
5 Did you	have you known your best friend?
6 Where	an e-mail address?
7 What kind of	broken your leg?
8 How many	did you get up this morning?
9 Have you got	enjoy primary school?
10 Can you	brothers have you got?
11 Why	like to work abroad?
12 What	like classical music?
13 Would you	do you want to learn English?
14 When	phones you most often?

b Write your answers to each question.

EXAMPLE

1 *Yes, I have/No, I haven't.* ....

2 ....

3 ....

4 ....

5 ....

6 ....

7 ....

8 ....

9 ....

10 ....

11 ....

12 ....

13 ....

14 ....

Short forms

3 Rewrite the sentences using short forms.

1 Peter is tired but his dog is not.
Peter's tired but his dog isn't.
....

2 If James does not want to go, I would love to.

....

....

3 I was not sure if I had seen her before.

....

....

4 I do not think Mark has been to New York, but I am sure Stephanie has.

....

....

....

5 We have got two cars already, and we have not got room for another.

....

....

....

Writing: Filling in a form

4 Here's an application form from someone who wants to work for *Thrillseekers*.

a Put the items in the box in the first column.

useful skills	qualifications	first names	title
relevant experience	daytime tel no.		date of birth
surname	address	occupation	

THRILLSEEKERS

.... *title*	Ms	
....	Willis	
....	Barbara Rebecca	
....	3/2/77	
....	45 King Street, Birmingham B17 9YT	
....	0121 384 7598	
....	trainee manager	
....	3 A-levels, BA in Spanish and Economics	
....	While at university I worked as a tour guide in London.	
....	I can speak French and Spanish. I can drive. I can cook.	

b Complete the third column with information about yourself. (You can invent your qualifications, skills, and experience if you want.)

1 Modern life

Talking about the present

1 Correct the verbs in these sentences.

EXAMPLES
I'm not wanting to go out.
I don't want to go out.
They're siting in the kitchen.
They're sitting in the kitchen.

1 I'm a teacher for three years.

....

2 **A** Where's David?

   B He plays tennis.

....

3 I'm sorry, I'm not understanding what to do.

....

4 Do you ever have been to New Zealand?

....

5 Richard worrys about his work, he never relaxs, and he don't gets home till 10.00.

....

....

6 She's usually getting up at 7.00, but this week she gets up at 6.00.

....

....

7 I've wrote a letter but I haven't send it yet.

....

8 We're working here since last year.

....

9 The government is cuting VAT, but increaseing income tax.

....

....

10 You're seeming very tired – are you having a lot of work to do?

....

....

2 Complete the interview. Put the verbs into the present simple, the present continuous, or the present perfect.

Mike Welcome to *Travelwise*. I'm Mike Sawyer. Today ...*I'm talking*.... (talk) to Tony Hollands. In the last six years he .... (be) on cycling trips all over the world. At the moment he .... (organize) a journey from Alaska to Mexico. Tell me, why .... (plan) this trip?

Tony I .... (not know), really. I .... (love) cycling since I was young, and I .... (always want) to go to North America.

Mike .... (do) a lot of extra cycling at the moment?

Tony Well, I normally .... (cycle) about 30 miles a day, but now I .... (do) about 80.

Mike You .... (need) £5,000 for your journey, and you .... (raise) £3,000 already. How?

Tony Well, I .... (just sell) my car and I .... (write) to over 100 companies. Twenty of them .... (decide) to sponsor me so far. And I .... (try) to sell the story of the trip to a newspaper at the moment.

Mike .... (have) any advice for listeners who .... (want) to do something like this?

Tony If you .... (not do) a long bicycle journey before, go on a short one first. If you .... (like) it, you .... (can) go anywhere. I .... (have) a wonderful time for the last six years!

3 **Put the verbs in brackets into the present simple or present continuous tense.**

1 **A** We ......'re going...... (go) to Paris tomorrow.

   B Oh, yes. Where .... you

   .... (stay)?

   A At a little hotel in Montmartre. We always

   .... (stay) there.

2 **A** Hi. I'm Isik. I'm from Turkey.

   B Hello. What .... you

   .... (do) here in England? Are
   you on holiday?

   A No, I .... (study) English at a
   language school.

   B Where .... you ....
   (live)? With a family?

   A No I .... (share) a room at the
   school with another girl.

   B Where .... you ....
   (live) in Turkey?

   A In Ankara. I .... (have) a flat in
   my parents' house.

3 **A** What .... you ....
   (do)?

   B Well I'm a student actually, but I've got a
   temporary job for the summer.

   A Oh, yes. What .... you

   .... (do)?

   B I .... (work) at a shoe factory.

4 **Make questions.**

a Write the words in the correct order.

1 do do you what
   What do you do?
   ....

2 lived present how address at have your you long
   ....?

3 many you times been abroad have how
   ....?

4 at raining it the is moment
   ....?

5 do up what get time usually you
   ....?

6 are what today you wearing
   ....?

7 ever anyone you famous have met
   ....?

b Answer the questions about yourself.

1 ....

2 ....

3 ....

4 ....

5 ....

6 ....

7 ....

Vocabulary: Using a dictionary

5 **Use your own dictionary (try to use an English–English dictionary if possible). Find this information.**

1 What part of speech is *mumps*? ....*noun*........

2 How is the verb *wind* pronounced?
   ....

3 On which syllable does the stress fall in *implicate*?
   ....

4 What do Americans call *a dustbin*? ....

5 Under which entry would you find these
   expressions?

   a close shave ....

   to have an idea ....

   to be a wet blanket ....

   to pick a fight with ....

6 Correct this sentence.

   John has a flu. ....

7 What does *skip* mean in this sentence?

   I'm going to skip the next lesson. ....

8 What's the difference between *practice* and

   practise? ....

Comparisons

6 Complete the chart with the comparatives of the adjectives.

adjective	comparative
fast	*faster*
fine	....
friendly	....
informal	....
good	....
bad	....

7 Complete these rules for making comparatives.

1 Most adjectives: .... *add -er* ....

2 Adjectives that end in *-e:* ....

3 Adjectives that end in consonant +*y:* ....

4 Adjectives with 2 or more syllables (except where the second syllable is *-y*): ....

5 Some adjectives like *good* and *bad*: ....
   ....

8 Complete the sentences. Use the adjectives in brackets and one of these forms.

Manners are	better than just as good as not as good as	they used to be.

1 I'm *not as fit as* ...... I was two years ago. (fit)

2 I'm .... when I was 14. (slim)

3 I'm .... my best friend. (old)

4 This exercise is .... exercise 4. (difficult)

5 My work this year is .... last year. (good)

6 Young people are .... they used to be. (polite)

7 Manners are .... they were 20 years ago. (bad)

8 Dogs are .... cats. (nice)

9 The streets were .... they are now. (clean and tidy)

10 The roads are .... they were when I was a child. (busy and dangerous)

11 Cars are .... they were then. (fast and powerful)

Idiomatic expressions

9 Complete the sentences with these expressions.

I'll give you that what have you was unthinkable cuts both ways can hardly hear myself think down to	on the whole wouldn't say there's anything wrong with that I must admit like to make out these days

1 The media *like to make out* that young people are all criminals or drug takers or ...., but I think that a lot of today's problems are .... the media themselves.

2 It's so noisy here, I ....

3 .... that life is freer today, and I don't think .... But we have to remember that freedom .... – people are also free to be less considerate if they want.

4 When I was at school, hitting a teacher ...., but you read about it all the time in the newspapers .... I think things have got worse ....

5 I .... that life is better now, but it's certainly a lot faster, ...

Pronunciation: The IPA

10 Write the words.

1 /dʒʌst/   ...... *just* ......

2 /wɜːd/   ....

3 /ˈweðə/   ....

4 /səˈdʒestʃən/ ....

5 /ˈfjuːtʃə/   ....

6 /naɪf/   ....

7 /jɔː/   ....

8 /ˈpiːpl/   ....

9 /θɪŋ/   ....

10 /tɔːk/   ....

Commenting

11 Complete the conversation with appropriate comments and questions. Try to use a different one each time.

Wendy	Where do you work, Barry?
Barry	I work for an airline.
Wendy	*Oh, really. What do you do?* ....
Barry	I'm a mechanical engineer.
Wendy	....
Barry	I check the planes before they take off.
Wendy	....
Barry	Well, it depends. We work shifts, you see, but I like to get the late shift from 5.00 till midnight, if I can.
Wendy	....
Barry	Well, then I have the day free. And anyway, a lot of the other guys have families so they prefer to be at home in the evenings.
Wendy	....
Barry	I go by car. Well, I have to, because the last train goes before I finish.
Wendy	....
Barry	Yes, it's great. And I get cheap travel with the airline, too.
Wendy	....
Barry	Yes, I go abroad two or three times a year.
Wendy	....

Vocabulary: Personality adjectives

12 Write down adjectives to match these descriptions. For some you may be able to give more than one adjective.

Someone who:	adjective(s)
1 likes to be with other people	*sociable*
2 talks a lot	....
3 is easily embarrassed	....
4 doesn't get excited easily	....
5 always expects the best	....
6 worries a lot	....
7 doesn't trust people	....
8 always likes to win	....
9 likes to work with other people	....
10 is very unhappy	....

Adverbs of frequency

13 Make true sentences about your life and opinions. Put adverbs of frequency from the box into the sentences.

never	hardly ever	sometimes
often	usually	always

1 I'm ∧ late for appointments.
    usually

2 I stay in bed till 11.00 on Sundays.

3 I go out on Saturday nights.

4 I can remember people's names.

5 I send postcards when I'm on holiday.

6 I don't fall asleep in lessons.

7 Politicians don't say what they really mean.

8 I have wanted to be a singer.

9 My English grammar is correct.

10 I've got a lot of money in the bank.

Writing: Personal letters

14 Here is a letter from Sandra to a friend.

a Write these items in the correct places.

11 November	Manchester	Flat 1
Dear	Love	M9 7TR

b Complete Sandra's letter. Use the tapescript on page 134 of the Student's Book to help you.

> .... Flat 1
>
> 6 Maiden Road
>
> ....
>
> ....
>
> ....
>
> .... June
>
> Just a quick note to let you know that I've moved. As you can see I'm now living in Manchester.
>
> I .... the university here.
>
> I .... university campus. I've got ...., but I .... every day, because ....
>
> I .... 10 o'clock, but then ....
>
> I ...., but I .... if it's raining. I'm really ....
>
> The course is ...., and Manchester's .... There's ....
>
> I hope you're well. Bye for now.
>
> ....
>
> Sandra

c Imagine you are living away from home for a short time. Write a letter to your parents or partner and tell them:

- how you are
- where you're staying
- what you're doing there
- what you do every day

2 Fortune

Talking about the past

1 **Match the grammar items to the correct tenses.**

has/have	past simple
had	past continuous
questions with *did*	present perfect
was/were	past perfect
past participles	
-*ing* forms	
negatives with *didn't*	

2 **Complete these sentences. Put the verb *to go* in the correct tense.**

1 Susan isn't here. She *'s gone* to the shops.

2 I .... to the park yesterday.

3 He was only a minute late, but the train
    ....

4 They .... on holiday three times last year.

5 **A** Where's Matthew?
    B He .... to London for the day.

6 The car broke down while I .... to the supermarket.

3 **Complete the questions.**

1 **A** What *were you doing* at 8 o'clock last night?
    B I was watching TV.

2 **A** .... Suzanna before?
    B Yes, I had. I met her about five years ago in Madrid.

3 **A** .... that letter yet?
    B No, he hasn't. He says he'll write it tomorrow.

4 **A** .... the accident?
    B No, I didn't, but my son saw it.

5 **A** Where .... when the accident happened?
    B He was standing over there by the gate.

6 **A** .... lunch yet?
    B No, we haven't. Would you like to join us?

7 **A** How long .... in India when you met him?
    B Oh, I think he'd lived there for over 20 years.

4 **Complete the text. Use these verbs in the past simple or the present perfect tense.**

crash (x2)	do (x2)	be	jump	get
not work	break (x2)	have to	not jump	

Elaine risks her life almost every day. She's a stunt woman. She does the dangerous parts in films.
'I *'ve been* .... a stunt woman for ten years now and I suppose that in those ten years I .... almost everything. I .... out of windows, I .... cars, and I .... most of the bones in my body at least once.

But I suppose the most dangerous thing that I .... ever .... was in a film called *Madness*. In one scene I .... jump over a wall on a motorbike. Well, unfortunately, I .... it wrong and I .... over the wall, I .... straight into it. I .... both my legs and three fingers. I .... with motorbikes since then.'

5 Complete the story with the correct tenses of the verbs in brackets.

- Paragraph 1: past simple or past continuous
- Paragraph 2: past simple or past perfect
- Paragraph 3: past simple or present perfect

Five years ago I .... *had to* .... (have to)

make a big decision. At the time I .... (work) for a small engineering company. However, things .... (not go) very well for the company and it .... (lose) money. One day while we .... (work) as normal, the boss .... (tell) us that the company .... (be) bankrupt. We .... (be) all unemployed.

That lunch-time we .... (go) to the pub as usual. We were all very depressed. I .... (work) at the company for over fifteen years and some of the people .... (be) there longer than that. Well, of course we .... (talk) about the problem. Then the landlord of the pub .... (hear) the news. He .... (say): 'Why don't you buy the company?' At first we all .... (laugh), but then we .... (start) to discuss it properly. We .... (know) the problems. The company .... (lose) a lot of customers, because it .... (not develop) new products. But finally we .... (decide) to go for it.

So we .... (buy) the company. The first few years .... (be) very difficult. But we .... (work) hard and we .... (have) a bit of luck. We finally .... (turn) the corner three years ago. Since then we .... (do) pretty well. Last year we .... (take on) four new people and so far this year we .... (take on) another ten. It .... (be) a big gamble six years ago, but I .... (not regret) it for a minute.

Vocabulary: Dealing with new words

6 Read the text. Find these things:

1	two kinds of vehicle	*juggernaut*
		....
2	the place where you see a doctor	....
3	a kind of shop	....
4	a kind of sport	....
5	a part of the body	....

Find words or expressions that mean:

6	to move to a later time	....
7	old	....
8	ran into	....
9	to get better	....
10	hurried	....
11	articles	....
12	looked quickly at	....
13	dangerous	....
14	a few days ago	....

The other day Rosy went to the doctor's. She'd hurt her wrist when she was rollerblading. She'd thought that it would just heal up, but it hadn't, so here she was for her appointment. She arrived at the surgery about ten minutes early, so she sat in the waiting room and flicked through a few of the magazines. They were all out of date, but there were a few interesting pieces. Suddenly, while she was sitting there, the doctor flew out of his room and left the building. The receptionist called Rosy over. 'I'm afraid the doctor's had to go out,' she said. 'There's been an accident in the High Street, you know, just in front of the ironmonger's.'
'Oh dear,' said Rosy, 'I hope it isn't serious.'
'Well, apparently one of those huge juggernauts has collided with a JCB. They shouldn't allow those great big things down the High Street. They're a menace. Anyway, I think it might be best to postpone your appointment.'

Vocabulary: *I survived!*

7 Put these words into the correct column.

fuselage clinic mouth lung resort
seatbelt aisle swamp pelvis jungle jaw
toe window cockpit throat wing elbow
ankle desert plain forehead nose tail
undercarriage thigh marsh suburb

parts of the body	parts of an aeroplane	places
	fuselage	

8 Complete the text with the items in the box.

we survived
set off for
on the other side of
bounced
took six passengers
to spare
to forget
had a feeling that

he was groaning
on holiday
fastened our seatbelts
flight
very excited
go for the weekend
terrible turbulence

When we were .....*on holiday*..... in the United States last
year we decided to .... to the Grand Canyon.
We .... the airport early in the morning and
checked in. Tim was ...., but I ....
I wasn't going to enjoy it. When I saw the plane, I nearly
died. It was very small and only .... and there
wasn't much room .... But we got into the
plane, ..., and took off. The first part of the
flight was OK, but over the Canyon itself we flew into
some .... The little plane rolled and
.... from side to side. Tim was ....
the aisle and .... : 'How much longer?' We
were both quite ill by the time we landed, but
.... I just wanted .... everything
about the flight. Then the pilot said: 'OK, folks. See you
tomorrow for the .... home.'

used to

9 Say what Sally used to do or didn't use to do.

1 She gave up smoking five years ago.

She ....*used to*......................... smoke.

2 She's started learning to play the violin.

She .... the violin.

3 She moved from Cambridge to Edinburgh last
year.

....

4 She changed her job, too. She's a chemist now.

....

5 When she was younger she listened to a lot of
pop music, but she's lost interest in it.

....

6 She's recently bought a cat. She's never had a pet
before.

....

7 She goes skiing now. She started two years ago.

....

8 She lives in the centre of the city so she doesn't
drive these days.

....

Responding to news

10 Write the expressions in the correct places in the conversation.

it must be nearly ten years	Yes, I suppose so
as I recall	I'm sure you must be
Well, well, well!	these things happen
this job came along	That sounds exciting!
Sounds great!	What about you?
the band split up	I don't believe it
Doesn't time fly?	what are you up to
things didn't work out	It's great to see you again

Charlie ....*Well, well, well!*.. Bill Needham!

Bill Charlie Cross! ....
What are you doing here?

Charlie Well, I work just round the corner from

here. ....,
Bill. When did we last meet?

Bill Oh, ..., I would think.

Charlie .... Ten years, eh.

Anyway, ... these days?

Bill I work for a TV company.

Charlie Wow! .... You
always wanted to be in show business,

.... Didn't
you use to play the drums with a band?

Bill Yes, that's right. We even made a

record, but ....

and ....

Charlie I'm sorry to hear that. I thought you
played pretty well.

Bill Well, ...

Charlie ....

Bill ....
What are you doing?

Charlie Me? I work in an electronics shop.
Well, actually I was unemployed until
about six months ago, but then

....,
and it's really interesting. So I'm really
happy about that.

Bill Yes, ...
Look, do you fancy going for a drink?

Charlie Sure. There's a place near here that has
really good beer.

Bill .... Come on.

Vocabulary: Phrasal verbs and idioms

11 Complete the sentences with these verbs in the correct tense.

pay off	start out
give up	fall short of
talk it over with	go for it
have a go	do for a living

1 I'd never played golf before, but I ......*had a go*......
and I really enjoyed it.

2 I'm afraid profits last year .... what
we expected. So I think we'll have to

.... the plans for a new office.

3 **A** What .... ?

B Well, I .... as a teacher but now I

work for the government.

4 I wasn't sure about going back to college, but in

the end I .... and I'm glad to say that

it ....

5 **A** Do you fancy going out for a meal on Friday?

B Yes. I'll .... Sally and get back to

you.

Writing: Linking words (1)

12 **Complete the story with these linking words.**

one day	and	while	that	after
soon	because	when	now	

Jim Reid liked diving. *While*......... he was diving in a

lake on a golf course ...., he made a discovery

.... would change his life, ... in the lake

he found thousands of golf balls. .... he looked

at them he found that they were in perfect

condition. .... thinking about it carefully he

decided to dive for golf balls full time. .... he

had his own factory .... his golf balls were

used all over the world. .... Jim Reid is a

millionaire.

13 **Look at the pictures and the information. Write the story of how the Swiss inventor, George de Mestral, invented Velcro. Use sentence linkers where possible.**

1 George de Mestral/ like/ hunting/ 1951/ hunt/ small seeds/ stick to trousers

2 home/ try/ pull/ seeds/ off/ difficult

3 get magnifying glass/ look closely/ small hooks on seed

4 seeds/ give/ George de Mestral/ idea/ develop Velcro

5 six years later/ own factory/ produce Velcro

6 Velcro/ be used for thousands of products/ inventor/ very rich

George de Mestral liked hunting. One day in 1951, while he was hunting, some small seeds stuck to his trousers.

....

....

....

....

....

....

....

....

....

....

....

....

....

....

....

Grammar check 1

1 **Write the questions and negative sentences.**

1 Where/ go

Where are you going?
....
We're going swimming.
We aren't going to the cinema.
....

2 Where/ George/ be

.... ?
He's been to the doctor's.
.... dentist's.

3 Where/ work

.... ?
I used to work for Clarkson's.
.... in a bank.

4 Where/ Claudia/ last week

.... ?
She was ill.
.... on holiday.

5 What time/ leave/ the party

.... ?
I left at one o'clock.
.... at midnight.

6 Where/ sit

.... ?
We were sitting by the door.
.... by the window.

7 When/ Jason/ get home

.... ?
He gets home at five.
.... half past four.

8 What/ watch

.... ?
I'm watching the news.
.... a film.

2 **Complete the sentences with go, goes, went, going, or gone.**

1 Where were you .....*going*.... with Simon?

2 Where does Mrs Smart .... on Fridays?

3 Kate has .... home.

4 We .... bowling yesterday.

5 Jim always .... to the football match on Saturdays.

6 Are you .... out with Mary?

3 **Put the verbs in brackets into the correct tense.**

A Why .....*do*...... you ....*want*.... (want) to work for South of the Border Expeditions?

B Well, I .... (love) travelling since I .... (be) a student back in the 1980s, and I .... always .... (want) to work with people.

A Which countries .... you .... (visit)?

B I .... (travel) round most of Europe and Latin America, and I .... (know) Mexico very well. I .... (spend) a year there before I .... (start) college.

A What languages .... you .... (speak)?

B Well, my Spanish is pretty good, and I .... (study) Portuguese in evening classes at the moment. I .... (try) Russian too for a while, but it .... (be) too hard so I .... (give up)!

A What's the worst thing that .... ever .... (happen) to you on your travels?

B Once I .... (fly) in a little six-seater – I .... never .... (be) in a small plane before – and a huge storm .... (hit) us. I .... (think) it was the end. When we finally .... (land) we .... all .... (shake) like a leaf.

A .... you .... (organize) an expedition yourself?

B Yes …

4 **Delete the incorrect verb form.**

While I **came** / **was coming** home three months ago, I **found** / **was finding** a wallet. I **saw** / **was seeing** it as I **have walked** / **was walking** through the park. It **was** / **has been** on a bench. I suppose it **has** / **had** fallen out of someone's pocket, while they **had sat** / **were sitting** on the bench. I **have looked** / **looked** in the wallet. It **contained** / **was containing** a lot of money but there was no name in it, so I **took** / **was taking** it to the police station. Nobody **reported** / **had reported** a lost wallet, so the police station **had kept** / **kept** it. I **have phoned** / **phoned** the police station three times since then, but nobody **has claimed** / **claimed** the wallet yet. If nobody claims it soon, it will be mine.

3 Your future

Talking about the future

1 Write the questions and negatives.

1 What time ...*will they be here?*...........................

They'll be here by 8.00.
They won't be here
.... by 7.00.

2 When .... ?
We're leaving tomorrow.
.... today.

3 What .... at university?
He's going to study History.
.... Geography.

4 How long .... ?
I'll be away for three days.
.... four days.

5 Where .... ?
They're going to live in Australia.
.... Canada.

6 When .... Mr Brown?
She's meeting him at 8.00.
.... him at 10.00.

2 A local factory has closed down. Say what plans the workers have, using the information and the most appropriate forms of the future.

1 retire/ buy a cottage.
I'm going to retire. I think I'll buy a cottage.

look for new jobs/ not be easy

2 We ...., but it
....

look for something here/ emigrate to Australia

3 I think I ....,
but if I can't find anything, I ....
probably ....

start a training course/ be useful

4 We .... next week.
We're sure it ....

join the army/ take a holiday

5 I ...., but I think I
.... first.

travel round the world/ leave

6 We ....
We .... on Monday.

3 Choose the most appropriate forms of the future. Delete the incorrect ones.

1 A What *are you doing / ~~will you do~~* this weekend?

   B I'm *going / going to go* to a concert in London. Do you fancy coming?

   A Maybe – I *'m going to / 'll* let you know.

   B OK. We *'re getting / 'll get* the train at 5.45.

2 A Kate's seventeen today.

   B *Will she / Is she going to* learn to drive?

   A Yes, she *'ll have / 's having* her first driving lesson tomorrow.

   B I hope she *'ll pass / 's passing* the test first time.

3 A I haven't received that report yet.

   B OK, I *'ll / 'm going to* fax you a copy.

   A Thanks. I *'ll give / 'm giving* you a call when I've read it.

   B Fine, but I *'ll have / 'm having* lunch out so I *won't be / 'm not being* back till two.

   A That's OK. I *won't finish / 'm not finishing* it before then.

4 A What *will you / are you going to* do when you leave school?

   B I *'ll / 'm going to* go to university. What about you?

   A Me too, but I'd like to go abroad first.

   B Oh yes? Ken *will / 's going to* do that. He *'ll / 's going to* work in Canada for a year.

Expressing probability

4 Make some predictions. Complete the sentences, using these expressions.

may	will probably/possibly
might	probably won't

1 The African elephant *may become extinct.* ....

2 .... pass my next test.

3 Robots ....

4 .... buy a new computer this year.

5 .... win the lottery.

6 The power of the United States ....
....

7 .... life on other planets.

8 .... sunny tomorrow.

9 ....
.... a major war in the next ten years.

10 .... a party for my next birthday.

First conditionals

5 Match the items in columns A and B. Make complete sentences using the first conditional.

A	B
the earth's climate/ warmer	racial conflicts
population/ younger	droughts and famine in Africa
large numbers of people/ move to find food	cost of medical care/ rise
the rain forest/ destroyed	more crime and drug problems
people/ have computers and videophones	not matter
petroleum/ run out	not need to go to offices
number of old people/ increase	many animals become extinct

EXAMPLE
If the earth's climate gets warmer there will be droughts and famine in Africa.

1 ....
   ....
   ....
   ....

2 ....
   ....
   ....

3 ....
   ....
   ....

4 ....
   ....
   ....

5 ....
   ....
   ....

6 ....
   ....
   ....

Vocabulary: The weather

6 Write the words in the correct column.
Some may go in more than one.

ice	bright	sleet	fog	dull	wind	dry
hail	warm	cloudy	storm	snow	thunder
cool	clear	frost	rain	sunshine

cold weather	wet weather	fine weather
ice		

7 Say what will happen to the weather.
Use these expressions.

| (I think) it should | it will probably | it might |

1

It's windy at the moment but I think it should calm
down later.
....

2

....
....

3

....
....

4

....
....

5

....
....

Making suggestions

8 Complete the sentences with appropriate verbs
in the correct form.

1 Shall we ..... *go* ...... for a walk?

2 Do you fancy .... a video?

3 Do you want .... a take-away meal?

4 How about .... Sam and Martha for lunch?

5 Would you like .... a meal?

6 Why don't we .... and watch TV?

7 We'd better be .... ready.

8 What about .... a bottle of wine?

9 Let's .... a party.

10 You'd better .... Jenny a ring.

Pronunciation: The IPA: Consonants

9 Connect the words to the correct symbols.

bath these other thin weather	/θ/ /ð/
which wish wash watch station	/ʃ/ /tʃ/
lose noisy race kiss loose	/s/ /z/
fuselage general juice measure hedge	/ʒ/ /dʒ/

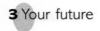

Conversations

10 **Use the information to make conversations. Try to use different expressions.**

1   **A** park?
    B raining
    A brighten up
    B wait half an hour

   A *Shall we go to the park?* ....
   B *But it's raining.* ....
   A *Yes, but it might brighten up soon.* ....
   B *Well, let's wait half an hour.* ....

2   **A** tennis?
    B weather?
    A sunny
    B get ready

   A ....
   B ....
   A ....
   B ....

3   **A** picnic/ tomorrow?
    B invite Carol?
    A good idea
    B ring

   A ....
   B ....
   A ....
   B ....

4   **A** go home?
    B foggy
    A drive carefully
    B wait/ brighter

   A ....
   B ....
   A ....
   B ....

5   **A** to town?
    B car/ not working
    A bus
    B OK/ time?

   A ....
   B ....
   A ....
   B ....

6   **A** ski/ next week?
    B grandparents/ come
    A pity
    B week after?
    A OK/ arrange

   A ....
   B ....
   A ....
   B ....
   A ....

7   **A** walk?
    B warm?
    A no/ jumper
    B stay at home

   A ....
   B ....
   A ....
   B ....

will and *would*

11 **Put in *will* ('ll) or *would* ('d).**

1   **A** How *would* you spend a year out?

   B Oh, I .... go abroad.

2   It .... be sunny tomorrow.

3   **A** .... you like a sandwich?

   B That .... be nice.

   A OK. I .... make you one.

4   **A** What .... your perfect partner be like?

   B Oh, she .... have to be intelligent most of all.

5   **A** .... you prefer to eat in tonight?

   B No, I .... rather go out.

   A OK. I .... book a table.

6   **A** How .... you spend your ideal day?

   B I .... spend it with my family.

Writing: Linking words (2): *but, however, although*

12 Study these rules.

> We can use *but*, *however*, and *although* to express contrast. *But* is used in a clause of the same sentence.
>
> **EXAMPLE**
> *John didn't like the film,* **but** *I loved it.*
>
> *However* is used in a new sentence. It can go at the beginning or end of the sentence, or after the subject. It is separated from the rest of the sentence by a comma (,).
>
> **EXAMPLE**
> *The world's oil will run out.* **However**, *scientists will produce oil from sunflowers.*
>
> *Although* is used in a clause of the same sentence. It is usually at the beginning of the sentence.
>
> **EXAMPLE**
> **Although** *it was raining, we went for a long walk.*

a Rewrite these sentences using *however* and *although*.

1 People will be able to work at home, but they may still choose to go to work.

....
....
....
....

2 People care about the rain forest, but it is still being destroyed.

....
....
....
....

3 The earth's climate is getting warmer, but we don't fully understand why.

....
....
....
....

4 Many species are in danger, but we are still destroying natural habitats.

....
....
....
....

b Now write two paragraphs about what you think will happen:

- in your future.
- in the world's future.

Use *but*, *however*, and *although*.

My future

....
....
....
....
....
....
....
....
....
....
....
....
....
....

The future of the world

....
....
....
....
....
....
....
....
....
....
....
....
....
....
....

4 Relationships

Relative clauses

1 **Complete the sentences with *who* or *which*.**

1 The woman ....*who*.... lives next door is a dentist.

2 The hotel .... caught fire has been rebuilt.

3 She has a job .... most people would hate.

4 Tony works for a company .... makes fridges.

5 That's the dog .... tried to bite me.

6 He's the kind of person .... loves an argument.

7 The government was defeated in the elections .... took place last week.

8 Did the assistant .... served you have blonde hair?

9 You should choose the clothes .... suit your personality.

10 I don't know the people .... live there.

2 **Complete the descriptions of these things. Use relative clauses.**

1 A nurse is *someone who is trained to look after sick or injured people.*

2 A digital watch is ....

3 Spaghetti ....

4 A snake ....

5 Extroverts ....

6 A wardrobe ....

7 An optimist ....

8 Socks ....

3 **Complete these statements with relative clauses.**

1 I like films *that have a happy ending.*

2 I don't like films ....

3 I like people ....

4 People .... annoy me.

5 I like animals ....

6 I'm afraid of animals ....

7 Days .... are the best.

8 I hate days ....

9 Food .... is my favourite.

10 I don't like food ....

4 **Delete the relative pronouns where possible.**

1 Here are some of the photos ~~that~~ we took.
2 This is the hotel which we stayed at.
3 These are two people that we met on the plane.
4 This is the waiter who served at our table.
5 That's the nightclub that we went to.
6 These are the two girls that I told you about.
7 This is the family that was in the next room.
8 This is the place that was in the postcard that I sent you.
9 Here's the tour guide who met us at the airport.
10 Would you like to see the video which we made?

5 **Combine these sentences using a relative clause with *that* or no relative pronoun.**

EXAMPLE
The woman is Hungarian. (She's coming tomorrow.)
The woman that's coming tomorrow is Hungarian.

1 The man has been sent to prison. (He robbed a bank.)

....

....

2 We've bought the car. (It has air-conditioning.)

....

....

3 The man was a police officer. (He phoned me yesterday.)

....

....

4 She stayed in the hotel. (I recommended it.)

....

....

5 The computer isn't powerful enough. (They bought it.)

....

....

6 I went to the restaurant. (It has a fixed price menu.)

....

....

7 The mountains were covered in snow. (We saw them.)

....

....

8 They're removing the tree tomorrow. (It fell on my house.)

....

....

9 We went to the film. (You told us about it.)

....

....

10 He wants the house. (It has three bedrooms.)

....

....

Vocabulary: *Successful small talk*

6 **Complete the text with these words.**

so	interested	those	sees	looking	go	
messages	carefully	way	themselves	secret		
off	important	on	well	herself	asked	
talk	up	hair	anyone	religion	allow	
soon	listening	where	that	obvious		
known	pays	said	keep	questions	to	

My aunt is one of .....*those*..... people who can talk to .... about anything. If she goes to a party .... she doesn't know any of the people, she just walks .... to the first person that she .... and introduces .... And yet she doesn't seem to .... about deeply .... things like politics or .... She always starts .... with something very .... like the other person's job. Very .... she's talking as if she's .... the other person for years. I .... her once what her .... was. She .... that the most important thing in a conversation was .... People love to talk about ...., so if you .... them to do ...., it's very easy to .... a conversation going. You have to listen .... and ask .... And you have to look ...., too. So don't keep .... at other things in the room while you're talking .... someone.

Another thing .... I've noticed is that she often .... people compliments. She says: 'I like your .... Which hairdresser do you .... to?' or 'You look very .... Have you been .... holiday?' Friendly .... like this seem to provide an easy .... into a conversation.

Vocabulary: Communicating

7 **Complete the sentences with the verbs in the box in the correct forms.**

agree   introduce   give   follow   speak   nod
listen   have   talk   say   understand   send
hear   ask   tell (x2)   get   think   express

1   Sarah .....*told*..... me a very good joke yesterday. I hadn't .... it before.

2   **A**   Did you .... Dennis to Mrs Novak at the party?

   B   Yes, I did and they .... a long conversation.

   A   Did he .... you what they .... about?

   B   He .... that she .... him a lot of questions about the new manager.

3   Thank you for .... your opinions, ladies and gentlemen. I have .... to all the arguments and I shall .... you my answer tomorrow.

4   **A**   I don't think we'll .... the results that we want if we .... the rules.

   B   Well, I'm afraid I can't .... with you there. It will .... the wrong message to head office. We'll have to .... of something else.

5   **A**   Can you .... Italian?

   B   Not really – I .... my head a lot but I don't actually .... much.

Question tags

8 **Add the question tags.**

1   We last met ten years ago, *didn't we?*

2   Let's have something to eat, ...

3   You can sing, ...

4   Colin lives in Paris now, ...

5   James used to have a beard, ...

6   Fiona isn't going out with Fred, ...

7   I'm always late, ...

8   You'd like a drink, ...

9   Sybil and Phil haven't moved yet, ...

10   We won't see you for a while, ...

9 **What would you say in these situations? Write appropriate questions with question tags.**

EXAMPLES

Does the plane leave at ten? (You think it does.)
The plane leaves at ten, doesn't it?
Has your friend seen the film? (You don't think he has.)
You haven't seen the film, have you?

1   Has Paul posted the letter? (You think he has.)

   Paul ....

   ....

2   Can Sally drive? (You think she can.)

   Sally ....

   ....

3   Does your friend still work at the shop? (You don't think she does.)

   You ....

   ....

4   Is it your turn next? (You think it is.)

   It's ....

   ....

5   Would your friend want to live in the country? (You don't think he would.)

   You ....

   ....

6   Does your friend's sister work in TV? (You think she does.)

   Your sister ....

   ....

7   Did your partner lock the front door? (You think so.)

   You ....

   ....

8   Are you going out tonight? (You don't think you are.)

   We ....

   ....

9   Was your friend born in the States? (You think she was.)

   You ....

   ....

10   Will the director be at the meeting? (You don't think he will.)

   The director ....

   ....

Pronunciation: Vowel sound pairs

10 Circle the two words in each line that have the same vowel sound.

1	(pot)	port	(what)
2	cat	have	cart
3	bin	been	mean
4	fill	feel	scene
5	pull	pool	wool
6	back	bark	half
7	full	fool	rule
8	sit	busy	seat
9	hat	heart	bath
10	caught	short	shot

Dates

11 Complete the table.

We write	We say
20 June	*the twentieth of June* ....
1 September	....
....	the fifth of March
19 December	....
....	the second of February
12 November	....
....	the tenth of May
23 July	....
....	the twenty-fourth of April
30 January	....

12 Write down ten important dates in your year. Say why they are important.

EXAMPLES
1 January   *New Year's Day*
4 February   *my sister's birthday*

1 ....
2 ....
3 ....
4 ....
5 ....
6 ....
7 ....
8 ....
9 ....
10 ....

Vocabulary: Christmas

13 Complete the crossword.

Across →
4 It used to be a stocking, but today this is more normal.
7 Santa Claus only comes when children are ....
8 things that make the room look bright and colourful
10 He brings the presents.
17 the meat that is normally eaten for Christmas dinner
18 things that contain party hats and jokes
19 People used to put candles on the tree but now they use these.

Down ↓
1 Father Christmas lives at the North ....
2 *Auld* .... *Syne*
3 the day after Christmas Day
4 People put these under the tree.
5 24 December is Christmas ....
6 your chance to buy things more cheaply after Christmas
9 Some people don't like Christmas. They're glad when it's ....
10 Christmas is a .... celebration.
11 Father Christmas comes down this.
12 the animals that pull the sleigh
13 There is a lot of this on Boxing Day.
14 Some people go here on Christmas morning.
15 things that you send to friends and relatives
16 something that you put on top of the tree

Writing: Paragraph organization

14 Read the paragraph giving advice about how to be a good listener.

a Number these items in the correct order to show the structure of the paragraph.

- [ ] advice
- [ ] examples
- [ ] general statement

any people don't listen properly, because they're too busy thinking about the next thing that they want to say themselves. Good conversationalists listen carefully and they show that they are listening, too. They ask questions, nod their head in agreement, or say things like, 'Oh that sounds exciting' or 'I bet you enjoyed that'.

b Number these sentences in the correct order to make a paragraph about visiting someone's house.

- [ ] Flowers, a bottle of wine, chocolates, or something from your own country are acceptable gifts.
- [ ] People in Britain often invite visitors to their homes.
- [ ] If you are invited to someone's house, you should take a small gift of some kind.

c Write some advice for people visiting your country. Write a paragraph about each of these topics.

- Greetings
- Smoking
- Topics to talk about

....
....
....
....
....
....
....
....
....
....
....
....
....
....
....
....
....
....
....
....
....
....
....
....
....
....
....
....
....
....

5 The law

The passive

1 **Put these sentences into the passive. Keep the same tense. Omit the agent if it is not necessary.**

1 The government has published the latest crime figures.

   The latest crime figures have been published.

2 Young people commit most crimes.

   ....

   ....

3 Last year the courts sent more people to prison.

   ....

   ....

4 The press had predicted an increase.

   ....

   ....

5 The figures will worry people.

   ....

   ....

6 The media are going to attack the government.

   ....

   ....

7 A special committee is studying the report.

   ....

   ....

8 They will present their ideas next month.

   ....

   ....

9 People would accept some big changes.

   ....

   ....

2 **Complete the police inspector's answers. Put the verbs in brackets into the passive in the appropriate tense.**

Reporter Can you give us any information about the incident?

Inspector Well, not a lot at the moment. A woman *was murdered*... (murder) at about 6

o'clock last night. She .... (find) by a cleaner at seven this morning.

We .... (call) to the scene by

a neighbour. The woman .... (identify) as Mrs Sarah Parker by the cleaner.

Reporter What have you done so far?

Inspector The room .... (search) for

clues. Some fingerprints .... (discover) on a door handle. The body

.... (take) to the mortuary. A

murder weapon .... (not find) yet.

Reporter What will happen now?

Inspector The body .... (examine) by a pathologist. The fingerprints

.... (feed) into a computer.

Witnesses .... (interview).

More information .... (give) to the newspapers as soon as we have it. Thank you, that's all for now.

3 Complete these newspaper reports. Put the verbs into the active or the passive.

escape	tie up	find	steal
enter	film	put	force

Over £1 million ......*was stolen*...... from a bank in West London yesterday. Three people .... the bank at 10.30. The bank staff .... to lie on the floor, while the thieves .... the money into bags. The staff .... and the thieves .... in a blue car. The incident .... by the bank's security cameras. The car .... four hours later in the river.

describe	hit	call	injure	believe
identify	not stop	kill	take	steal

A dog .... and its owner .... yesterday when they .... by a car on a pedestrian crossing. The car ...., but it .... by two witnesses as a red VW. An ambulance .... to the scene and the man .... to the Royal Hospital. Last night his condition .... as 'serious'. The police .... that the car ....

shoot	give	hurt	intend
damage	plant	happen	explode
not reach	try	say	

A shop and several offices .... yesterday when a bomb .... Nobody .... in the explosion, which .... at about five o'clock. A telephone warning .... to the police, but they .... the bomb in time. It .... by a group called Freedom International. Two months ago a member of the same group .... when she .... to put a bomb on a train. The police .... that today's explosion .... to show that the group was still active.

Vocabulary: Crime and the law

4 What are these crimes?

a Say what crime the people are charged with.

1 You deliberately set fire to a factory. ...*arson*......

2 You took someone's son and demanded money. ....

3 You drove at 100 mph where the limit was 60 mph. ....

4 You tried to bring heroin into the country. ....

5 You stole something from a shop. ....

b Give definitions of these crimes.

1 Burglary ...*is when someone breaks into a house and steals things.*......

2 Vandalism ....

....

3 Blackmail ....

....

4 Smuggling ....

....

5 Assault ....

....

6 Hijacking ....

....

5 Complete the sentences with appropriate verbs in the correct form.

1 The judge will ....*pass*..... sentence tomorrow.

2 I don't think the people who were found guilty .... the crime.

3 How did the detective .... the crime?

4 If you .... the law, you might be .... to prison.

5 The witness had to .... evidence for over two hours.

6 And then he was .... for another two hours.

7 The woman was .... for murder but she was found not guilty.

8 My house was .... while I was on holiday.

6 Complete the text with these words.

> trips   drug traffickers   more   neglected   own
> USA   vandalism   afraid   rewards   better
> difference   prison   hurt   crime   looked   year
> group   victim   expect   treat   purpose
> arrested   thugs   childhood   cane   fined
> vandalized   punishment   law-abiding   way
> afford   strict

In 1994 an 18-....*year*....-old American teenager, Todd Newman was .... in Singapore. With a .... of friends he had .... several cars. For this .... he was beaten six times with a .... He was also sent to .... for two months and .... £1,400. The case created a lot of debate in the .... Some people felt that the .... was too hard. They felt it was wrong to .... people like this. But other people .... at the clean streets and .... society of Singapore and compared it to their own cities where .... control the streets and decent people are .... to go out after dark. We send young .... to homes where they have their .... televisions. We give them .... like computers and .... to other countries, which many ordinary families can't .... We try to understand them, because they have been .... or abused in their .... We try to give them a .... in life. In Singapore, on the other hand, the law is .... People are expected to know the .... between right and wrong and criminals can .... tough treatment. But which society has got .... crime? And remember that every crime has a .... More robbery, more assault, more .... means more victims – more people who are .... If we look at it this ...., which society really treats people .... ?

Modal verbs and the passive

7 Complete the instructions with modal verbs and the passive.

1 Baggage ....*must not be left*.... (must not/ leave) unattended at any time. Any unattended baggage .... (will/ remove) and .... (may/ destroy).

2 Vehicles .... (must not/ park) on the yellow lines. This entrance .... (must/ keep) clear at all times.

3 The camera .... (should not/ leave) in direct sunlight. It .... (should/ keep) in its case when not in use.

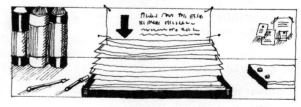

4 Essays .... (should/ place) in the tray. Marked essays .... (can/ collect) on Friday.

5 Hard hats .... (must/ wear) at all times. Hats for visitors .... (can/ obtain) at reception.

Questions in the passive

8 Someone's car has been broken into. Complete the conversation with the insurance company. Use the information to make questions in the appropriate tense. The answers will indicate the correct tense.

Insurance clerk Well, can I take some details of the incident, please?

When was the car broken into? ....
(When/ car/ break into)

Motorist Three days ago on 4 March.

Insurance clerk ....
at the time?
(Where/ it/ park)

Motorist In Gresham Street.

Insurance clerk .... ?
(When/ damage/ notice)

Motorist When I came back to the car at about three o'clock.

Insurance clerk .... ?
(How long/ park/ there)

Motorist Oh, it had been there about two hours, I suppose.

Insurance clerk ....
to the vehicle?
(What damage/ do)

Motorist The window had been smashed.

Insurance clerk And .... ?
(anything/ steal)

Motorist Yes, the radio had been stolen.

Insurance clerk ....
to the police?
(incident/ report)

Motorist Yes, it has.

Insurance clerk .... ?
(When/ report)

Motorist I reported it immediately.

Insurance clerk And .... ?
(vehicle/ repair/ yet)

Motorist I took it to the garage, but it hasn't been done yet.

Insurance clerk So .... ?
(when/ it/ repair)

Motorist Tomorrow.

Pronunciation: /ɜ:/

9 Circle the two words in each line that have the /ɜ:/ sound.

1	worth	north	birth
2	beard	heard	occurred
3	fir	fur	fear
4	stir	steer	prefer
5	year	learn	turn
6	pulled	world	curled
7	sir	curl	cruel
8	bird	fired	girl
9	worm	storm	burn
10	ford	third	word

Prepositions

10 Put in the correct prepositions.

1 He was sentenced ..*to*.... three years .... prison .... assault.

2 Many people thought that the sentence was an insult .... the victim.

3 The lorry was parked .... a bend and other vehicles couldn't get ....

4 The sound .... the shot came .... the direction .... the living room.

5 I was .... bed .... the time of the murder. I had gone .... bed early because I was tired.

6 When I looked .... the window they were standing .... the middle .... the garden next .... the statue.

7 Three weeks ago we went .... their house .... dinner.

8 I saw you. You had the gun .... your hand. You shot him .... the head and then you tried to get rid .... the gun.

Writing: Linking words (3): Sequence linkers

11 Complete the text about solving a crime with these linkers.

after that	the first job	finally	first
until	where	then	

......*First*..... the scene of the crime is sealed off.

.... nothing is touched .... the forensic scientists and the photographer arrive. .... is to photograph the scene. .... evidence is collected. .... the evidence is taken away to the laboratory .... it will be examined.

12 Describe what happens when a car is illegally parked. Use sequence linkers.

1   sticker/ windscreen/ traffic warden
    tow-away truck/ call

2   car/ check/ any damage/ record

3   car/ lift/ tow-away truck

4   car/ take/ car pound
    collect/ owner

A car has been parked on a bend on double yellow lines.

First a sticker is put on the windscreen by a traffic warden.

....
....
....
....
....
....
....
....
....
....
....
....

Grammar check 2

1 Complete these sentences with question tags.

1 You haven't eaten, *have you?*

2 We went there on holiday, ...

3 Lydia always looks good, ...

4 Let's go dancing, ...

5 I'm going with you, ...

6 Jack can't ski, ...

7 Those people shouldn't be here, ...

8 You won't be late, ...

2 Put these sentences into the passive. Keep the same tense. Omit the agent if it is not necessary.

1 An American company makes these computers.
These computers are made by an American company.

2 Compuspeak wrote the program.
....

3 Someone has left a disk in the disk drive.
....

4 People should make backup copies.
....

5 Children mustn't use these machines.
....

3 Put the verbs in brackets into the active or passive in the past simple tense.

A man ....*fell*.... (fall) 220 feet from a tower and
.... (survive). He .... (save)
because he .... (land) on a car roof.
The car's roof .... (crush), but the man
just .... (get up) and ....
(walk away). His elbow .... (break),
but otherwise he .... (not injure). Later
the man .... (take) to hospital by his
father and his elbow .... (X-ray).

4 Delete the incorrect verb form.

1 'What *are you doing* / ~~will you do~~ tomorrow?'
'We*'ll go* / *'re going* to town.'
2 'I*'ll* / *'m going* to watch a film in a minute.'
'Good idea. I*'ll* / *'m going to* join you.'
3 'I think I*'ll have* / *'m having* a bath.'
'Don't be long. The Robinsons *will come* / *are coming* at eight.'
4 In the future people *will have* / *are having* computers as small as a watch.

5 Combine these sentences using a relative clause with *who* or *which*.

1 They went to a café. (It had tables outside.)
They went to a café which had tables outside. ☐

2 The forest was going to be cut down. (The scientists were studying it.)
....
.... ☐

3 The woman's a millionaire. (You met her yesterday.)
....
.... ☐

4 She asked the man to be quieter. (He lives in the flat upstairs.)
....
.... ☐

5 The plane was going to Rio. (It was hijacked.)
....
.... ☐

6 The boy was arrested. (He set fire to the factory.)
....
.... ☐

7 Did you hire the video? (I told you about it.)
....
.... ☐

8 The men escaped. (They kidnapped the President's son.)
....
.... ☐

6 Tick the boxes in exercise 5 if you can leave out *who* or *which*.

7 Make these statements less definite, using the words in brackets.

1 It will be cold tomorrow. (probably)
It will probably be cold tomorrow.

2 We'll be a bit late. (could)
....

3 The lecture won't start on time. (may)
....

4 Mike won't be there. (probably)
....

5 We'll get a lift home. (might)
....

6 Travel

First conditionals

1 **Complete the sentences. Put the verbs in brackets into the correct tense.**

INTERNATIONAL
Insurance services

1 If you ......*lose*........ (lose) your credit card, we ....*will send*.... (send) a new one within 24 hours.

2 If you .... (require) medical help, we .... (contact) a local doctor or hospital.

3 An air ambulance .... (be provided) if you .... (have to) be brought back to this country.

4 If you .... (be arrested), our legal team .... (give) you advice.

5 An interpreter .... (be provided) if you .... (not understand) the local language.

6 We .... (pay) your legal costs if you .... (be charged) with an offence.

7 But if you .... (be fined), we .... (not pay) the fine for you.

8 However, we .... (lend) you the money for the fine if you .... (not have) enough.

Second conditionals

2 **Express these situations using a second conditional.**

EXAMPLE

He misses his favourite programmes. He should buy a video recorder.
He wouldn't miss his favourite programmes if he bought a video recorder.
She doesn't have a car. She doesn't go out in the evenings.
If she had a car she would go out in the evenings.

1 They don't go abroad. They're afraid of flying.

....

....

2 Frank doesn't read a lot. He can't find the time.

....

....

3 I feel embarrassed at parties. I don't know what to say.

....

....

4 Peter is overweight. He eats too much.

....

....

5 Sarah doesn't study hard. She hates school.

....

....

6 The office is cold. People leave the door open.

....

....

7 I can't translate this. I don't speak Japanese.

....

....

First and second conditionals

3 **Complete the sentences. Use the first or second conditional forms.**

1 **A** Good morning. This is Capital Radio. It's 7 o'clock on Monday 3 June.

   B Oh no. If it ..*was*........ (be) Sunday, I .*would be able to*..... (be able to) stay in bed.

2 **A** Good luck with the interview!

   B Thanks. If I .... (get) this job, we .... (go out) and celebrate this evening.

3 **A** It's a lovely day. I'm going for a walk.

   B I .... (join) you if I .... (not have) so much work to do, but I've got to finish it.

4 **A** When will you be back?
   B Well, I'm hoping to get the 9.00 train, but if I .... (miss) it, I .... (give) you a ring.

5 **A** If you .... (be) rich, where .... you .... (live)?
   B In a big house by the beach.

6 **A** If it .... (not be raining), I .... (go) for a cycle ride.

   B Yes, but it will brighten up soon. If it .... (be) fine this afternoon, we .... (go out) then.

7 **A** Are they here yet?
   B No, but if the traffic .... (be) bad, they .... (be) late.

   A Yes, I suppose so. But .... you .... (call) me as soon as they .... (arrive)?
   B Yes, of course.

8 **A** Are you looking forward to your holiday?

   B Not really. If I .... (have) my way, we .... (stay) at home, but everyone else wants to go away.

   A Oh, I'm sure you .... (enjoy) it when you .... (get) there.

9 **A** .... you still .... (be) here when I .... (get back)?

   B I don't know. If I .... (finish) this, I .... (leave) at four as usual.

10 **A** I think I .... (ask) the boss for a pay rise when he .... (come back) from lunch.

   B Well, if I .... (be) you I .... (not ask) him today. He isn't in a very good mood.

Time clauses

4 **Make sentences with the information.**

EXAMPLE
send the report/ as soon as/ it/ be finished
I'll send the report as soon as it's finished.

1 have a party/ when/ you/ get back

   We ....

2 have a shower/ before/ go out

   I think I ....

3 look after the house/ while/ you/ be away

   We ....

4 continue/ until/ reach a decision

   The meeting ....

5 take a holiday/ after/ exams/ be over

   I ....

6 leave/ as soon as/ taxi/ arrive

   We ....

7 tell you/ when/ post/ come

   I ....

8 not lock the doors/ until/ leave

   We ....

Vocabulary: Phrasal verbs

5 **Delete the incorrect sentences. In some cases both are correct.**

1 We decided to set off early.
   ~~We decided to set early off.~~

2 Could you turn off the radio, please?
   Could you turn the radio off, please?

3 No, switch on it again.
   No, switch it on again.

4 I'm listening to it.
   I'm listening it to.

5 They didn't turn up till ten o'clock.
   They didn't turn till ten o'clock up.

6 I can't go out tonight.
   I can't go tonight out.

7 I'm looking after my little sister.
   I'm looking my little sister after.

8 John put forward his suggestions.
   John put his suggestions forward.

9 We talked them over.
   We talked over them.

10 We decided to go for plan A.
   We decided to go plan A for.

6 What are the people doing? Use these verbs.

put up	put off	put away
put down	put out	put on

1 *He's putting the box down.*
....

2 ....
....

3 ....
....

4 ....
....

5 ....
....

6 ....
....

Vocabulary: Travel

7 Complete the words. The vertical word is a popular British tourist attraction.

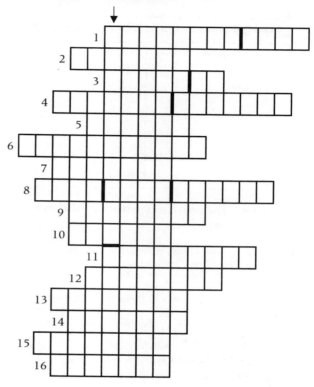

1   You need this to get on a plane.
2   someone who is on holiday
3   You do this before you get on a plane.
4   This includes travel and accommodation.
5   You can have a single or a return of this.
6   the place that you are going to
7   bags and suitcases
8   This goes to another continent.
9   You stand on this when you wait for a train.
10 You need this if you want to take holiday snaps.
11 someone who travels on a plane, train, etc.
12 You need this to enter or leave a country.
13 Lufthansa and KLM are these.
14 A train or bus stops here.
15 You pack your clothes in this.
16 not from your own country

8 **Put these words in the correct column.**

| plane | bus | car | train | coach |
| boat | horse | bike | ship | taxi |

You get on and off a	You get in and out of a
plane	

9 **Complete the sentences with one of these verbs or expressions.**

| be on | go ... for | have | go on |
| spend | enjoy | take | book |

1 Where do you usually ....*spend*.... your holidays?

2 We always .... to Italy .... our holidays.

3 I won't be here next week, I'm .... a holiday.

4 **A** Where's John?

   B He .... holiday.

5 **A** Have you .... your holiday in Australia yet?

   B Yes, I did it last week.

6 Welcome back. Have you .... a nice holiday?

7 **A** Is anybody in next door?

   B No, they've .... holiday.

8 **A** Did you .... your holiday?

   B Yes, it was great.

Checking in

10 **Complete the conversation at the check-in desk.**

Passenger *Do I check in here for* .... Buenos Aires?

Clerk Yes. Could I .... ?

Passenger Yes, here you are.

Clerk .... ?

Passenger My passport? Oh yes, here it is.

Clerk .... ?

Passenger Yes, these two suitcases.

Clerk .... the cases yourself?

Passenger Yes, I did.

Clerk .... any electrical items?

Passenger No, they don't.

Clerk .... ?

Passenger Non-smoking, please.

Clerk .... ?

Passenger Oh, er, a window seat, please.

Clerk Here's ....
.... is at 16.40 at gate 3.
....

Passenger Thank you.

11 **What will the people have to do? Complete what the check-in clerk says.**

EXAMPLE
I'm afraid your ticket isn't valid for this flight.
You'll have to go to the airline ticket counter.

1 I'm afraid your luggage is overweight. You'll
....

2 There are no window seats left, I'm afraid.
....

3 I'm sorry, but all the non-smoking seats are taken. ....

4 I'm afraid you're only allowed one piece of hand baggage. ....

Writing: Linking words (4)

12 **Look at these sentences and the paragraph.**

- British holidaymakers are deserting European destinations for faraway places such as the Caribbean.

- A holiday in the Caribbean can cost little more than a holiday in the Canary Islands.

- Long-haul flights are cheaper.

- Local labour costs are low.

- Travellers are becoming more sophisticated.

- Travellers are looking for somewhere more exotic.

- At one time a holiday in Europe was considered something special.

- Now it's become normal.

- Places like the USA, Jamaica, Egypt, India, and South Africa have all become regular holiday destinations.

British holidaymakers are deserting European destinations for faraway places such as the Caribbean. A holiday <u>here</u> can cost little more than a holiday in the Canary Islands, because long-haul flights are cheaper and local labour costs are low. Travellers are also becoming more sophisticated and are looking for somewhere more exotic. At one time a holiday in Europe was considered something special, but now it's become normal. So places like the USA, Jamaica, and South Africa have all become regular holiday destinations.

a Underline all the ways which have been used to link the sentences.

b Find examples of these things.

1. a linker that shows a cause   *because*
2. a linker that shows a result   ....
3. a linker that shows a contrast   ....
4. two verbs with the same subject   ....
   ....
5. a place reference   ....

c Which of the linking words could you replace with these? (A change in punctuation may be necessary.)

1. however   ....
2. as a result   ....
3. in addition   ....
4. as   ....

13 **Rewrite these sentences as a paragraph. Use these linkers.**

although	as	and	so
also	however	because	where

- The trend is causing concern in many Mediterranean countries.

- Tourism is a vital part of the economy.

- Millions of jobs depend upon it.

- Long-haul holidays bring employment to poorer countries.

- Some people are concerned about the effects upon the environment.

- The trend will continue.

- The trend will develop.

- Places like the Caribbean can guarantee year-round sunshine.

- People can escape from the dreary British winter to tropical sunshine.

- Tour operators like this.

- It spreads the holiday season over the whole year instead of just the summer months.

The trend is causing concern in many Mediterranean countries where tourism is a vital part of the economy, ...

....

....

....

....

....

....

....

....

....

....

....

....

....

....

....

....

7 Entertainment

Present perfect simple and continuous

1 **What have they been doing?**

a Look at the pictures. Complete the dialogues, using the information.

have a party	celebrate my promotion
work late	watch a horror movie.
fix the car	work out the accounts

1 **A** You look tired, Arthur.
  B *I've been working late.* ....

2 **A** You look worried, Mary.
  B ....

3 **A** Your flat's in a terrible mess, Jason.
  B ....

4 **A** Peter, your hands are covered in oil.
  B ....

5 **A** You look happy, Meg.
  B ....

6 **A** You look scared.
  B ....

b Say how the situations in the pictures have arisen.

1   *Arthur looks tired because he's been working late.*
2   ....
3   ....
4   ....
5   ....
6   ....

2 **Delete the incorrect verb form (in some sentences both forms are correct).**

1 I've always **wanted** / ~~**been wanting**~~ to play the piano.
2 She's **worked / been working** here for years.
3 He's **watched / been watching** TV for two hours.
4 I'm tired. I've **studied / been studying** all evening.
5 She's **decorated / been decorating** the house, but she hasn't finished yet.
6 Have you ever **won / been winning** anything on the lottery?
7 I've **lived / been living** here since last year.
8 Paul McCartney has **written / been writing** hundreds of songs.
9 Has Mr Terrill **arrived / been arriving**? I've **waited / been waiting** for half an hour.
10 Have you **finished / been finishing** that book?

3 **Match the items from columns A and B. (Each item in A goes with more than one item in B.)**

A	B
I've been to the cinema three times	for ages.
	in the last week.
	lately.
I saw him	last month.
	the other day.
She's been waiting for a bus	since 2.00.
	a couple of minutes ago.

4 **Change the underlined parts of the sentences so that they are grammatically correct.**

1 He<u>'s lived</u> here until he got married.
   ....*lived*..

2 I <u>don't see</u> him since Monday.
   ....

3 **A** Sorry I'm late. <u>Are you waiting</u> long?
   ....

   B No, I<u>'ve arrived</u> ten minutes ago.
   ....

4 I <u>haven't seen</u> James yesterday.
   ....

5 She<u>'s been working</u> here until 1993.
   ....

6 Your hands are filthy! What <u>did you do</u>?
   ....

7 I <u>didn't go</u> to the bank recently.
   ....

5 **Complete the interview. Put the verbs in brackets into the past simple, present perfect simple, or present perfect continuous tense. In some cases more than one tense is possible.**

Reporter Today, West Side Radio, the area's first local radio station, ..*has been broadcasting*.. (broadcast) for ten years. I .... (come) down to the radio station to interview one of the people who .... (make) the station a success – DJ, Frank Frankham. How long .... you .... (work) for West Side Radio?

DJ I .... (be) with West Side ever since it .... (start), but I .... (not be) a DJ all that time. I .... (be) an assistant producer at first. Then one day about five years ago the normal DJ .... (not come) in, so I .... (stand in) for him. Well, I obviously .... (do) a good job, because they .... (ask) me to be a DJ and I .... (present) my own show ever since.

Reporter Why do you think West Side Radio .... (be) successful?

DJ Well, I think it's because it .... (become) part of the local community. Last week, for instance, there was a big traffic jam in the city centre and we .... (report) that, and I'm sure that .... (help) a lot of people. And one of my colleagues .... just .... (talk) about a local music festival that's happening next week.

Reporter And you .... (also run) several campaigns about local issues.

DJ Yes, that's right. Earlier this year we .... (have) a campaign about traffic in the city. Our current campaign is about the plans for the new market. We .... (run) it for about two weeks now. People .... (phone) us with their views and we .... (pass) these ideas on to the local council.

Vocabulary: Entertainment

6 **Find these things in the wordsquare.**

9 kinds of music
9 kinds of film

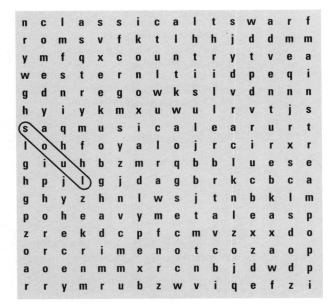

n	c	l	a	s	s	i	c	a	l	t	s	w	a	r	f
r	o	m	s	v	f	k	t	l	h	h	j	d	d	m	m
y	m	f	q	x	c	o	u	n	t	r	y	t	v	e	a
w	e	s	t	e	r	n	l	t	i	i	d	p	e	q	i
g	d	n	r	e	g	o	w	k	s	l	v	d	n	n	n
h	y	i	y	k	m	x	u	w	u	l	r	v	t	j	s
s	a	q	m	u	s	i	c	a	l	e	a	r	u	r	t
l	o	h	f	o	y	a	l	o	j	r	c	i	r	x	r
g	i	u	h	b	z	m	r	q	b	b	l	u	e	s	e
h	p	j	l	g	j	d	a	g	b	r	k	c	b	c	a
g	h	y	z	h	n	l	w	s	j	t	n	b	k	l	m
p	o	h	e	a	v	y	m	e	t	a	l	e	a	s	p
z	r	e	k	d	c	p	f	c	m	v	z	x	x	d	o
o	r	c	r	i	m	e	n	o	t	c	o	z	a	o	p
a	o	e	n	m	m	x	r	c	n	b	j	d	w	d	p
r	r	y	m	r	u	b	z	w	v	i	q	e	f	z	i

7 **Complete the text with these words.**

certainly   behaviour   believed   concerts
drugs   famous   alcohol   write   spoilt
defeated   drums   clubs   when   develop
huge   born   stage   entertainment   hits
guitarist   found out   art   treated   successful
copies   years   skyscraper   brought up   know
teenager   music   black   bass   broke up
superstar

Eric Clapton is one of the most *successful* rock stars
of all time. He has sold millions of .... of his
records and has appeared in live .... all over
the world. Many people regard him as the greatest
.... ever.

Clapton was .... in 1945 in a small town near
London. When he was only two .... old his
mother left him. She went abroad and Eric was
.... by his grandparents. Until he was nine he
.... that they were his parents and it was a
terrible shock when he .... that they weren't.
In the 1980s he told his biographer: 'It explains a lot
of my .... throughout my life. Because I still
don't .... who I am.'

But his grandparents .... him well. In fact they
probably .... him. When he was a ....
they bought him his first guitar and when he left
school they paid for him to go to .... college.
But Eric had already become interested in ....
and he started playing the guitar in pubs and
.... in London. At that time groups like the
Rolling Stones were starting to play blues, which up
to then had only been played by .... musicians
in the United States.

Clapton first became .... when he started a
group called Cream, with Jack Bruce on ....
guitar and Ginger Baker on ...., in 1966. The
group only lasted two years but they had a ....
impact on rock music. They changed rock and roll
from just .... into serious music.

After Cream .... , Clapton formed a new group
called Derek and the Dominoes. He had several
..............., most notably *Layla* and *I Shot the Sheriff*.
Clapton showed that he could not only play the
guitar and sing but could also .... excellent
songs. But while on .... he was the brilliant
guitar-playing ...., his private life was falling
apart. He became addicted to drugs and ....
At one point he was spending over £1,500 a day on
.... Then in 1991 his four-year-old son,
Conor, died .... he fell from the window of a
New York ....

Eric Clapton has .... had his problems, but he
has survived. He finally .... his addiction and
has continued to .... as an artist. Perhaps he
has finally found out who he is.

(not) want someone to

8 **Say what the people want or don't want.**

EXAMPLE

She doesn't want him to leave his coat on the floor.

1 ....

....

2 ....

....

3 ....

....

4 ....

....

5 ....

....

6 ....

....

7 ....

....

8 ....

....

Expressing opinions

9 **Look at these opinions.**

a Rewrite the opinions using these expressions.

I (don't) think	I (don't) believe	I would say
I maintain	In my opinion	

Note: When we express a negative opinion with the verbs *think* or *believe* we usually make *think* or *believe* negative and the statement positive.

1 Violence on TV doesn't affect children.

> *I don't think violence on TV affects children.*

2 People should be able to watch what they like.

> ....

3 Animals shouldn't be used for experiments.

> ....

4 Drugs should be legalized.

> ....

5 It's wrong to eat meat.

> ....

b Say whether you agree with the opinions. Give your reasons.

EXAMPLE

1 *I agree with this. Children can tell the difference between real life and what happens on television.*

2 ....

....

....

3 ....

....

....

4 ....

....

....

5 ....

....

....

Pronunciation: Syllables

10 **Write the number of syllables in each word.**

looked	*1*	society	.....
wanted	.....	believed	.....
ideal	.....	diet	.....
station	.....	died	.....
create	.....	million	.....
dream	.....	everything	.....
neglected	.....	unnecessary	.....
violence	.....	studio	.....

Writing: A review

11 **Number these parts of a review in the correct order.**

☐ He writes a letter to the company accepting the job and he gives it to his son, Bobby, to post.

☐ My award goes to young Justin Time, who plays Bobby.

☐ Bobby isn't too pleased, because he'd rather play football with his friends, but he sets off on the long walk to the post office.

☐ *1* Local playwright Hanna Godber has given her home town a chance to see her most successful play, *The Letter*, at the Lexford Playhouse.

☐ *The Letter* is on for just one more week, so don't miss it.

☐ The story is set in the 1930s.

☐ Unaware of its importance, Bobby gives them the letter and runs off happily to play football.

☐ The play is excellent, and the lighting, scenery, and sound effects are all very good. The cast perform it brilliantly.

☐ If you want to know what happens next, you'll have to go and see the play for yourself, but believe me, you won't regret it.

☐ John Barlow, who has been out of work for several months, is offered a job by a large engineering firm.

☐ On the way he meets two older boys who offer to post the letter for him.

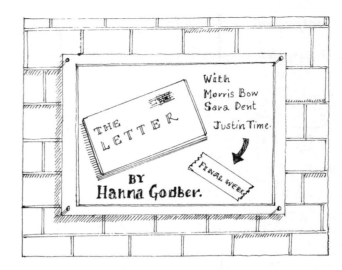

12 **Write a review of a play or film you have seen. Follow this format:**

- The name of the play or film
- The story and the main characters
- The performances/ the set/ the special effects
- Your opinion

....
....
....
....
....
....
....
....
....
....
....
....
....
....
....
....
....
....
....
....

8 Time out

Question forms

1 **Make questions to fit the answers, using the information.**

1 *Where has David gone?*
   ....
   (Where/ David/ go)
   He's gone to the shops.

2 ....
   (see/ the news/ last night)
   No, I didn't.

3 ....
   (Simon and Mary/ at the party)
   No, they weren't.

4 ....
   (play/ the piano)
   Yes, I can.

5 ....
   (do/ anything/ this evening)
   No, I'm not.

6 ....
   (What/ Kelly/ do)
   She's an engineer.

7 ....
   (like/ a drink)
   Yes, I would, please.

8 ....
   (Where/ the woman/ sit)
   She was sitting by the door.

9 ....
   (How long/ live/ there)
   He'd lived there for over fifty years.

10 ....
   (What/ do)
   We've been having a game of cricket.

11 ....
   (When/ be/ back)
   I'll be back on Tuesday.

12 ....
   (used to/ go out with/ Clara)
   Yes, I did.

Indirect questions

2 **Say what the people don't know. Use these expressions.**

doesn't know isn't sure	can't remember has no idea

1 *She doesn't know*
   what time it is.

2 ....
   ....

3 ....
   ....

4 ....
   ....

5 ....
   ....

6 ....
   ....

7 ....
   ....

8 ....
   ....

3 Write indirect questions about the missing information in the article, using *We don't know, I wonder, I'd like to know.*

Super-pigeon wins in record time

A racing pigeon called ▮▮▮ arrived home last night, after flying ▮▮▮ miles across Europe in just ▮▮▮ hours. The bird was released in northern ▮▮▮ at ▮▮▮ o'clock on Wednesday morning, along with ▮▮▮ other pigeons. The weather was ▮▮▮, perfect for flying, and the winner's average speed was ▮▮▮ mph. The pigeon's owner, ▮▮▮ -year-old pensioner Oswald Gosling, said: '▮▮▮ of my life!'

1 *I'd like to know what the pigeon's name is.*
2 ....
3 ....
4 ....
5 ....
6 ....
7 ....
8 ....
9 ....
10 ....

Vocabulary: Sport

4 With which sports do you associate these things? Write the words next to the sports. Some words go with more than one sport.

a goal	a court	a racquet	a course	a pitch
clubs	a track	a race	a rink	a net	a piste
a stick	skates	poles	a shuttlecock	

football — *a goal, a pitch, a net* ....
tennis — ....
golf — ....
athletics — ....
rugby — ....
basketball — ....
badminton — ....
skiing — ....
motor racing — ....
cycling — ....
volleyball — ....
hockey — ....
ice skating — ....

5 Answer the questions.

1 Which of the sports have you played or done?
....

2 Which are the most popular in your country?
....

3 How many of the sports above:
use a ball? ....
are team games? ....
are normally played indoors? ....

6 Match the verbs in A with the items in B. (Some verbs may go with more than one item.)

A	B
score	a ball
	a game
hit	a goal
	a match
win	a race
	an opponent
beat	the other team

Vocabulary: Compound nouns

7 **What do you call these things?**

1. a knife that is used in the kitchen *a kitchen knife*
2. a shop that sells toys ....
3. games for a computer ....
4. a bike for exercise ....
5. an expert on fitness ....
6. a presenter who works on radio ....
7. a restaurant that serves pizzas ....
8. a magazine about cars ....
9. a shop that sells fish and chips ....
10. shoes that you wear for tennis ....

Polite requests

8 **Some people are asking a politician some questions. Rewrite the questions using the expressions in the box.**

I'd like to know	I want to know
Can you tell us	Do you know

1. Will you increase taxes again?
   Can you tell us if you will increase taxes again?

2. What is your policy on education?
   ....

3. Why have you cut spending on hospitals?
   ....

4. How long do we have to wait for a new road?
   ....

5. Does the government intend to cut unemployment benefit?
   ....
   ....

6. Is the government going to do anything about youth crime?
   ....
   ....

7. Do you agree with capital punishment?
   ....

8. What will you do for old people?
   ....

Airport dialogues

9 **Use the information to make polite dialogues.**

EXAMPLE
where/ excess baggage counter
there/ next/ ticket counters
Excuse me. Could you tell me where the excess baggage counter is?
Yes, it's over there next to the ticket counters.

1. flight from Paris/ late
   two-hour delay
   ....
   ....
   ....

2. where/ change/ money
   there/ near/ passport control
   ....
   ....
   ....

3. how much/ watch
   £159
   ....
   ....
   ....

4. how/ get/ train station
   down/ escalator/ left
   ....
   ....
   ....

5. possible/ change/ ticket/ flight/ tomorrow
   see/ ticket/ please
   ....
   ....
   ....

6. how much/ hand baggage/ allowed
   one piece
   ....
   ....
   ....

7. can/ send/ fax
   business lounge/ upstairs
   ....
   ....
   ....

Adjectival expressions with numbers

10 **What would you call these?**

1 a car that costs fifty thousand dollars
   a fifty-thousand-dollar car....................................

2 a delay of forty minutes
   ....

3 a lesson that lasts forty-five minutes
   ....

4 a flight that lasts twenty-four hours
   ....

5 a swim that's four kilometres long
   ....

6 a team of six men
   ....

Vocabulary: Triathlete

11 **Complete the text with these words.**

> couch potato whatever exercise diet mile
> trainers health fun preparing rest back
> jog great weightlifting energy gruelling
> participant cycle forward meat heats
> sweets dedicated backside entrants unfit
> win tired life event serious swim
> fastest gym

It's 5.30 am, and while the .....*rest*..... of us are still snoring in our beds Susan Wates is putting on her .... and getting ready for her morning .... around the streets of East London. Two hours later she's back home and while she's .... breakfast for her family she's already looking .... to the evening and another two hours of ....

Every day, ... the weather, she exercises for four hours. Once a week she also does an hour of running and .... at the local .... club. That's followed by a long swim. On Sundays – just for .... – she goes for an extra ten-.............. run or cycle ride. Susan doesn't smoke, drink, or eat ...., and she's very careful about her .... She very rarely eats ...., chocolate, or ice cream.

Just reading about Susan's .... schedule makes most people feel ...., so why does she do it? 'Well, you probably won't believe it but I used to be a real .... – overweight and .... I hated myself. Then one day I said to myself, 'You've got to get off your .... and do something with your ....' So I went to a ...., started training, and well, I just felt so .... I found that the more I trained the more .... I had.'

Now Susan is in .... training. She is going to enter the selection .... for the Ironman triathlon in Hawaii. The .... consists of a four-kilometre ...., a 42-kilometre run, and a 180-kilometre .... race .... to back, so you've got to be very .... 'I know I won't ....,' says Susan, 'but just to be a .... will be terrific.' And in case you think Susan is unusual, the triathlon is one of the .... growing sports in the world, and the Ironman race has thousands of .... every year.

Writing: Formal letters

12 John Clarke of 16 St John's Walk, London SE13 6GH is writing to the Hotel Belmont. Write these items in the correct places. (Some of the items are not used.)

the second of August

John Clarke

Yours faithfully

16 St John's Walk

The Reservations Manager

Dear Reservations Manager

Hotel Belmont
The Parade
Birmingham
B4 7JB

Mr John Clarke

Dear Sir or Madam

2 August

Love

London SE13 6GH

Yours sincerely

16 St John's Walk
....

....

....

....

....

....

....

....

....

I wish to reserve a double room for the nights of 3–5 September. Could you please tell me whether you have a room available for those nights and what the rate will be?

Thank you for your attention.

....

John Clarke

....

13 You work for Weldon International. Your boss has left this message on your answerphone. Write the letter. Provide an address in your country for Weldon International.

Could you write to the Belmont Hotel and book a meeting room for the Birmingham group on, oh, when is it? Oh yes, 26 April. OK? Oh, and can they provide lunch and give us an idea how much it will cost? Thanks.

Grammar check 3

1 Put the verbs in brackets into the correct tense.

1 **A** What time's the next bus?
B It's at 12.00. If you ....._hurry_..... (hurry) you
....._'ll get_...... (get) it.

2 I'm bored with revising. If I .... (not have)
an exam tomorrow, I .... (go out).

3 If I .... (be) the prime minister, I ....
(ban) all exams.

4 I'm going to the post office. If you ....
(give) me those letters, I .... (post) them.

5 I .... (be) careful if I .... (be) you.

6 **A** I can't get my car started.
B I .... (give) you a lift if you ....
(want).

2 Rewrite the sentences using the conjunctions in brackets.

1 Ken will arrive and then we'll start. (as soon as)
We'll start as soon as Ken arrives.

2 I'll have a drink and then we'll go. (before)
....

3 It hasn't stopped raining so I'll wait. (until)
....

4 I'll do it but I haven't got time now. (when)
....

5 Jack will phone and then we'll book the
restaurant. (after)
....

6 First the taxi will come and then we'll lock up
the house. (as soon as)
....

3 Correct these questions.

1 Who did win the tennis match?
Who won the tennis match?

2 When does starts the film?
....

3 Why they did it?
....

4 What at you are looking?
....

5 Do you can swim?
....

4 Put the verbs into the past simple, the present perfect, or the present perfect continuous.

1 **A** I ...._'ve lost_.... (lose) my glasses. I can't find them
anywhere. I've .... (look for)
them for hours.
B Don't worry. I .... (do) the same
thing the other week, but I ....
(find) them a few days later.

2 We're too late. The train .... (go).
Why .... you .... (take) so long to
get ready?

3 **A** Where .... you .... (be)?
B We .... (play) tennis.

4 The newspaper .... (not arrive) yet.
It's the second time this week it .... (be)
late. It .... (come) late on Tuesday, too.

5 What have the people been doing? Use the verbs in the box.

swim	read	watch a film	jog

1 **Mandy** My feet hurt.
Jane Mine, too.
They ...._'ve been jogging._...............................

2 **Carl** My eyes are tired.
He ....

3 **Susan** I've got water in my ears.
She ....

4 **Mr Brown** That was exciting, wasn't it?
They ....

6 Complete the requests.

1 Where's the computer gone?
Do you know ...._where the computer's gone_.... ?

2 Have you got a fax machine?
Could you tell me ....
.... ?

3 What time does the museum open?
I'd like to know ....
....

4 Did anyone phone yesterday?
Do you know ....
.... ?

9 All in the mind?

-ing forms

1 Describe the picture. Write sentences, using the information.

EXAMPLE
vampire/ stand/ door
There's a vampire standing behind the door.

1 witch/ cook/ something horrible

....

2 ghost/ walk/ wall

....

3 skeletons/ play/ cards

....

4 spider/ crawl/ table

....

5 mad professor/ play/ organ

....

6 monster/ watch/ TV

....

7 face/ look/ window

....

2 Look at the picture again. What can the couple see, hear, and smell? Write two sentences for each verb, using the words in the box.

EXAMPLE
They can see two skeletons playing cards.

burn	wolf	wall	organ	table	cook

1 (see) ....
....

2 (see) ....
....

3 (smell)..
....

4 (smell)..
....

5 (hear)...
....

6 (hear)...
....

-ing forms and infinitives

3 **Complete the sentences with the correct form of the verbs in brackets. In some cases both forms are possible.**

1 **A** I've stopped ....*smoking*...... (smoke).

   B Lucky you. I've tried .... (stop) several times, but I've never managed .... (give up) yet.

   A Oh, if you really want .... (stop), you can.

2 **A** Did you remember .... (lock) the door before we left?

   B I think so, but I can't remember .... (do) it.

3 We had forgotten .... (buy) a newspaper, so we stopped .... (get) one.

4 **A** Are you good at .... (keep) in touch with people?

   B Not really. I don't mind .... (telephone), but I can't stand .... (write) letters.

5 **A** Have you finished .... (write) that report?

   B Yes, but I didn't really enjoy .... (do) it.

   A Never mind, it's done now, so do you fancy .... (go out) somewhere this evening?

   B That would be nice. What do you feel like .... (do)?

   A Would you like .... (try) that new club in the Square?

   B OK. Let's start .... (get) ready.

6 **A** Could you stop .... (make) all that noise, please?

   B But I like .... (play) the drums.

   A Well if you carry on .... (play) that loudly, there's going .... (be) trouble.

-ing forms and past participles

4 **Complete the story. Use these verbs in either the -ing form or the past participle (-ed form).**

speak appear replace place point
produce explain burn sit call in come
shout stare open amaze dig up scrub
frighten groan terrify lock up

One day in August 1971 an old woman and her young grandchild were ...*sitting*... in the kitchen of their house in the village of Belmez, in southern Spain. Suddenly the child started .... and .... at the floor. When the old woman looked down at the tiles, she was .... at what she saw. There was a human face .... at her. The face was terribly sad. .... the floor couldn't remove the face. In fact its eyes only started .... wider. The .... tiles were .... by the owner of the house, but three weeks later the family saw another face .... in the new concrete floor.

Experts were .... After .... the floor they found a medieval cemetery under the house. The faces continued ...., so microphones were .... in the house. When people listened to the recordings they heard voices .... in strange languages. There were other voices .... in terrible pain. The kitchen was ...., but four more faces appeared in different parts of the house. Then, as suddenly as it had started, the house stopped .... faces. The mystery has never been .... The experts could only suggest that some .... incident, such as .... witches, had happened there long ago.

after/ before/ while + -ing

5 In which of these sentences can you use the -ing construction? Tick (✓) the boxes if you can.

☑ 1 After the old woman saw the face, she tried to scrub it away.

☐ 2 While the child was playing on the floor, a face appeared.

☐ 3 Before he called in the experts, the owner replaced the tiles.

☐ 4 While the people were listening to the voices, they felt very frightened.

☐ 5 After they closed the kitchen, the family thought they would see no more faces.

☐ 6 After the owner closed the kitchen, other faces appeared.

☐ 7 After they had dug up the floor, they found a medieval cemetery.

☐ 8 Before the owner closed the kitchen, the experts put microphones there.

6 Rewrite the sentences you have ticked, using the -ing construction.

After seeing the face, the old woman tried to scrub it away.

....

....

....

....

....

....

Vocabulary: Strong adjectives

7 Complete the table with adjectives from the box.

brilliant	exhausted	terrified	huge	bad
ugly	freezing	surprising	fascinating	difficult

Base	Strong
tired	_exhausted_
....	hideous
frightened	....
cold	....
....	amazing
big	....
interesting	....
....	impossible
....	awful
good	....

8 Complete these sentences with very, absolutely, or adjectives from the table above.

1 The town was _fascinating_ , and the view from our hotel window was .... magnificent.

2 **A** The film was .... interesting, wasn't it?

B Well, the special effects were absolutely ...., but the acting wasn't ....

....

3 **A** You look absolutely ....

B I am. I just want to go to bed.

4 **A** Was the exam .... difficult?

B It was worse than difficult – it was ....

....

5 That dress is .... hideous.

Verb phrases with -ing

9 Study these rules.

> Look at this sentence.
> **She** closed the door and (**she**) breathed deeply.
> The subject of the two clauses is the same, so we can replace She closed with Closing.
> **Closing** the door, she breathed deeply.
> If the subject of the two clauses is different we can't do this.
> **She** closed the door and **the phone** started to ring.
> ~~Closing the door, the phone started to ring.~~

a In which of these sentences could you use the -ing form? Tick (✓) the boxes if you can.

☑ 1 Jason put on his jacket and set off home.

☐ 2 She thought that it was his phone number and she dialled it.

☐ 3 I was sitting in a café on holiday and I saw my neighbour.

☐ 4 The _Titanic_ was sailing from England to New York and it sank.

☐ 5 The iceberg made a hole in the ship's side and it sank.

☐ 6 The passenger pulled the emergency cord and the train stopped.

b Rewrite the sentences you have ticked here, using the -ing construction.

Putting on his jacket, Jason set off home.

....

....

....

....

....

....

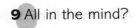

Vocabulary: Phrasal verbs

10 Complete the dialogues. Put the verbs into the correct tense.

turn up	find out	walk past
turn out	bump into	call up

1 **A** Guess who I ...*bumped into*... the other day. Ken Smart.

   B Really! It's a small world.

   A Yes, he .... at a party I was at.

   Anyway, we got talking and it .... that he works just round the corner from you.

   B Wow! That's a coincidence. Did you .... exactly where he works?

   A Yes, at Simpsons.

   B How strange. I must .... there at least twice a day and I've never seen him. I'll have to .... him .... sometime.

call up	pin up	set off
break down	pull up	look at

2 **A** My car ...*broke down*... last week.

   B Oh dear. What did you do?

   A Well I .... the engine, but I couldn't see anything wrong, so I .... to find a garage.

   B And did you find one?

   A Yes, but there was a notice .... on the door saying 'Closed for two weeks'.

   B That's bad luck.

   A Well, yes, but then this really smart sports car .... and the driver asked me if I needed any help.

   B What did you say?

   A Well, I said yes, so he .... another garage on his mobile phone.

Agreeing and disagreeing

11 Agree with these statements.

1 'I can't stand noisy people.' *'Neither can I.'*

2 'I've got two sisters.' '........................'

3 'I hate getting up early.' '........................'

4 'I can speak Spanish.' '........................'

5 'I don't like waiting in queues.' '........................'

6 'I've never been to India.' '........................'

7 'I watched TV last night.' '........................'

8 'I wasn't very good at maths at school.'
   '........................'

12 Disagree with these statements.

1 'I wanted to be a doctor when I was a child.'
   ..*'Oh, I didn't.'*..

2 'I like dogs.' '........................'

3 'I thought the story about the faces was interesting.' '........................'

4 'I hadn't heard it before.' '........................'

5 'I didn't play volleyball yesterday.'
   '........................'

6 'I won't be on holiday next week.'
   '........................'

7 'I'm going to the cinema.' '........................'

8 'I'd like to go on a cruise.'
   '........................'

Pronunciation: The vowel -o-

13 Circle the two words in each line that have the same vowel sound.

won	come	dome
mother	bother	brother
phone	son	done
do	ago	so
boy	nose	noise
four	short	hour
goes	does	toes
among	some	home
move	love	prove
gone	front	once
our	tour	sour
short	cost	score

Writing: A ghost story

14 Use the pictures and the information. Write the
story. Use linking words and strong adjectives
where possible.

1 In the 1880s/ Lord Dufferin/ stay with friends in
Ireland
One night/ wake up suddenly/ hear/ someone/
call/ name

In the 1880s Lord Dufferin was staying ....

....

....

....

....

....

....

....

....

....

2 get out of bed/ go to window
see/ shape/ move/ across lawn

He got ....

....

....

....

....

....

....

....

3 go outside/ see/ man/ carry coffin
call out/ man turn round
man/ very ugly face
man/ disappear/ Lord Dufferin/ feel/ man/ walk
through him

He went outside ....

....

....

....

....

....

4 Several years later/ in hotel in Paris/ wait for lift
lift operator/ ugly man
Lord Dufferin/ horrified/ not get into the lift

Several years later he was ....

....

....

....

....

5 lift/ go up/ to fifth floor/ cable snap
lift/ crash/ everyone inside/ kill

Then, as the lift ....

....

....

....

....

10 Your health

Modal verbs

1 Complete the sentences with these verbs. Each is used only once.

must	may	might	should
shouldn't	can	can't	

1   We ...*should*... do something to reduce air

    pollution in cities.

2   When it's hot some people .... breathe

    properly, because the pollution is so bad.

3   People .... use their cars so much.

4   Public transport .... be improved, so that

    people .... leave their cars at home.

5   If nothing is done soon, it .... be too late.

6   Thousands of people .... die if we get a

    very hot summer.

2 Put in *to* where necessary.

1   We ought ...*to*... leave soon.

2   I can't .... make the football match tonight.

3   Do you want .... go to the party?

4   Well, we could .... go back tomorrow.

5   You aren't allowed .... drive till you're
    seventeen.

6   There's someone at the door. I'll have .... call
    you back.

7   The shops were so crowded I wasn't able ....
    get what I wanted.

8   I think it might .... rain today.

9   You may .... get a phone call today.

10   I need .... go to the shops.

11   Oh, it's 10.00. I must .... go.

12   What would you like .... do today?

3 Match the sentences in A and B.

A	B
She must come.	She hasn't got the time.
She may come.	She has no choice.
She should come.	It's not necessary.
She can't come.	I think she'd enjoy it.
She doesn't have to come.	I don't know for certain.
He might leave.	He'll be in trouble if he does.
He shouldn't leave.	It's all right if he does.
He mustn't leave.	But I don't think he will.
He ought to leave.	We need help with this work.
He can leave.	It would be better for him if he does.

4 Complete the sentences with your own ideas.

1   I might ....

    ....

2   I mustn't ....

    ....

3   People shouldn't ....

    ....

4   The government ought to ....

    ....

5   Next week I may ....

    ....

6   I think our teacher should ....

    ....

7   I can't ....

    ....

8   When I'm 75 I'll have to ....

    ....

9   When I was a child I had to ....

    ....

10   In ten years time I'll be able to ....

    ....

Vocabulary: Medical terms

5 Label the items.

1 *a bandage* .... 2 ....

 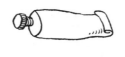

3 .... 4 ....

5 .... 6 ....

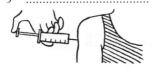

7 .... 8 ....

9 .... 10 ....

6 Complete the sentences with an appropriate word where necessary.

1 I've got a ....*sore*.... throat and ....
temperature.

2 There have been 6,000 .... of flu this
winter.

3 Have we got any .... ? I've got ....
headache.

4 My father has .... high blood pressure.

5 The doctor wrote me a .... for ....
antibiotics.

6 You've got .... cholesterol. I'm going to put
you on .... low-fat ....

7 You might have .... fracture – you should
have .... to make sure.

8 I've got .... pain in my side here. I think
it's .... indigestion.

9 I've got .... cold, but my sister's got
.... flu.

10 She's got .... nasty cough. She needs
.... cough ....

Possibility

7 Here are some of the things that people worry about when they go on holiday. Say what the worries are. Use *could*, *may*, or *might* and these words.

weather	delayed	crash	mugged
lose	break in	ill	accident

1 *Someone might break
into the house.* .... 2 ....

3 .... 4 ....

5 .... 6 ....

BA 315 CAIRO DELAYED
DK 907 MILAN DELAYED
UA 525 NEW YORK DELAYED
BA 103 TOKYO DELAYED

7 .... 8 ....

Vocabulary: Research

8 **Replace the underlined words and expressions with words and expressions of similar meaning.**

In the early 1950s an American <u>scientist</u>/
researcher.............., Professor Ancel Keys, first noted a

<u>link</u>/ .... between diet and heart disease.

<u>A study of</u>/ .... the diets of men in seven

countries <u>revealed</u>/ .... that people eating

a Mediterranean diet, such as those in Italy and

Spain, <u>ran a smaller risk of dying</u>/ ....

....

from heart disease than people in the USA or

Northern Europe. At first the research team thought

<u>there was a possibility</u>/ .... that fat in the

diet <u>could</u>/ .... be causing the difference.

However, <u>according to Professor Keys</u>/ ....

....

the difference did not <u>appear</u>/ .... to be

<u>linked</u>/ .... to the amount of fat. The

<u>results</u>/ .... of the study <u>seemed</u>/

.... to indicate that it was the type of fat

that made the difference. The Mediterranean diet is

rich in monounsaturated fats, such as olive oil,

which it is <u>believed</u>/ .... to reduce levels

of cholesterol in the blood. More recent studies have

<u>confirmed</u>/ .... these findings.

At the doctor's

9 **Write the conversation.**

> Hmm, yes. Does it itch?
> I'll give you a prescription for some ointment. Put it on twice a day.
> Thank you, doctor. Goodbye.
> I see. Just slip your shirt off. How long have you had the rash?
> Goodbye.
> Good morning. What seems to be the problem?
> Continue the treatment for a week after the rash has disappeared.
> Yes, it does.
> Good morning, doctor.
> I've got a rash under my arm.
> Well, you've got a bit of an infection there.
> About two weeks.

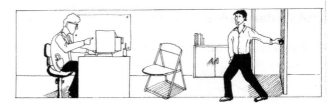

1 **Patient** _Good morning, doctor._....................................

  Doctor _Good morning. What seems to be the problem?_

2 **Patient** ....

  Doctor ....

3 **Patient** ....

  Doctor ....

  Patient ....

4 **Doctor** ....

5 **Doctor** ....

6 **Doctor** ....

  Patient ....

  Doctor ....

must, mustn't, and *needn't*

10 Read the instructions and complete the sentences with *must, mustn't,* or *needn't.*

> Don't leave disks in the disk drive.
> Keep disks in their files.
> You can use my disks if you want.
> Don't put drinks near the computer.
> You can leave the computer on, if you want.
> Lock the door when you leave.

1 You ..*mustn't*.. leave disks in the disk drive.

2 You .... keep disks in their files.

3 You .... use your own disks.

4 You .... put drinks near the computer.

5 You .... switch the computer off.

6 You .... lock the door when you leave.

Pronunciation: The vowel *-i-*

11 Tick (✓) the pairs of words that have the same vowel sound.

✓	miss	kiss
☐	alive	olive
☐	title	little
☐	drive	active
☐	pill	fill
☐	mile	while
☐	office	mice
☐	nice	price
☐	give	arrive
☐	hi-fi	sci-fi
☐	thin	line
☐	tired	bird
☐	think	drink
☐	item	high
☐	office	pine
☐	third	birthday

Vocabulary: The cost of health

12 Complete the text with the words in the box.

> skiing money should injure health
> treatment question drugs children
> unemployed refuse provide spending
> longer old worse costs would ageing
> priority taxes patient life-threatening
> chances case developed choices
> after who

The ....*case*.... of Child B has raised the difficult .... of which patients should get .... when the amount of money available to .... authorities is limited. Of course, it .... be good if anyone could receive any .... that they need, but unfortunately this is not possible. So what .... we spend money on – old people or ...., people who do important jobs or the ...., people with conditions that are not .... or only on emergencies? What should we do about people who .... themselves in some way, such as people .... smoke, eat too much or take ...., people with dangerous hobbies such as rock climbing or .... ? And what about the treatment? Should we .... to pay for anything that .... more than, say, £10,000, or should we only .... treatment when the .... of survival are good?

Doctors will always have to make .... about what treatment any .... should receive. Health .... already takes a huge share of .... And the problem will only get ...., as new kinds of treatment are .... Many countries also have the problem of an .... population. There will be more .... people and they will live .... Who is going to provide the .... that will be needed to look .... them?

Writing: A letter of apology

13 Complete Roger's letter with these words.

touch	for	so	Green	it	Tim	able
afraid	had	well	anyway	fortunately		best
party	sorry	downstairs	May			

88 .....*Green*..... Lane

Oxford

OX5 9PL

23 ....

Dear .... and Yolande,

I'm very .... we weren't .... to

come to your .... on Saturday. I'm

.... Tania fell .... and hurt her arm,

.... she .... to go to the hospital

.... an X-ray. ...., she hasn't

broken ...., but it's still very painful.

..............., I hope the party went .... I'll

be in .... again soon.

All the ....,

Roger

14 You have arranged to go and stay with your friends Ellen and Joe next weekend. However, you forgot that you have an exam next Monday. You'll have to stay at home revising at the weekend. Write to Ellen and Joe, apologizing for not being able to go, and explaining why. Suggest another weekend. Use *will/won't be able to* and *will/won't have to.*

11 Priorities

make, let, and get

1 Mrs James is a head teacher. Here are some events from her day. Say what she made, let, or got people (to) do.

1 *She got her husband to take their son to school.*

2 ....

3 ....

4 ....

5 ....

6 ....

7 ....

2 What have you made, let, or got someone (to) do recently? Write two things for each verb.

EXAMPLE
I let my friend borrow my camera.

....
....
....
....
....
....
....
....
....

Causative *have*

3 **What have these people had done?**

WESTWORLD COMPUTERS	**ALPHA** CLEANING SERVICES
Mr Oldcorn computer repair: £127	Mrs Jones for cleaning carpets: £37.50

1 *Mr Oldcorn has had his computer repaired.*

2 ....

....

R.J. Turner **Decorators** Mr White for repainting house: £268	*Bathroom Heaven* Ms Hardy decorating bathroom: £387

3 ....

....

4 ....

....

QuickChange **TYRES** Ms Riley tyre replacement: £45	**ABLE** Construction Mr Ridge building new garage: £2,700

5 ....

....

6 ....

....

Bruce's Garage Mr Downham for fitting new engine: £986	**HEATING** CENTRAL John Fleming gas fire installation £220

7 ....

....

8 ....

....

do and *have something done*

4 **Rewrite the sentences. Keep the same tense.**

EXAMPLES

John's car is going to be repaired. He's going to do it himself.
John's going to repair his car.
John's car is going to be repaired. He's going to take it to the garage.
John's going to have his car repaired at the garage.

1 Fatma's films have been developed at the local chemist's shop.

Fatma ....

....

2 Some flowers were planted in Mrs Peck's garden. She did it herself.

Mrs Peck ....

....

3 Mr Nye's front door will be painted. A painter will do it.

Mr Nye ....

....

4 Brenda's hair has been dyed. She did it herself.

Brenda ....

....

5 Colin's suit has been cleaned at the dry cleaner's.

Colin ....

....

Vocabulary: Noun formation

5 **Complete the boxes.**

	verb	noun		verb	noun
creat	*e*	*ion*	examin		
surviv			injur		
deci			suggest		
agree			produc		
protect			introduc		
destr			imagin		

Vocabulary

6 Complete the crossword.

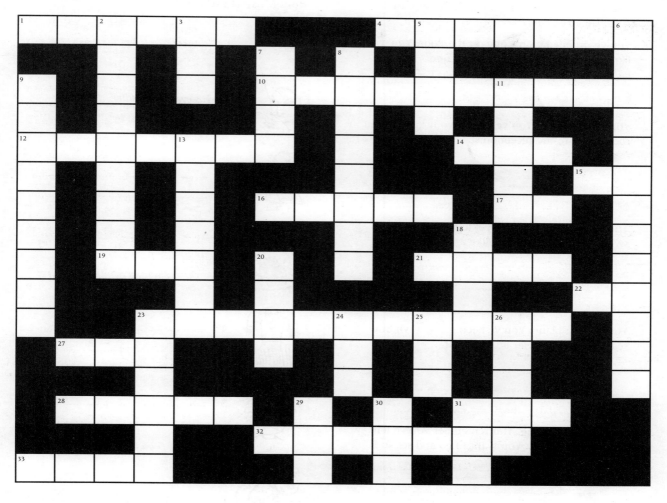

Across →

1 If you make a reduction, you .... something.
4 to import illegally
10 teenage
12 let go
14 toilet
15 I got Mary ..... tell me her secret.
16 A soap .... is a kind of TV programme.
17 **A** I like animals.
   B ..... do I.
19 Di-Di didn't want to leave, ... she?
21 When you hurt yourself you feel this.
22 What do you spend your money ..... ?
23 clever
27 *be able to* replaces this verb in the future tense.
28 You .... a toilet.
31 Orang-utans are a kind of ....
32 very fast
33 a very young person or animal

Down ↓

2 I had my films .... at the chemist's.
3 Martin's had his hair ....
5 Pleased to .... you.
6 unusual
7 Donna didn't want to eat her dinner, but her mum .... her finish it.
8 I rang the ....
9 If you agree on something you have an ....
11 You .... a border.
13 leave forever
18 Animals are often kept in this.
20 You'll soon get .... to your new home.
23 The runner is recovering from his ....
24 My dad .... me drive his car the other day.
25 Could you .... Barry to work late this evening?
26 A baby wears this.
29 The trousers were too long so I .... them shortened.
30 The police officer stopped the man and made .... empty his bag.
31 every

Dealing with problems

7 What would you say in these situations? You should attract attention, state the problem, then make a request.

1 You've dropped your knife on the floor. You'd like the waiter to get you a clean one.
Excuse me, I've dropped my knife on the floor. Could
you get me a clean one, please?
....

2 You're in a hotel. You've locked your key in your room. Talk to the receptionist.
....
....
....

3 You bought a radio last week but one of the switches is broken. You'd like a new radio.
....
....
....

4 You're on a plane. You've been given a window seat, but you'd prefer an aisle seat.
....
....
....

5 You're in a meeting. You remember you've left your car unlocked. You want to go and see to it.
....
....
....

6 You're in a restaurant. Your glass isn't clean. You'd like a new one.
....
....
....

7 You're in a restaurant. You aren't satisfied with the service. You'd like to speak to the manager.
....
....
....

8 You were at the cinema last night. You think you left your umbrella there. Phone the box office.
....
....
....

need + -ing

8 Look at the pictures and write what needs doing. Use these verbs.

comb	repair	mark
cut	test	wash

1 *His eyes need testing.*
....

2 ....
....

3 ....
....

4 ....
....

5 ....
....

6 ....
....

Pronunciation: *-ea-*

9 Circle the two words in each line which have the same vowel sound.

1	(head)	bead	(bread)
2	easy	heavy	leave
3	real	read	rear
4	early	hear	heard
5	weak	clean	ear
6	earth	dead	leather
7	seal	seat	bear
8	bean	fear	clean
9	death	breath	breathe
10	beneath	weather	east

Expressions

10 **Complete the dialogues with these expressions.**

> workload
> in the first place
> he can't find the time for it
> We don't want a repeat
> he's let us down
> she's still learning the ropes
> chap
> this is the limit
> I think he means it
> It's holding everything up
> Sorry to disturb you
> has got a good name
> the deadline
> putting things off
> I should have known better

1 **A** Hello. *Sorry to disturb you,* ....
   but I was just wondering how our new
   advertising manager is getting on.

   B Well, ...
   at the moment, but I think she's doing fine.

   A Good. ....
   of the problems we had with the ....
   who was doing it before.

   B I don't think that's very likely. Sonja ....
   .... in her field.

2 **A** Has Charlie done that survey yet? ....
   ....
   We'll never meet ....
   if he doesn't get it done soon.

   B Yes, I know. I spoke to him yesterday. He
   says ....

   A What? Oh ....
   This is the second time ....
   on something important.

   B Well, he says his .... is too heavy.

   A Oh, that's just an excuse for ....
   ....

   B I'm not so sure. He's threatened to resign
   again and .... this time.

   A Well, I don't believe it. ....
   ....
   than to get him to do it ....

Writing: Punctuation

11 **Rewrite these sentences with the correct
punctuation and capital letters.**

EXAMPLE
johns been waiting for half an hour said sharon
'John's been waiting for half an hour,' said Sharon.

1 weve released more than fifty apes said dr willie
   smits but theres another two hundred at the
   wanariset centre

   ....
   ....
   ....
   ....

2 whats the time said sally sleepily is it five oclock
   yet im hungry

   ....
   ....
   ....

3 is that kens girlfriend asked fiona
   yes it is said alison shes french you know

   ....
   ....
   ....

4 sandras parents went to italy in june said larissa

   ....
   ....

5 on the left you can see the houses of parliament
   said the guide and on your rights westminster
   abbey

   ....
   ....
   ....

6 id like to know he whispered what youve done
   with the childrens money

   ....
   ....

7 how often have you been here before demanded
   the customs officer

   ....
   ....
   ....

Grammar check 4

1 **Complete the text with the correct form of these verbs.**

point	stand	sit	say	laugh
lie	fall	blow	shout	

I had a strange dream the other night. I was in a room. There were two women ....*sitting*.... on chairs. I saw one of the women .... to two doors and I heard her .... : 'Choose.' I opened one of the doors and I found myself .... on top of a tower. There was a strong wind .... I could hear people .... and there was someone .... very loudly: 'Wrong door. Wrong door.' Then I felt myself .... When I woke up I was .... on the floor.

2 **Rewrite the sentences using** *while, after,* **or** *before* **+** *-ing.*

1 Liam almost fell asleep while he was driving.
   Liam almost fell asleep while driving.

2 After he stopped he opened his window.
   ....

3 He had a rest before he continued his journey.
   ....

4 But after he almost fell asleep again, he checked into a hotel.
   ....

5 Before he went to bed he phoned his wife.
   ....

3 **Complete the sentences with the** *-ing* **form, the infinitive, or the infinitive with** *to.*

1 Would you like ......*to leave*...... (leave) now?

2 Oh no. I've forgotten .... (switch off) the computer.

3 Do you remember .... (play) here when you were younger?

4 How do you fancy .... (go out)?

5 You ought .... (take) a break.

6 You must .... (look) after yourself.

7 She made them .... (wait) for hours.

8 The photocopier's stopped .... (work).

9 I'll get the mechanic .... (fix) the car.

10 The windows need .... (clean).

4 **Agree with these statements.**

1 Mark wants to stay longer. ...*So do I.*...

2 I can't sing very well. ....

3 I'll send her some flowers. ....

4 Pat worked late yesterday. ....

5 I've never seen him before. ....

5 **Disagree with these statements.**

1 I haven't been to Barcelona. ...*Oh, I have.*...

2 I had a good weekend. ....

3 I wouldn't stay here. ....

4 I'm going to the lecture. ....

5 I won't be here tomorrow. ....

6 **Rewrite these sentences using the future with** *will.*

1 I must go.
   I'll have to go.

2 Neil can't make it.
   ....

3 We needn't take the exam.
   ....

4 I can see you next week.
   ....

7 **Write what Teresa** *must, mustn't,* **or** *needn't* **do.**
Don't bring your passport. You won't need it. Don't forget your ticket. Be at the airport by 6.00. You won't need any cash.

1 She ....*needn't bring*............ her passport.

2 She .... her ticket.

3 She .... by 6.00.

4 She .... any cash.

8 **What did these people have done?**

1 Harry took his coat to the cleaners.
   He ....*had*.... his coat ......*cleaned*...... .

2 Denise took a key to the key-cutting shop.
   She ....

3 Jill and Marie went to the photographers.
   They ....

4 Mrs Garratt went to the opticians.
   She ....

12 News

Reported speech

1 **Look at the speech bubbles and complete the dialogues.**

> I've passed my driving test. I'm going to buy a car when I can afford it. I'll use my parents' car till then.

1 **A** Andrea said *that she had passed her driving test.*

B That's good news.

A And she said ....

B What's she going to do till then?

A She said ....

> I'm playing tennis this evening. I didn't play this Monday because John had broken his racquet.

2 **A** Is Tim coming to the cinema?

B No, he said ....

A I thought he played on Mondays.

B Yes, that's right, but he said ....

....

> I'd like to get a new job. I just don't enjoy what I'm doing in my present job.

3 **A** I saw Pauline the other day. She didn't look

very happy. She said ....

....

B Oh, why's that?

A She said ....

....

Reported questions

2 **Report what the people asked.**

1 **Helena**   Have you seen my keys, Dad?

Helena asked her dad whether he had

seen her keys.

2 **Fred**   Had you ever been to Australia before your recent trip, Peter?

Fred asked Peter ....

....

....

3 **Sandra**   Where are you going, Ken?

Sandra asked ....

....

4 **Police officer**   How long will you be away, Mrs Cassidy?

The police officer ....

....

5 **Mr Hoyle**   Where have you put the disks, Roberta?

....

....

6 **Receptionist**   Would you prefer a double or a single room, Mrs Carlucci?

....

....

7 **Managing Director**   Why did you leave your last job, Mr Walsh?

....

....

8 **Helen**   Do you like living in London, Dean?

....

....

Reported speech

3 **Read the dialogues and write the original conversations.**

a What did Sam and Frank say?

Sam	*Hello, Frank. Have you heard? Lena and I are getting married.*
Frank	....
Sam	....
	....

Frank	I phoned Sam yesterday. He told me that he and Lena were getting married.
Maggie	Oh, wonderful! Did he say when?
Frank	Well, I asked him when the big day would be, but he said they hadn't fixed the date yet. But he said we'd be the first to know.

b What did Jane and Betty say?

Jane	....
	....
Betty	....
	....
Jane	....
	....
	....

Betty	I saw Jane yesterday. She told me she'd got a new job. She said she was working at the Clyde bank now.
Deborah	Did you ask her why she'd left her old job?
Betty	Yes. She said she had applied for promotion, but she hadn't got it, so she'd decided to leave.

c What did Sandra and Sanjit say?

Sandra	....
Sanjit	....
Sandra	....
	....
Sanjit	....
Sandra	....

David	Where's Peter?
Sanjit	Oh, haven't you heard? Sandra told me that he'd had an accident.
David	Oh dear.
Sanjit	I asked her whether he was all right and she said he'd broken his leg and he couldn't walk.
David	Did you ask her how it had happened?
Sanjit	Yes, I did, but she said she didn't know.

Vocabulary: Phrasal verbs

4 **Complete the dialogues using the verbs in the box. (Some verbs are used more than once.)**

get	turn	put	kick	go	pull
come	pick	run	grow	look	head

1 She ..*put*.... on her coat and ...*went*..... out, but it was raining, so she .... back and .... up her umbrella.

2 **A** Can you .... the TV off, please?

   B But it's the football match and they're just .... off.

   A .... it down then. It's too loud.

3 **A** Oh, there isn't anywhere to park.

   B Just .... in a minute. I'll .... out and .... for a parking space.

   A It's all right. That car's .... out. I think I'll be able to .... in there.

4 I .... up in a small town and I got very bored. I decided to .... away. I .... for the city, but I soon .... back, because my money .... out.

5 **Complete the sentences with these verbs.**

get away with	put up with	get round to
grow out of	get out of	set off for
make up for	stand up for	get back to

1 **A** Have you fixed that shelf yet?

   B No, but don't worry. I'll ...*get round to*..... it.

2 I forgot our wedding anniversary, so I had to book a holiday to .... it.

3 Children .... shoes so quickly.

4 You have to .... your rights. If people try to push you around, don't let them .... it.

5 The flight's at 12.40, so what time should we .... the airport?

6 I tried to .... going to the meeting, but I still had to go.

7 I can't afford a new computer, so I'll just have to .... my old one for now.

8 Well, it was nice to talk to you, but I suppose I'd better .... work.

Indirect commands/requests

6 What did the people ask or tell someone to do?

1 The teacher asked
   Paul to close the window .

2 Sally's father told
   ....
   ....
   ....

3 The painter ....
   ....
   ....

4 The driving instructor
   ....
   ....

5 The flight attendant
   ....
   ....

6 She ....
   ....

7 Tom's grandfather
   ....
   ....

8 The dentist ....
   ....
   ....

Vocabulary: Reported speech verbs

7 Here are some things that people said to John Clarke. Report what they said. Use these words.

advise	order	beg	warn

1 His sister: Please don't join the army.
   His sister begged him not to join the army.
   ....

2 The sergeant: Collect all your equipment.
   ....

3 William Ross: Please don't shoot.
   ....

4 His father: Forget about William Ross.
   ....

5 His father: Don't try to talk to Ross's wife.
   ....

6 His mother: Send the diary back.
   ....

7 Mrs Ross: Please give me the diary.
   ....

8 The boy: Put your hands up.
   ....

Vocabulary: *say* or *tell*

8 Put in *said* or *told*.

1 John .... he was going out.

2 I .... you to leave me alone.

3 Have I .... you what happened yesterday?

4 The manager .... we could all go home.

5 Has Isobel .... anything to you about the party?

6 The police officer .... the boys to go home.

7 Sally .... a very funny joke yesterday.

8 Frank .... he'd finished the job.

9 My father .... me a story.

10 You should have .... the truth.

Reported speech: A news report

9 Look at what the people said. Complete the news report.

A scientist: The earthquake happened at 4.13 in the morning. It measured 6.5 on the Richter scale.

The fire chief: Fires have broken out all over the city.

The police department: Most of the major roads are damaged. Please stay at home, if possible. Don't drive unless you have to.

A doctor: Hundreds of patients are waiting for treatment.

The Mayor: We will do everything we can to get the city back to normal.

Here is the news. There has been a serious earthquake in San Francisco. A scientist said that *the earthquake had happened at 4.13 in the morning.* She said that it ....

....

The earthquake has caused major problems for the emergency services. The city's fire chief said that

....

Transport has been badly hit. A spokesman for the police department said ....

.... He asked people ....

.... and he advised ....

.... Local hospitals are full. A doctor said ....

....

As the city tries to deal with the damage the Mayor said that they ....

....

Pronunciation: Silent letters

10 Write the words in the correct column. Some do not go in any column.

| talk who clerk knife comb school cake |
| chemistry blank bomb chimney scientist |
| what calm where walk hour knee |
| doubt want climb ghost half debt |

silent *c*	silent *h*	silent *k*
silent *l*	**silent *w***	**silent *b***
talk		

Vocabulary: Nouns used as adjectives

11 Change the expressions, using nouns used as adjectives.

1 shoes with high heels
  high-heeled shoes ....

2 a shirt with long sleeves
  ....

3 a man with a beard
  ....

4 a dog with a short tail
  ....

5 a house with five bedrooms
  ....

6 paper with lines
  ....

7 a bat with long ears
  ....

8 an envelope with a stamp and an address on
  ....

Writing: Reference

12 **Look at the text.**

In 1961 Viv Nicholson won £153,000. (That) was a lot of money (then), and (it) would be worth over £2 million today. (She) announced that she was going to 'spend, spend, spend', and (that) is exactly what she and (her) husband did. (They) lived a life of luxury, and after a few years of (this) (the whole lot) had all gone. (The big winner) had only one regret. Her husband had bought a sports car, and (he) was killed when he crashed (it).

Who or what do the circled items refer to?

That	_£153,000_	They	....
then	....	this	....
it	....	the whole lot	....
She	....	The big winner	....
that	....	he	....
her	....	it	....

13 **Complete the story with these words and expressions. (Some are used more than once.)**

each other	the Asian factory worker	the other
his	their	they	Mrs Mohidin	hers
the family	she	Mr and Mrs Mohidin	both
the money	her	all of it	he	my

Hands off my money!

Mukhtar and Sayeeda Mohidin couldn't believe it. _Their_ .... dream had come true. .... had won the £18 million jackpot in the National Lottery. .... gave up .... £240 a week job and .... bought a new and expensive house near London.

Today, less than six months later, ... are suing .... Mukhtar and Sayeeda have accused .... of giving too much money to .... relatives. Now Sayeeda has gone to court to claim that half the money should be .... husband maintains that .... is .... since .... bought the ticket with .... own money.

A friend said .... had changed everything, but yesterday .... claimed that there was no problem. 'I am living happily with .... husband and family,' .... said.

14 **Write a newspaper story about a lottery winner, using reference where possible.**

I'm giving it all away, says woman – husband disagrees

Two weeks ago, Monica Wells won £8 million in the lottery. Now, ...

....

....

....

....

....

....

....

....

....

....

....

....

....

....

....

....

....

13 Regrets

Third conditionals

1 Ben and Clara have just got married. It all started when Ben overslept one morning. Complete the spaces with these sentences.

> Oh, they're towing that guy's car away.
> Will you marry me?
> Excuse me. Your car's been towed away, I'm afraid.
> I hope the car will be all right there on the double yellow lines.
> Thanks very much, Clara. Look. Are you doing anything this evening?
> I'm going to be late for my appointment.
> It's my lunch break. Can I give you a lift to the pound?

1   *I'm going to be late for my appointment.*

2   ....
    ....

3   ....
    ....

4   ....
    ....

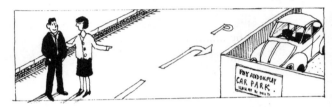

5   ....
    ....

6   ....
    ....

7   ....
    ....

2 **Complete the sentences with the correct form of the verbs in brackets.**

1   If Ben *hadn't overslept* (not oversleep), he

wouldn't have been (not be) late for his

appointment.

2   If he .... (not be) late for his

appointment, he .... (have)
time to find a parking space.

3   He .... (not leave) the car on

double yellow lines if he ....
(find) a parking space.

4   The car .... (not be) towed

away if he .... (not leave) it
on double yellow lines.

5   But if the car .... (not be)

towed away, he .... (not
meet) Clara.

6   And if he .... (not meet)

Clara, she .... (not give) him
a lift to the pound.

7   Ben .... (not ask) Clara out if

she .... (not give) him a lift to
the pound.

8   And they .... (not start) going

out together if Ben .... (not
ask) her out.

9   So Ben and Clara .... (not

get) married if Ben .... (not
oversleep) one morning.

should/shouldn't have

4 **Say what the people should or shouldn't have done.**

1   Carol left her bag in the car and it was stolen.

   Carol shouldn't have left her bag in the car................

2   The footballer kicked the goalkeeper and he was
sent off.

   ....

   ....

3   Mr Warren didn't look before he crossed the road
and he was knocked down.

   ....

   ....

4   Nina shouted at her little brother and he cried.

   ....

5   John didn't have the car serviced and it broke
down.

   ....

6   Mr and Mrs Jarvis didn't pay the phone bill and
the phone was cut off.

   ....

   ....

7   Mary left her books at school and she couldn't do
her homework.

   ....

   ....

8   Alan didn't buy a ticket for the train and he was
fined.

   ....

Vocabulary: Animals

3 **Write the names of these animals in the correct column.**

fly   bee   lion   ant
dog   mosquito
dolphin   snake   pigeon
shark   lizard   cow
octopus   elephant
worm   horse   wasp
frog   pig   duck   tiger
parrot   ostrich   sheep
bat   eagle   monkey
owl   bear   chicken
tuna   crocodile
tortoise   spider
salmon   cat   butterfly
whale   trout

mammals	birds	fish	insects	reptiles/ amphibians	others
			fly		

Jasna's story

5 **Complete the story with these words and expressions.**

a life of her own	like thousands of others
daily work	for centuries
money for nothing	tried to get her
dreamed of	to a sudden end
a couple of years later	in the town square
She finally realized	in the magazines
All she had to do	to the big city
no money left	It seemed as if
it was just her imagination	

It was a small town *like thousands of others* and life
had hardly changed there .... The
people weren't poor. They did their ....
and in the evenings they sat .... and
talked. But Jasna .... being rich and
famous. She wanted to be a fashion model like the
ones she had seen ...., and she decided
to leave the small town. Her boyfriend, Miro, and
her parents .... to stay, but she wouldn't
listen to them. She wanted to have ....
So one day she said goodbye to her family and to
Miro and went .... Jasna was an
attractive young woman and she soon got some
small modelling jobs. At a fashion show
.... she met Hans Becker. He became her
manager and soon Jasna had a big house and lots of
new friends. .... she had everything.
.... was be photographed wearing
beautiful clothes. It seemed like ....

But one day it came .... Jasna and
Becker were involved in a car crash. Jasna was badly
injured and Becker died. Then Jasna discovered that
Becker had gambled away all her money. There was
.... She had nothing but debts and her
modelling career was over. And perhaps
........................, but she didn't seem to have so many
friends any more. She was alone. ....
that her only true friends were back in her home
town, but she felt so ashamed that she couldn't go
back.

6 **Complete these sentences with your own ideas.**

1 If Jasna hadn't read the fashion magazines,

....

2 ....,
she would have married Miro.

3 ....,
she wouldn't have met Hans Becker.

4 If Becker hadn't become her manager,

....

5 ....,
she wouldn't have been injured.

6 If Becker hadn't gambled, ...

....

7 If she hadn't been injured, ...

....

8 ....,
she would have gone back home.

7 **How would you like the story to end? Write an
ending.**

....
....
....
....
....
....
....
....
....
....
....
....
....

Vocabulary: Colloquial expressions

8 The underlined expressions in this conversation are wrong. Delete them and write the correct expressions.

A I crashed my car the other day and broke all the lights on the back.

B It's a bit rough/ *That's a bit rough.*

A Yes, and when the garage told me how much it was going to cost, I was stunning/ ....

....

B Did it cost a bit quite/ ....

.... ?

A You're saying to me/ ....

....

It cost me an arm and a hand/

....

The lights were over £50 each.

B You joke/.................................... .

A I'm not. I phoned the insurance company, but they weren't many

helps/ ....

....,

because it was my fault.

B Oh well, that's the way it does/

....

sometimes.

A Yes, I suppose/............................. .

Anyway, I think it's my circle/

....

Do you want the same again?

Talking about a holiday

9 **Complete the conversation with these expressions.**

> I wasn't in too good a mood   Something similar happened
> we've been away   Did you have a good time?
> funnily enough   we were hanging around at the airport
> when we finally got there   I can tell you
> I haven't seen you around for a while.   we did in the end   Oh dear
> I hope it didn't spoil your holiday too much   Nor was my husband

A Hi. *I haven't seen you around for a while.* ....

B Well, ... for a couple of weeks, in Jamaica.

A Oh, very nice. ....

B Well, ...

A Why? What was the problem?

B The flight was delayed, so .... for ages.

A .... How long did you have to wait?

B About seven and a half hours. ....

by the time we took off. ....

We won't be travelling with that company again, ...

A Well, ...

B No, it was OK ....

A .... to my sister's family last year.

They were going to Jamaica, too, ...

B Oh really, what happened?

Expressing interest

10 **Write the response to these statements.**

1 We're moving house.

   Are you? Where are you moving to? ....

2 Simon's had an accident.

   ....

3 I saw Bill yesterday.

   ....

4 Jim would leave tomorrow if he could.

   ....

5 Zara works for me now.

   ....

6 Terry and Brenda have split up.

   ....

7 That big house on the corner is for sale.

   ....

Vocabulary: Collocations

11 Match the verbs in column A with the nouns in column B.

A	B
tell	a match
knit	a meal
change	people
offer	a jumper
cook	a gun
claim	into tears
deceive	lies
win	compensation
fire	a wheel
burst	a reward

Vocabulary: Adjectives

12 Write the negative forms of these adjectives.

1	happy	*unhappy*
2	honest	....
3	polite	....
4	careful	....
5	correct	....
6	natural	....
7	useful	....
8	lucky	....
9	expensive	....
10	patient	....
11	important	....
12	reliable	....
13	efficient	....
14	usual	....
15	sensitive	....
16	satisfied	....
17	convenient	....
18	tolerant	....
19	dependent	....
20	healthy	....

Writing: A letter of complaint

13 Complete the text of the letter with these expressions.

However	I was amazed	I am writing to complain	as a result
I would be grateful if	I appreciate that		and unfortunately
I feel that	While we were on holiday		

> 70 Bramble Drive
> Exeter EX3 9JY
>
> 14 February
>
> Snowtours
> 192 Turner Street
> London SW8 9GG
>
> Dear Sir or Madam
> I am writing to complain .... about the insurance cover on our recent skiing holiday in the USA. .... my daughter decided to try snowboarding .... broke her arm. After taking her to hospital .... to find that our travel insurance did not cover us for snowboarding. The treatment, ..., cost us over $2,000.
>
> .... I should have read the insurance cover first. ...., many people these days go snowboarding and .... ski insurance should cover people for it. .... you would explain to me why snowboarding is not covered in the policy.
>
> Yours faithfully
>
> Brendan Frost

14 Look at the situation in exercise 9 above. Think of some more details for the story. Write a letter of complaint to the travel company, Suntime, 4 Brook Road, London NW14 7NM. Ask for compensation. Follow the format for a formal letter.

14 Success

Verb forms

1 Delete the incorrect verb forms.

One summer the Grant family – David, Kate, and their three children – ~~have decided~~ / *decided* to follow their dream and travel round the world. They *have sold / sold* their house in Scotland, bought a caravan and a horse, and set *off / up*. They *thought / were thinking* that the whole trip *will / would* take two years. Now, six years later, they *have reached / reached* the west coast of the USA.

Their days *are starting / start* very early and they are on the road by six o'clock. After *travel / travelling* for about fifteen miles in the morning, they stop. The children *can't / mustn't* go to school, so in the afternoons they have lessons from their parents. They *doesn't / don't* watch television in the evenings. They *read usually / usually read* or play games.

They *have had / had* many adventures on their journey so far. While they *travelled / were travelling* through Italy the caravan broke *out / down*. Fortunately, a man *recognized / has recognized* the caravan from an article which David *has / had* written for a magazine. He took the family to his house and repaired the caravan. He also helped them when one of the children became ill and *must / had to* go to hospital.

In Mongolia someone tried *stealing / to steal* their horse and then in China they *were arrested / arrested*. The authorities *said / told* them that they shouldn't have received a visa and *made / let* them leave the country.

Now they are in California and they *are getting / get* ready to set off across the USA and Canada. For the last few days they *have visited / have been visiting* San Francisco. Eventually, they *are returning / will return* to Britain. They *are looking / look* forward to seeing Britain again, but they *aren't knowing / don't know* what life will be like. The trip hasn't been easy, but the Grants *did / would do* it all again if they *had / would have* the chance.

Causative *have*

2 Say what the Grant family had done.

EXAMPLE
caravan/ make/ Scotland
They had the caravan made in Scotland.

1 caravan/ repair/ Italy

  ....

2 photographs/ take/ Slovenia

  ....

3 the horse/ take/ America/ by plane

  ....

4 money/ send out/ to different places

  ....

Question forms

3 Mrs Grant is being interviewed in California. Make questions with the verbs in brackets in appropriate tenses.

Interviewer Where *were you living* ....
(live) before you started your journey?

Mrs Grant In Scotland.

Interviewer How long ....
(journey/ take) so far?

Mrs Grant Six years.

Interviewer How far ....
(travel) in a day?

Mrs Grant About 15 miles.

Interviewer What ....
(do) for the last few days?

Mrs Grant Visiting San Francisco.

Interviewer ....
(get) ready to cross the USA now?

Mrs Grant Yes, we are – and Canada.

Interviewer ....
(return) to Britain after that?

Mrs Grant Yes, eventually.

Interviewer ....
(look) forward to it?

Mrs Grant Yes, but we don't really know what to expect.

Interviewer ....
(do) it all again?

Mrs Grant Oh yes, we would.

Indirect questions

4 Here are some more questions for the Grants, but they don't know the answers. Complete the sentences.

EXAMPLE
What will life be like back in Britain?
They don't know what life will be like back in Britain.

1 Will we feel at home there?

  They wonder ....

2 Where will we live?

  They aren't sure ....

3 Has the place changed much?

  They have no idea ....

  ....

4 Can we sell our story to a newspaper?

  They aren't sure ....

  ....

5 What do other people think of us?

  They don't know ....

  ....

Prepositions

5 Put in the correct prepositions.

1 Joanne had tears *.in.* her eyes as she said goodbye ..... Eric. She knew that she was ..... love .... him.

2 I'll be ..... a conference ..... London ..... the weekend.

3 A lot ..... people like to get married ..... church even though they don't go ..... church regularly.

4 I don't live ..... the country these days. I've got a flat ..... town.

5 **A** How did the boss react ..... the news?
  B I think he was rather pleased ..... me.

6 What are we doing all this work ..... ? I can't see the point ..... it. I sometimes feel that life is passing us ..... .

7 Mr Allan was charged ..... assault because he fired a gun ..... two burglars. He had to pay one ..... them £2,000 ..... compensation ..... his injuries.

8 There was no water ..... the village so the women walked ..... the river ..... pots ..... their heads.

Vocabulary: *What is success?*

6 Find words in the wordsquare to match the definitions.

E	B	R	E	F	L	E	C	T	A
R	Y	H	N	R	S	B	I	F	E
E	F	U	N	E	R	A	L	A	O
C	F	M	A	S	W	C	L	R	S
T	L	D	R	O	D	K	N	E	M
O	I	R	T	L	O	W	E	W	L
R	B	U	N	V	L	A	P	E	S
Y	P	M	E	E	F	T	O	L	T
P	A	C	K	E	D	E	J	L	W
D	Z	E	H	P	A	R	I	S	H
A	M	A	Z	E	M	E	N	T	E
R	L	O	U	N	D	E	A	S	T

1   when someone is buried   *funeral*
2   quiet and unexciting   ....
3   an isolated place   ....
4   the area served by a church   ....
5   a priest's house   ....
6   decide   ....
7   great surprise   ....
8   think   ....
9   full of people   ....
10 goodbye   ....

Responding

7 Match the items in A and B to make dialogues.

A	B
I think that hunting should be banned.	Lucky you. I wish I could.
Ouch! You just hit me in the eye.	Well, thank you very much for coming. See you again.
Right. Shall we make a start on the cleaning?	Yes, I suppose so.
Did you have a nice Christmas?	Mmm, that would be nice.
I think I'll be off now.	Oh, I'm terribly sorry. Are you all right?
Shall I post these letters?	Not at all. Help yourself.
Well, it's my round. What would you like?	Certainly. I'm just putting you through.
Do you mind if I take some of this paper?	Not so bad. What about you?
Could I possibly speak to Mr Andrews, please?	Me neither.
I don't feel tired at all.	I'll have a gin and tonic, please.
I think I might have the day off tomorrow.	I'm afraid I have to disagree with you there.
Shall we have a night out?	Yes please, if you wouldn't mind.

Dialogues

8 Make the dialogues.

1   **A**   Suggest going abroad for a holiday this year.
    B   Accept and ask where A would like to go.
    A   Suggest a place.
    B   Accept – you've always wanted to go there.
    A   Offer to go to the travel agency and get some information.
    B   Thank A.

    A   *Shall we go abroad for a holiday this year?*

    B   *Yes, that would be nice. Where would you like to go?*

    A   ....

    B   ....

    A   ....
        ....

    B   ....

2   **A**   Phone to speak to Harry Brown.
    B   Tell A that Harry is not there. Offer to take a message.
    A   Identify yourself. Ask Harry to call you back.
    B   Ask if A will be in all day.
    A   Say whether you will.
    B   Say that you will pass the message on.

    A   ....

    B   ....
        ....

    A   ....
        ....

    B   ....

    A   ....

    B   ....

3   **A**   Say that you must go because you have a job interview.
    B   Wish A luck.
    A   Thank B and say how you feel about the interview.
    B   Reassure A and tell him/her not to worry.
    A   Thank B.

    A   ....
        ....

    B   ....

    A   ....
        ....

    B   ....

    A   ....

Vocabulary: Synonyms

9 Replace the underlined items with words or expressions from the box.

> your abilities a light sleeper was unfair to me
> messy suits want to avoid pulled it off
> very punctual improving a bully
> rather ill-mannered I'm very tense

1 I didn't think we would get that new contract, but we succeeded/ *pulled it off* .

2 Sarah's desk is always so untidy/ ....
   and she's not very polite/ ....

3 Colin is never late/ ....

4 I don't like that man. He treated me very badly/ .... when I first joined the team. He's always pushing people around/ ....

5 You'd better leave now, if you don't want to meet/ .... the director.

6 I didn't like this job at first but things are getting better/ .... now.

7 You'll find this job will certainly test what you can do/ ....

8 Do you think this colour looks good on/ .... me?

9 I need a quiet room. I'm easily woken up/ ....

10 I don't feel very relaxed/ .... today.

Vocabulary: Verbs

10 Complete the sentences with appropriate verbs in the correct form.

1 Fiona didn't ....*give*.... me a chance to explain.

2 I wanted to .... the late film on TV, but I .... asleep.

3 Could you .... me a favour, please?

4 I can't .... people who are always late.

5 I .... very nervous before my interview yesterday.

6 John .... down a good job in Hollywood and decided to .... for a quiet life in his home town.

7 Don't .... the boss too seriously. He .... angry very easily, but he never .... a grudge.

Writing: Your personal preface

11 Imagine you are writing a book setting down your ideas about life. Write a personal preface for the book. Use this format.

- your childhood and your family life
- your ambitions as a child
- how you changed as you grew up
- any important turning points which made you stop and think about your life
- how you feel about your life now

....
....
....
....
....
....
....
....
....
....
....
....
....
....
....
....
....
....
....
....
....
....
....
....
....
....
....
....

Grammar check 5

1 **Report what the people said. Use** *said, asked,* **or** *told.*

1 **Felicity** Are you going to lunch, Tim?
   Felicity asked Tim if he was going to lunch.

2 **Mr Clapham** Could you phone the travel
   agency, please, Molly?

   ....

3 **Samantha** I really enjoyed my holiday.

   ....

4 **Mrs Usher** I won't be late.

   ....

5 **Daniel** Don't leave the CDs on the floor, Bill.

   ....

6 **Bob** What do you do on Sundays, Kate?

   ....

7 **Jenny** Please don't leave, Rob.

   ....

8 **Teacher** Leave your boots outside, boys.

   ....

2 **Complete the sentences with** *said* **or** *told.*

1 I .... you to wait outside.

2 Johann .... he was leaving.

3 Valerie .... goodbye to her friends.

4 Have I .... you the joke about the dog?

5 Sally .... she was OK.

3 **Look at what these people did. What would
you say to them?**

1 Victoria left the cage open and the bird escaped.
   *You shouldn't have left the cage open. If you hadn't left
   it open the bird wouldn't have escaped.*

2 Terry put his drink on top of the TV. It was
   knocked over.

   ....

   ....

3 Sarah ate so much at a party that she was sick.

   ....

   ....

4 Ian didn't lock his bike up and it was stolen.

   ....

   ....

4 **Complete the text. Put the verbs in brackets
into the correct tense.**

———— COMING HOME ————

I woke up while the flight attendant .....*was serving*....
(serve) breakfast. The plane .... (cross)
the Channel, and when I .... (look) out
of the window, I .... (can) see ships far
below me. I .... (come) home after a
long time abroad. I .... (be) away for
twenty years. I .... (not know) what to
expect. I .... (wonder) whether things
.... (change) much.

The plane .... (land) and the bus
.... (take) us to the terminal building.
After I .... (collect) my luggage, I
.... (walk) out of the baggage hall. I
didn't know whether anyone .... (be)
there to meet me. But when I ....
(appear), I .... (have) a big surprise.
Almost half my family was there. It was wonderful.

'You .... (not recognize) the old town,'
my sister told me. 'Almost everything ....
.... (change) since you last ....
.... (see) it. They .... (build)
a new shopping centre near the park. The old town
hall .... (be destroyed) by a fire about
five years ago. They .... (build) a new
one at the moment. They .... (build) it
for the past three years in fact, but they
.... (not finish) it yet.'

I .... (be) back for nearly a month now.
And my sister was right. The place looks very
different, but strangely enough it still
.... (feel) the same, because the people
that I .... (love) are here. I ....
.... (leave) again in a few weeks' time,
but I know that even if I .... (be) away
for twenty years again, this .... always
.... (be) my home.

Answer key

Starting out

Exercise 1

a My name's Jack Roberts and I'm from South Africa. I *came* to Britain about eight years ago and *looked for* a job. I was working in a supermarket for a while, then one day I *met* Marie at a party. She *told* me that she *had* always *wanted* to travel and I *said* that I *would love* to travel, too, and, well one thing *led* to another and we *decided* to set up *Thrillseekers*. We*'ve made* about forty trips now, but we *know* that each trip *will bring* new experiences. Mind you, they *won't* all *be* pleasant experiences. Our vehicle *has been stolen* three times and we *were caught* in a war last year. But we always *survive*, so *don't worry*! You*'re going to have* a great time. So, *put* all your bags in the van. We*'re leaving* in half an hour.

b 1 *decided*
   2 *came*
   3 will bring, you're going to have, we're leaving
   4 looked for
   5 know
   6 we're leaving
   7 were caught
   8 would love
   9 put
   10 don't worry
   11 have made
   12 had ... wanted
   13 was working

Exercise 2

a
	A	B
1	*Have you ever*	*broken your leg?*
2	Do you	like classical music?
3	How long	have you known your best friend?
4	Who	phones you most often?
5	Did you	enjoy primary school?
6	Where	would you most like to live?
7	What kind of	food do you like best?
8	How many	brothers have you got?
9	Have you got	an e-mail address?
10	Can you	type?
11	Why	do you want to learn English?
12	What	are you doing this evening?
13	Would you	like to work abroad?
14	When	did you get up this morning?

Exercise 3

1 *Peter's tired but his dog isn't.*
2 If James doesn't want to go, I'd love to.
3 I wasn't sure if I'd seen her before.
4 I don't think Mark's been to New York, but I'm sure Stephanie has.
5 We've got two cars already, and we haven't got room for another.

Exercise 4

a
title	Ms
surname	Willis
first names	Barbara Rebecca
date of birth	3/2/77
address	45 King Street, Birmingham, B17 9YT
daytime tel no.	0121 384 7598
occupation	trainee manager
qualifications	3 A-levels, BA in Spanish and Economics
relevant experience	While at university I worked as a tour guide in London.
useful skills	I can speak French and Spanish. I can drive. I can cook.

1 Modern life

Exercise 1

1 I've been a teacher for three years.
2 **A** Where's David?
   B He's playing tennis.
3 I'm sorry, I don't understand what to do.
4 Have you ever been to New Zealand?
5 Richard worries about his work, he never relaxes, and he doesn't get home till 10.00.
6 She usually gets up at 7.00, but this week she's (been) getting up at 6.00.
7 I've written a letter, but I haven't sent it yet.
8 We've been working here since last year.
9 The government is cutting VAT, but increasing income tax.
10 You seem very tired – have you got/do you have a lot of work to do?

Exercise 2

Mike Welcome to *Travelwise*. I'm Mike Sawyer. Today I*'m talking* to Tony Hollands. In the last six years he *has been* on cycling trips all over the world. At the moment he *is organizing* a journey from Alaska to Mexico. Tell me, why *are you planning* this trip?

Tony I *don't know*, really. I've *loved* cycling since I was young, and I*'ve always wanted* to go to North America.

Mike *Are you doing* a lot of extra cycling at the moment?

Tony Well, I normally *cycle* about 30 miles a day, but now I*'m doing* about 80.

Mike You*'ll need* £5,000 for your journey, and you *have raised* £3,000 already. How?

Tony Well, I've *just sold* my car and I*'ve written* to over 100 companies. Twenty of them *have decided* to sponsor me so far. And I*'m trying* to sell the story of the trip to a newspaper at the moment.

Mike *Have you got/Do you have* any advice for listeners who *want* to do something like this?

Tony If you *haven't done* a long bicycle journey before, go on a short one first. If you *like* it, you *can* go anywhere. I *have had* a wonderful time for the last six years!

Exercise 3

1 **A** We*'re going* to Paris tomorrow.
   B Oh, yes. Where *are you staying*?
   A At a little hotel in Montmartre. We always *stay* there.
2 **A** Hi. I'm Isik. I'm from Turkey.
   B Hello. What *are you doing* here in England? Are you on holiday?
   A No, I*'m studying* English at a language school.
   B Where *are you living*? With a family?
   A No I*'m sharing* a room at the school with another girl.
   B Where *do you live* in Turkey?
   A In Ankara. I*'ve got/have* a flat in my parents' house.
3 **A** What *do you do*?
   B Well I'm a student actually, but I've got a temporary job for the summer.
   A Oh, yes. What *are you doing*?
   B I*'m working* at a shoe factory.

Exercise 4

a 1 *What do you do?*
   2 How long have you lived at your present address?
   3 How many times have you been abroad?
   4 Is it raining at the moment?
   5 What time do you usually get up?
   6 What are you wearing today?
   7 Have you ever met anyone famous?

Exercise 5

1 *noun*
2 /waɪnd/
3 the first syllable /ˈɪmplɪkeɪt/
4 a garbage can/trash can
5 *a close shave* – close
   to have an idea – idea
   to be a wet blanket – wet
   to pick a fight with – pick
6 *John has flu.*
7 to miss
8 *practice* is a noun, *practise* is a verb

Exercise 6

adjective	comparative
fast	*faster*
fine	finer
friendly	friendlier
informal	more informal
good	better
bad	worse

Exercise 7

1 Most adjectives *add -er*.
2 Adjectives that end in *-e* add *-r*.
3 Adjectives that end in consonant + *-y* change to *-ier*.
4 Adjectives with 2 or more syllables (except where the second syllable is *-y*) add *more*.
5 Some adjectives like *good* and *bad* are irregular.

Exercise 8

Possible answers
1 I'm *not as fit as* I was two years ago.
2 I'm *just as slim as* when I was 14.
3 I'm *older than* my best friend.
4 This exercise is *just as difficult as* exercise 4.
5 My work this year is *not as good as* last year.
6 Young people are *just as polite as* they used to be.
7 Manners are *worse than* they were 20 years ago.
8 Dogs are *nicer than* cats.

9 The streets were *just as clean and tidy as* they are now.
10 The roads are *busier and more dangerous than* they were when I was a child.
11 Cars are *faster and more powerful than* they were then.

Exercise 9

1 The media *like to make out* that young people are all criminals or drug takers or *what have you*, but I think that a lot of today's problems are *down to* the media themselves.
2 It's so noisy here, I *can hardly hear myself think*.
3 I *must admit* that life is freer today, and I don't think *there's anything wrong with that*. But we have to remember that freedom *cuts both ways* – people are also free to be less considerate if they want.
4 When I was at school, hitting a teacher *was unthinkable*, but you read about it all the time in the newspapers *these days*. I think things have got worse *on the whole*.
5 I *wouldn't say* that life is better now, but it's certainly a lot faster, *I'll give you that*.

Exercise 10

1	*just*	6	knife
2	word	7	your
3	weather	8	people
4	suggestion	9	thing
5	future	10	talk

Exercise 11

Possible answers

Wendy Where do you work, Barry?
Barry I work for an airline.
Wendy *Oh, really. What do you do?*
Barry I'm a mechanical engineer.
Wendy *What does that involve?*
Barry I check the planes before they take off.
Wendy *What hours do you work?*
Barry Well, it depends. We work shifts, you see, but I like to get the late shift from 5.00 till midnight, if I can.
Wendy *Why do you like working late?*
Barry Well, then I have the day free. And anyway, a lot of the other guys have families so they prefer to be at home in the evenings.
Wendy *How do you get to work?*
Barry I go by car. Well, I have to, because the last train goes before I finish.
Wendy *Do you like working for the airline?*
Barry Yes, it's great. And I get cheap travel with the airline, too.
Wendy *Do you go abroad much?*
Barry Yes, I go abroad two or three times a year.
Wendy *Wow! That sounds fun!*

Exercise 12

1	sociable	6	anxious
2	talkative	7	suspicious
3	self-conscious	8	competitive
4	calm	9	co-operative
5	optimistic	10	miserable

Exercise 13

Possible answers
1 I'm *usually* late for appointments.
2 I *sometimes* stay in bed till 11.00 on Sundays.
3 I *always* go out on Saturday nights.
4 I can *never* remember people's names.
5 I *usually* send postcards when I'm on holiday.
6 I don't *often* fall asleep in lessons.
7 Politicians don't *always* say what they really mean.
8 I have *always* wanted to be a singer.
9 My English grammar is *sometimes* correct.
10 I've *hardly ever* got a lot of money in the bank.

Exercise 14

Possible answers

Flat 1
6 Maiden Road
Manchester
M9 7TR

11 November

Dear June
Just a quick note to let you know that I've moved. As you can see I'm now living in Manchester. I*'m studying at* the university here. I *don't live on the* university campus. I've got *a flat in the city*, but I *usually go into the university* every day, because *I like to work in the library*.
I *get in at* 10 o'clock, but then *I often stay till 9 or 10 at night*. I *usually cycle to the* university, but *I get the bus* if it's raining. I'm really *enjoying myself*. The course is *interesting*, and Manchester's *a great city*. There's lots *to do*.
I hope you're well. Bye for now.
Love
Sandra

2 Fortune

Exercise 1

has/have	present perfect
had	past perfect/past simple
questions with *did*	past simple
was/were	past continuous/past simple
past participles	present perfect and past perfect
-ing forms	past continuous
negatives with *didn't*	past simple

Exercise 2

1 Susan isn't here. She*'s gone* to the shops.
2 I *went* to the park yesterday.
3 He was only a minute late, but the train *had gone*.
4 They *went* on holiday three times last year.
5 **A** Where's Matthew?
  B He*'s gone* to London for the day.
6 The car broke down while I *was going* to the supermarket.

Exercise 3

1 **A** What *were you doing* at 8 o'clock last night?
  B I was watching TV.
2 **A** *Had you met* Suzanna before?
  B Yes, I had. I met her about five years ago in Madrid.
3 **A** *Has he written* that letter yet?
  B No, he hasn't. He says he'll write it tomorrow.
4 **A** *Did you see* the accident?
  B No, I didn't, but my son saw it.
5 **A** Where *was he* when the accident happened?
  B He was standing over there by the gate.
6 **A** *Have you had* lunch yet?
  B No, we haven't. Would you like to join us?
7 **A** How long *had he lived/been living* in India when you met him?
  B Oh, I think he'd lived there for over 20 years.

Exercise 4

Elaine risks her life almost every day. She's a stunt woman. She does the dangerous parts in films. 'I*'ve been* a stunt woman for ten years now and I suppose that in those ten years I *'ve done* almost everything. I*'ve jumped* out of windows, I*'ve crashed* cars, and I*'ve broken* most of the bones in my body at least once.

But I suppose the most dangerous thing that I *have* ever *done* was in a film called *Madness*. In one scene I *had to* jump over a wall on a motorbike. Well, unfortunately I *got* it wrong and I *didn't jump* over the wall, I *crashed* straight into it. I *broke* both my legs and three fingers. I *haven't worked* with motorbikes since then.'

Exercise 5

Five years ago I *had to* make a big decision. At the time I *was working* for a small engineering company. However, things *were not going* very well for the company and it *was losing* money. One day while we *were working* as normal, the boss *told* us that the company *was* bankrupt. We *were* all unemployed.
That lunch-time we *went* to the pub as usual. We were all very depressed. I *had worked* at the company for over fifteen years and some of the people *had been* there longer than that. Well, of course we *talked* about the problem. Then the landlord of the pub *heard* the news. He *said*: 'Why don't you buy the company?' At first we all *laughed*, but then we *started* to discuss it properly. We *knew* the problems. The company *had lost* a lot of customers, because it *hadn't developed* new products. But finally we *decided* to go for it.
So we *bought* the company. The first few years *were* very difficult. But we *worked* hard and we *had* a bit of luck. We finally *turned* the corner three years ago. Since then we *have done* pretty well. Last year we *took on* four new people and so far this year we *have taken on* another ten. It *was* a big gamble six years ago, but I *haven't regretted* it for a minute.

Exercise 6

1	*juggernaut*, JCB
2	surgery
3	ironmonger's
5	rollerblading
4	wrist
6	postpone
7	out of date
8	collided
9	heal up
10	flew
11	pieces
12	flicked through
13	a menace
14	the other day

Exercise 7

parts of the body	parts of an aeroplane	places
mouth	*fuselage*	clinic
lung	seatbelt	resort
pelvis	aisle	swamp
jaw	window	jungle
toe	cockpit	desert
throat	wing	plain
elbow	tail	marsh
ankle	undercarriage	suburb
forehead	nose	
nose		
thigh		

Exercise 8

When we were *on holiday* in the United States last year we decided to *go for the weekend* to the Grand Canyon. We *set off for* the airport early in the morning and checked in. Tim was *very excited*, but I *had a feeling that* I wasn't going to enjoy it. When I saw the plane, I nearly died. It was very small and only *took six passengers* and there wasn't much room *to spare*. But we got into the plane, *fastened our seatbelts*, and took off. The first part of the flight was OK, but over the Canyon itself we flew into some *terrible turbulence*. The little plane rolled and *bounced* from side to side. Tim was *on the other side of* the aisle and *he was groaning*: 'How much longer?' We were both quite ill by the time we landed, but *we survived*. I just wanted *to forget* everything about the flight. Then the pilot said: 'OK, folks. See you tomorrow for the *flight home.*'

Exercise 9

1 She *used to* smoke.
2 She *didn't use to* play the violin.
3 She used to live in Cambridge.
4 She didn't use to be a chemist.
5 She used to listen to a lot of pop music.
6 She didn't use to have a cat.
7 She didn't use to go skiing.
8 She used to drive to the centre of the city.

Exercise 10

Charlie	*Well, well, well!* Bill Needham!
Bill	Charlie Cross! *I don't believe it.* What are you doing here?
Charlie	Well, I work just round the corner from here. *It's great to see you again*, Bill. When did we last meet?
Bill	Oh, *it must be nearly ten years*, I would think.
Charlie	*Doesn't time fly?* Ten years, eh. Anyway, *what are you up to* these days?
Bill	I work for a TV company.
Charlie	Wow! *That sounds exciting!* You always wanted to be in show business, *as I recall.* Didn't you use to play the drums with a band?
Bill	Yes, that's right. We even made a record, but *things didn't work out* and *the band split up.*
Charlie	I'm sorry to hear that. I thought you played pretty well.
Bill	Well, *these things happen.*
Charlie	Yes, *I suppose so.*
Bill	*What about you?* What are you doing?
Charlie	Me? I work in an electronics shop. Well, actually I was unemployed until about six months ago, but then *this job came along* and it's really exciting. So I'm really happy about that.
Bill	Yes, *I'm sure you must be.* Look, do you fancy going for a drink?
Charlie	Sure. There's a place near here that has really good beer.
Bill	*Sounds great!* Come on.

Exercise 11

1 I'd never played golf before, but I *had a go* and I really enjoyed it.
2 I'm afraid profits last year *fell short of* what we expected. So I think we'll have to *give up* the plans for a new office.
3 **A** What *do you do for a living*?
   B Well, I *started out* as a teacher but now I work for the government.
4 I wasn't sure about going back to college, but in the end I *went for it* and I'm glad to say that it *paid off.*
5 **A** Do you fancy going out for a meal on Friday?
   B Yes. I'll *talk it over with* Sally and get back to you.

Exercise 12

Jim Reid liked diving. *While* he was diving in a lake on a golf course *one day*, he made a discovery *that* would change his life, *because* in the lake he found thousands of golf balls. *When* he looked at them he found that they were in perfect condition. *After* thinking about it carefully he decided to dive for golf balls full time. *Soon* he had his own factory *and* his golf balls were used all over the world. *Now* Jim Reid is a millionaire.

Exercise 13

George de Mestral liked hunting. One day in 1951, while he was hunting, some small seeds stuck to his trousers. When he got home he tried to pull the seeds off, but it was very difficult. He got out a magnifying glass and looked closely at one of the seeds. After a while he noticed small hooks on the seed. The seeds gave George de Mestral an idea and he started to develop Velcro. Six years later, his own factory was producing Velcro. Velcro is used for thousands of products and it has made its inventor very rich.

Grammar check 1

Exercise 1

1 *Where are you going?*
   We aren't going to the cinema.
2 Where has George been?
   He hasn't been to the dentist's.
3 Where did you use to work?
   I didn't use to work in a bank.
4 Where was Claudia last week?
   She wasn't on holiday.
5 What time did you leave the party?
   I didn't leave at midnight.
6 Where were you sitting?
   We weren't sitting by the window.
7 When does Jason get home?
   He doesn't get home at half past four.
8 What are you watching?
   I'm not watching a film.

Exercise 2

1 Where were you *going* with Simon?
2 Where does Mrs Smart *go* on Fridays?
3 Kate has *gone* home.
4 We *went* bowling yesterday.
5 Jim always *goes* to the football match on Saturdays.
6 Are you *going* out with Mary?

Exercise 3

A Why *do* you *want* to work for South of the Border Expeditions?
B Well, I *'ve loved* travelling since I *was* a student back in the 1980s, and I *'ve always wanted* to work with people.
A Which countries *have* you *visited*?
B I *'ve travelled* round most of Europe and Latin America, and I *know* Mexico very well. I *spent* a year there before I *started* college.
A What languages *do* you *speak*?
B Well, my Spanish is pretty good, and I *'m studying* Portuguese in evening classes at the moment. I *tried* Russian too for a while, but it *was* too hard so I *gave up*!
A What's the worst thing that *has* ever *happened* to you on your travels?
B Once I *flew* in a little six-seater – I *had* never *been* in a small plane before – and a huge storm *hit* us. I *thought* it was the end. When we finally *landed* we *were* all *shaking* like a leaf.
A *Have* you *organized* an expedition yourself?
B Yes …

Exercise 4

While I *was coming* home three months ago, I *found* a wallet. I *saw* it as I *was walking* through the park. It *was* on a bench. I suppose it *had* fallen out of someone's pocket, while they *were sitting* on the bench. I *looked* in the wallet. It *contained* a lot of money but there was no name in it, so I *took* it to the police station. Nobody *had reported* a lost wallet, so the police station *kept* it. I *have phoned* the police station three times since then, but nobody *has claimed* the wallet yet. If nobody claims it soon, it will be mine.

3 Your future

Exercise 1

1 What time *will they be here*? They won't be here by 7.00.
2 When *are we leaving*? We're not/We aren't leaving today.
3 What *is he going to study* at university? He's not/He isn't going to study Geography.
4 How long *will you be away*? I won't be away for four days.
5 Where *are they going to live*? They're not/They aren't going to live in Canada.
6 When *is she meeting* Mr Brown? She's not/She isn't meeting him at 10.00.

Exercise 2

1 *I'm going to retire. I think I'll buy a cottage.*
2 We're going to look for new jobs, but it won't be easy.
3 I think I'm going to look for something here, but if I can't find anything, I'll probably emigrate to Australia.
4 We're going to start a training course next week. We're sure it will be useful.
5 I'm going to join the army, but I think I'm going to take a holiday first.
6 We're going to travel round the world. We're leaving on Monday.

Exercise 3

1 **A** What *are you doing* this weekend?
   B I'm *going* to a concert in London. Do you fancy coming?
   A Maybe – I *'ll let* you know.
   B OK. We *'re getting* the train at 5.45.
2 **A** Kate's seventeen today.
   B *Is she going* to learn to drive?
   A Yes, she *'s having* her first driving lesson tomorrow.
   B I hope she *'ll pass* the test first time.

3   **A** I haven't received that report yet.
   B OK, I'*ll fax* you a copy.
   A Thanks. I'*ll give* you a call when I've read it.
   B Fine, but I'*m having* lunch out so I *won't be* back till two.
   A That's OK. I *won't finish* it before then.
4   **A** What *are you going to* do when you leave school?
   B I'*m going to* go to university. What about you?
   A Me too, but I'd like to go abroad first.
   B Oh yes? Ken'*s going to* do that. He'*s going to* work in Canada for a year.

Exercise 4

Possible answers
1 The African elephant *may become extinct.*
2 I may pass my next test.
3 Robots will probably take over the world.
4 I'll probably buy a new computer this year.
5 I might win the lottery.
6 The power of the United States will probably become even greater.
7 There may be life on other planets.
8 It probably won't be sunny tomorrow.
9 There probably won't be a major war in the next ten years.
10 I might have a party for my next birthday.

Exercise 5

1 If the population gets younger there will be more crime and drug problems.
2 If large numbers of people start moving to find food there will be racial conflicts.
3 If the rain forest is destroyed many animals will become extinct.
4 If people have computers and videophones there will be no need to go to offices.
5 If petroleum runs out it won't matter.
6 If the number of old people increases the cost of medical care will rise.

Exercise 6

cold weather	wet weather	fine weather
ice	sleet	bright
sleet	fog	dry
wind	dull	warm
storm	wind	clear
snow	hail	sunshine
frost	cloudy	
	storm	
	thunder	
	cool	
	rain	

Exercise 7

Possible answers
1 *It's windy at the moment but I think it should calm down later.*
2 Its sunny at the moment but it might get cloudy later.
3 It's cold at the moment but it will probably get warmer later.
4 It's raining at the moment but it might become drier later.
5 It's dull at the moment but it might brighten up later.

Exercise 8

1 Shall we *go* for a walk?
2 Do you fancy *hiring* a video?
3 Do you want *to buy* a take-away meal?
4 How about *asking* Sam and Martha for lunch?
5 Would you like *to cook* a meal?
6 Why don't we *sit* and watch TV?
7 We'd better be *getting* ready.
8 What about *buying* a bottle of wine?
9 Let's *have* a party.
10 You'd better give Jenny a ring.

Exercise 9

/θ/	/ð/
bath	these
thin	other
	weather

/ʃ/	/tʃ/
wish	which
wash	watch
station	

/s/	/z/
race	lose
kiss	noisy
loose	

/ʒ/	/dʒ/
fuselage	general
measure	juice
	hedge

Exercise 10

Possible answers
1   **A** *Shall we go to the park?*
   B *But it's raining.*
   A *Yes, but it might brighten up soon.*
   B *Well, let's wait half an hour.*
2   **A** Shall we have a game of tennis?
   B What's the weather like?
   A It's sunny.
   B OK, let's get ready.
3   **A** Shall we go somewhere and have a picnic tomorrow?
   B Yes, I'd love to. Shall we invite Carol?
   A Yes, that's a good idea.
   B I'll give her a ring.
4   **A** Shall we go home now?
   B But it's very foggy.
   A We'll drive carefully.
   B Let's wait, it may get brighter soon.
5   **A** Why don't we go into town?
   B The car's isn't working.
   A We could go by bus.
   B OK, what time does it go?
6   **A** How about going skiing next week?
   B We can't, my grandparents are coming.
   A Oh, that's a pity.
   B What about going the week after?
   A Yes, OK. Let's arrange it.
7   **A** Shall we go for a walk?
   B Is it warm out?
   A No, you'll need a jumper.
   B I think I'll stay at home then.

Exercise 11

1   **A** How *would* you spend a year out?
   B Oh, I'*d* go abroad.
2 It'*ll* be sunny tomorrow.
3   **A** *Would* you like a sandwich?
   B That *would* be nice.
   A OK. I'*ll* make you one.
4   **A** What *would* your perfect partner be like?
   B Oh, she'*d* have to be intelligent most of all.
5   **A** *Would* you prefer to eat in tonight?
   B No, I'*d* rather go out.
   B OK. I'*ll* book a table.
6   **A** How *would* you spend your ideal day?
   B I'*d* spend it with my family.

Exercise 12

1 People will be able to work at home. However, they may still choose to go to work.
2 Although people care about the rain forest, it is still being destroyed.
3 The earth's climate is getting warmer. However, we don't fully understand why.
4 Although many species are in danger, we are still destroying natural habitats.

4 Relationships

Exercise 1

1 The woman *who* lives next door is a dentist.
2 The hotel *which* caught fire has been rebuilt.
3 She has a job *which* most people would hate.
4 Tony works for a company *which* makes fridges.
5 That's the dog *which* tried to bite me.
6 He's the kind of person *who* loves an argument.
7 The government was defeated in the elections *which* took place last week.
8 Did the assistant *who* served you have blonde hair?
9 You should choose the clothes *which* suit your personality.
10 I don't know the people *who* live there.

Exercise 2

Possible answers
1 A nurse *is someone who is trained to look after sick or injured people.*
2 A digital watch is a watch which shows the time by numbers rather than hands.
3 Spaghetti is a type of pasta which is very popular in Italy.
4 A snake is a long animal which doesn't have legs.
5 Extroverts are lively, cheerful people who like to be with others.
6 A wardrobe is a large cupboard which is used for storing clothes.
7 An optimist is a person who always expects the best to happen.
8 Socks are things which you wear on your feet.

Exercise 4

1 Here are some of the photos ~~that~~ we took.
2 This is the hotel ~~which~~ we stayed at.
3 These are two people ~~that~~ we met on the plane.
4 This is the waiter who served at our table.
5 That's the nightclub ~~that~~ we went to.
6 These are the two girls ~~that~~ I told you about.
7 This is the family that was in the next room.
8 This is the place that was in the postcard that I sent you.
9 Here's the tour guide who met us at the airport.
10 Would you like to see the video ~~which~~ we made?

Exercise 5

1 The man *that* robbed a bank has been sent to prison.
2 The car (that) we've bought has air-conditioning.
3 The man that phoned me yesterday was a police officer.
4 She stayed in the hotel (that) I recommended.
5 The computer (that) they bought isn't powerful enough.
6 The restaurant (that) I went to has a fixed price menu.
7 The mountains (that) we saw were covered in snow.
8 The tree that fell on my house will be removed tomorrow.
9 We went to the film (that) you told us about.
10 He wants the house that has three bedrooms.

Exercise 6

My aunt is one of *those* people who can talk to *anyone* about anything. If she goes to a party *where* she doesn't know any of the people, she just walks *up* to the first person that she *sees* and introduces *herself*. And yet she doesn't seem to *talk* about deeply *important* things like politics or *religion*. She always starts *off* with something very *obvious* like the other person's job. Very *soon* she's talking as if she's *known* the other person for years. I *asked* her once what her *secret* was. She *said* that the most important thing in a conversation was *listening*. People love to talk about *themselves*, so if you *allow* them to do so, it's very easy to *keep* a conversation going. You have to listen *carefully* and ask *questions*. And you have to look *interested*, too. So don't keep *looking* at other things in the room while you're talking *to* someone.
Another thing *that* I've noticed is that she often *pays* people compliments. She says: 'I like your *hair*. Which hairdresser do you *go* to?' or 'You look very *well*. Have you been *on* holiday?' Friendly *messages* like this seem to provide an easy *way* into a conversation.

Exercise 7

1 Sarah *told* me a very good joke yesterday. I hadn't *heard* it before.
2 **A** Did you *introduce* Dennis to Mrs Novak at the party?
   B Yes, I did and they *had* a long conversation.
   A Did he *tell* you what they *talked* about?
   B He *said* that she *asked* him a lot of questions about the new manager.
3 Thank you for *expressing* your opinions, ladies and gentlemen. I have *listened* to all the arguments and I shall *give* you my answer tomorrow.
4 **A** I don't think we'll *get* the results that we want if we *follow* the rules.
   B Well, I'm afraid I can't *agree* with you there. It will *send* the wrong message to head office. We'll have to *think* of something else.
5 **A** Can you *speak* Italian?
   B Not really – I *nod* my head a lot but I don't actually *understand* much.

Exercise 8

1 We last met ten years ago, *didn't we?*
2 Let's have something to eat, *shall we?*
3 You can sing, *can't you?*
4 Colin lives in Paris now, *doesn't he?*
5 James used to have a beard, *didn't he?*
6 Fiona isn't going out with Fred, *is she?*
7 I'm always late, *aren't I?*
8 You'd like a drink, *wouldn't you?*
9 Sybil and Phil haven't moved yet, *have they?*
10 We won't see you for a while, *will we?*

Exercise 9

1 Paul has posted the letter, hasn't he?
2 Sally can drive, can't she?
3 You don't still work at the shop, do you?
4 It's my turn next, isn't it?
5 You wouldn't want to live in the country, would you?
6 Your sister works in TV, doesn't she?
7 You did lock the front door, didn't you?
8 We aren't going out tonight, are we?
9 You were born in the States, weren't you?
10 The director won't be at the meeting, will he?

Exercise 10

1 pot	what
2 cat	have
3 been	mean
4 feel	scene
5 pull	wool
6 bark	half
7 fool	rule
8 sit	busy
9 heart	bath
10 caught	short

Exercise 11

We write:	**We say:**
20 June	*the twentieth of June*
1 September	the first of September
5 March	the fifth of March
19 December	the nineteenth of December
2 February	the second of February
12 November	the twelfth of November
10 May	the tenth of May
23 July	the twenty-third of July
24 April	the twenty-fourth of April
30 January	the thirtieth of January

Exercise 13

Across
4 pillowcase
7 asleep
8 decorations
10 Father Christmas
17 turkey
18 crackers
19 lights

Down
1 Pole
2 *Lang*
3 Boxing Day
4 presents
5 Eve
6 sales
9 over
10 family
11 chimney
12 reindeer
13 sport
14 church
15 cards
16 angel

Exercise 14

a 1 general statement
  2 examples
  3 advice

b 1 People in Britain ...
  2 If you are invited ...
  3 Flowers, a bottle of wine, ...

5 The law

Exercise 1

1 *The latest crime figures have been published.*
2 Most crimes are committed by young people.
3 More people were sent to prison last year.
4 An increase had been predicted (by the press).
5 People will be worried (by the figures).
6 The government are going to be attacked by the media.
7 The report is being studied (by a special committee).
8 Their ideas will be presented next month.
9 Some big changes would be accepted.

Exercise 2

Reporter Can you give us any information about the incident?
Inspector Well, not a lot at the moment. A woman *was murdered* at about 6 o'clock last night. She *was found* by a cleaner at seven this morning. We *were called* to the scene by a neighbour. The woman *was identified* as Mrs Sarah Parker by the cleaner.
Reporter What have you done so far?
Inspector The room *has been searched* for clues. Some fingerprints *have been discovered* on a door handle. The body *has been taken* to the mortuary. A murder weapon *has not been found* yet.
Reporter What will happen now?
Inspector The body *will be examined* by a pathologist. The fingerprints *will be fed* into a computer. Witnesses *will be interviewed*. More information *will be given* to the newspapers as soon as we have it. Thank you, that's all for now.

Exercise 3

Over £1 million *was stolen* from a bank in West London yesterday. Three people *entered* the bank at 10.30. The bank staff *were forced* to lie on the floor, while the thieves *put* the money into bags. The staff *were tied up* and the thieves *escaped* in a blue car. The incident *was filmed* by the bank's security cameras. The car *was found* four hours later in the river.

A dog *was killed* and its owner *was injured* yesterday when they *were hit* by a car on a pedestrian crossing. The car *didn't stop*, but it *was identified* by two witnesses as a red VW. An ambulance *was called* to the scene and the man *was taken* to the Royal Hospital. Last night his condition *was described* as 'serious'. The police *believe* that the car *was stolen*.

A shop and several offices *were damaged* yesterday when a bomb *exploded*. Nobody *was hurt* in the explosion, which *happened* at about five o'clock. A telephone warning *was given* to the police, but they *didn't reach* the bomb in time. It *was planted* by a group called Freedom International. Two months ago a member of the same group *was shot* when she *tried* to put a bomb on a train. The police *said* that today's explosion was *intended* to show that the group was still active.

Exercise 4

a 1 *arson*
   2 kidnapping
   3 speeding
   4 drug trafficking
   5 shoplifting
b 1 Burglary *is when someone breaks into a house and steals things.*
   2 Vandalism is when someone breaks or damages something for fun.
   3 Blackmail is when someone demands money with threats.
   4 Smuggling is bringing something into a country illegally.
   5 Assault is when someone attacks and hurts another person.
   6 Hijacking is when someone forces a pilot to fly a plane to a different destination.

Exercise 5

1 The judge will *pass* sentence tomorrow.
2 I don't think the people who were found guilty *committed* the crime.
3 How did the detective *solve* the crime?
4 If you *break* the law, you might be *sent* to prison.
5 The witness had to *give* evidence for over two hours.
6 And then he was *questioned* for another two hours.
7 The woman was *tried* for murder but she was found not guilty.
8 My house was *burgled* while I was on holiday.

Exercise 6

In 1994 an 18-*year*-old American teenager, Todd Newman, was *arrested* in Singapore. With a *group* of friends he had *vandalized* several cars. For this *crime* he was beaten six times with a *cane*. He was also sent to *prison* for two months and *fined* £1,400. The case created a lot of debate in the *USA*. Some people felt that the *punishment* was too hard. They felt it was wrong to *treat* people like this. But other people *looked* at the clean streets and *law-abiding* society of Singapore and compared it to their own cities where *drug traffickers* control the streets and decent people are *afraid* to go out after dark. We send young *thugs* to homes where they have their *own* televisions. We give them *rewards* like computers and *trips* to other countries, which many ordinary families can't *afford*. We try to understand them, because they have been *neglected* or abused in their *childhood*. We try to give them a *purpose* in life. In Singapore, on the other hand, the law is *strict*. People are expected to know the *difference* between right and wrong and criminals can *expect* tough treatment. But which society has got *more* crime? And remember that every crime has a *victim*. More robbery, more assault, more *vandalism* means more victims – more people who are *hurt*. If we look at it this *way*, which society really treats people *better*?

Exercise 7

1 Baggage *must not be left* unattended at any time. Any unattended baggage *will be removed* and *may be destroyed*.
2 Vehicles *must not be parked* on the yellow lines. This entrance *must be kept* clear at all times.
3 The camera *should not be left* in direct sunlight. It *should be kept* in its case when not in use.
4 Essays *should be placed* in the tray. Marked essays *can be collected* on Friday.
5 Hard hats *must be worn* at all times. Hats for visitors *can be obtained* at reception.

Exercise 8

Insurance clerk Well, can I take some details of the incident, please? *When was the car broken into?*
Motorist Three days ago on 4 March.
Insurance clerk *Where was it parked* at the time?
Motorist In Gresham Street.
Insurance clerk *When did you notice the damage?*
Motorist When I came back to the car at about three o'clock.
Insurance clerk *How long was it/had it been parked there?*
Motorist Oh, it had been there about two hours, I suppose.
Insurance clerk *What damage was done/had been done* to the vehicle?
Motorist The window had been smashed.
Insurance clerk And *had anything been stolen?*
Motorist Yes, the radio had been stolen?
Insurance clerk *Has the incident been reported* to the police?
Motorist Yes, it has.
Insurance clerk *When did you report it?*
Motorist I reported it immediately.
Insurance clerk And *has the vehicle been repaired yet?*
Motorist I took it to the garage, but it hasn't been done yet.
Insurance clerk So *when will it be repaired?*
Motorist Tomorrow.

Exercise 9

1	worth	birth
2	heard	occurred
3	fir	fur
4	stir	prefer
5	learn	turn
6	world	curled
7	sir	curl
8	bird	girl
9	worm	burn
10	third	word

Exercise 10

1 He was sentenced *to* three years *in* prison *for* assault.
2 Many people thought that the sentence was an insult *to* the victim.
3 The lorry was parked *on* a bend and other vehicles couldn't get *past*.
4 The sound *of* the shot came *from* the direction *of* the living room.
5 I was *in* bed *at* the time of the murder. I had gone *to* bed early because I was tired.
6 When I looked *out of* the window they were standing *in* the middle *of* the garden next *to* the statue.
7 Three weeks ago we went *to* their house *for* dinner.
8 I saw you. You had the gun *in* your hand. You shot him *in* the head and then you tried to get rid *of* the gun.

Exercise 11

First the scene of the crime is sealed off. *Then/After that* nothing is touched *until* the forensic scientists and the photographer arrive. *The first job* is to photograph the scene. *After that/Then* evidence is collected. *Finally* the evidence is taken away to the laboratory *where* it will be examined.

Exercise 12

A car has been parked on a bend on double yellow lines. First a sticker is put on the windscreen by a traffic warden. Then she calls the tow-away truck on her mobile phone. When the tow-away truck arrives the first job is to check the car for any damage and this is recorded. After that the car is lifted onto the tow-away truck and taken to the car pound. Finally, the car is collected by the owner.

Grammar check 2

Exercise 1

1 You haven't eaten, *have you?*
2 We went there on holiday, *didn't we?*
3 Lydia always looks good, *doesn't she?*
4 Let's go dancing, *shall we?*
5 I'm going with you, *aren't I?*
6 Jack can't ski, *can he?*
7 Those people shouldn't be here, *should they?*
8 You won't be late, *will you?*

Exercise 2

1 *These computers are made by an American company.*
2 The program was written by Compuspeak.
3 A disk has been left in the disk drive.
4 Backup copies should be made.
5 These machines mustn't be used by children.

Exercise 3

A man *fell* 220 feet from a tower and *survived*. He *was saved* because he *landed* on a car roof. The car's roof *was crushed*, but the man just *got up* and *walked* away. His elbow *was broken*, but otherwise he *wasn't injured*. Later the man *was taken* to hospital by his father and his elbow *was X-rayed*.

Exercise 4

1 'What *are you doing* tomorrow?'
   'We're *going* to town.'
2 'I'm *going* to watch a film in a minute.'
   'Good idea. I'*ll* join you.'
3 'I think I'*ll* have a bath.'
   'Don't be long. The Robinsons *are coming* at eight.'
4 In the future people *will have* computers as small as a watch.

Exercise 5

1 *They went to a café which had tables outside.*
2 The forest which the scientists were studying was going to be cut down.
3 The woman who you met yesterday is a millionaire.
4 She asked the man who lives in the flat upstairs to be quieter.
5 The plane which was hijacked was going to Rio.
6 The boy who set fire to the factory was arrested.
7 Did you hire the video which I told you about?
8 The men who kidnapped the President's son escaped.

Exercise 6

2, 3, and 7 should be ticked.

Exercise 7

1 *It will probably be cold tomorrow.*
2 We could be a bit late.
3 The lecture may not start on time.
4 Mike probably won't be there.
5 We might get a lift home.

6 Travel

Exercise 1

1 If you *lose* your credit card, we *will send* a new one within 24 hours.
2 If you *require* medical help, we *will contact* a local doctor or hospital.
3 An air ambulance *will be provided* if you *have to* be brought back to this country.
4 If you *are arrested*, our legal team *will give* you advice.
5 An interpreter *will be provided* if you *don't/do not understand* the local language.
6 We *will pay* your legal costs if you *are charged* with an offence.
7 But if you *are fined*, we *won't/will not pay* the fine for you.
8 However, we *will lend* you the money for the fine if you *haven't got/don't have* enough.

Exercise 2

1 If they weren't afraid of flying, they'd go abroad.
2 If Frank had more time, he'd read a lot.
3 I wouldn't feel embarrassed at parties if I knew what to say.
4 Peter wouldn't be overweight if he didn't eat so much.
5 If Sarah didn't hate school, she would study harder.
6 The office wouldn't be cold if people didn't leave the door open.
7 If I could speak Japanese I could/would be able to translate this.

Exercise 3

1 **A** Good morning. This is Capital Radio. It's 7 o'clock on Monday 3 June.
   B Oh no. If it *was* Sunday, I*'d be able to* stay in bed.
2 **A** Good luck with the interview!
   B Thanks. If I *get* this job, we*'ll go out* and celebrate this evening.
3 **A** It's a lovely day. I'm going for a walk.
   B I*'d join* you if I *didn't have* so much work to do, but I've got to finish it.
4 **A** When will you be back?
   B Well, I'm hoping to get the 9.00 train, but if I *miss* it, I*'ll give* you a ring.
5 **A** If you *were* rich, where *would* you *live*?
   B In a big house by the beach.
6 **A** If it *wasn't raining*, I*'d go* for a cycle ride.
   B Yes, but it will brighten up soon. If it*'s* fine this afternoon, we*'ll go out* then.
7 **A** Are they here yet?
   B No, but if the traffic*'s/is* bad, they*'ll be* late.
   A Yes, I suppose so. But *will* you *call* me as soon as they *arrive*?
   B Yes, of course.
8 **A** Are you looking forward to your holiday?
   B Not really. If I *had* my way, we*'d stay* at home, but everyone else wants to go away.
   A Oh, I'm sure you*'ll enjoy* it when you *get* there.
9 **A** Will you still *be* here when I *get back*?
   B I don't know. If I *finish* this, I*'ll leave* at four as usual.
10 **A** I think I*'ll ask* the boss for a pay rise when he *comes back* from lunch.
   B Well, if I *were* you I *wouldn't ask* him today. He isn't in a very good mood.

Exercise 4

1 We'll have a party when you get back.
2 I think I'll have a shower before I go out.
3 We'll look after the house while you're away.
4 The meeting will continue until we reach a decision.
5 I'll take a holiday after the exams are over.
6 We'll leave as soon as the taxi arrives.
7 I'll tell you when the post comes.
8 We won't lock the doors until we leave.

Exercise 5

The correct sentences are
1 We decided to set off early.
2 Could you turn off the radio, please?
   Could you turn the radio off, please?
3 No, switch it on again.
4 I'm listening to it.
5 They didn't turn up till ten o'clock.
6 I can't go out tonight.
7 I'm looking after my little sister.
8 John put forward his suggestions.
   John put his suggestions forward.
9 We talked them over.
10 We decided to go for plan A.

Exercise 6

1 *He's putting the box down.*
2 She's putting a coat on.
3 He's putting a shelf up.
4 She's putting the meeting off until tomorrow.
5 He's putting the candle out.
6 He's putting his jacket away.

Exercise 7

1 boarding card
2 tourist
3 check in
4 package holiday
5 ticket
6 destination
7 luggage
8 long-haul flight
9 platform
10 camera
11 passenger
12 passport
13 airlines
14 station
15 suitcase
16 foreign

The tourist attraction is *Buckingham Palace.*

Exercise 8

You get on and off a:	You get in and out of a:
plane	car
bus	taxi
train	
coach	
boat	
horse	
bike	
ship	

Exercise 9

1 Where do you usually *spend* your holidays?
2 We always *go* to Italy *for* our holidays.
3 I won't be here next week, I'm *taking* a holiday.
4 **A** Where's John?
   B He*'s on* holiday.
5 **A** Have you *booked* your holiday in Australia yet?
   B Yes, I did it last week.
6 Welcome back. Have you *had* a nice holiday?
7 **A** Is anybody in next door?
   B No, they've *gone on* holiday.
8 **A** Did you *enjoy* your holiday?
   B Yes, it was great.

Exercise 10

Passenger	*Do I check in here for* Buenos Aires?
Clerk	Yes. Could *I see your ticket, please?*
Passenger	Yes, here you are.
Clerk	*Could I also see your passport, please?*
Passenger	My passport? Oh yes, here it is.
Clerk	*Thank you. Do you have any luggage?*
Passenger	Yes, these two suitcases.
Clerk	*Did you pack* the cases yourself?
Passenger	Yes, I did.
Clerk	*Do they contain* any electrical items?
Passenger	No, they don't.
Clerk	*Fine. Would you like smoking or non-smoking?*
Passenger	Non-smoking, please.
Clerk	*And would you prefer a window or an aisle seat?*
Passenger	Oh, er, a window seat, please.
Clerk	Here's *your boarding card, ticket, and passport. Boarding* is at 16.40 at gate 3. *Have a pleasant flight.*
Passenger	Thank you.

Exercise 11

Possible answers
1 I'm afraid your luggage is overweight. You'll *have to pay excess baggage.*
2 There are no window seats left, I'm afraid. *You'll have to sit in an aisle seat.*
3 I'm sorry, but all the non-smoking seats are taken. *You'll have to sit in the smoking section.*
4 I'm afraid you're only allowed one piece of hand baggage. *You'll have to check in the other bag with the rest of your luggage.*

Exercise 12

a British holidaymakers are deserting European destinations for faraway places such as the Caribbean. A holiday <u>here</u> can cost little more than a holiday in the Canary Islands, <u>because</u> long haul-flights are cheaper <u>and</u> local labour costs are low. Travellers are also becoming more sophisticated <u>and</u> are looking for somewhere more exotic. At one time a holiday in Europe was considered something special, <u>but</u> now it's become normal. <u>So</u> places like the USA, Jamaica, and South Africa have all become regular holiday destinations.

b 1 *because*
  2 so
  3 but
  4 are becoming, are looking for
  5 here
c 1 but
  2 so
  3 and
  4 because

Exercise 13

Possible answer
The trend is causing concern in many Mediterranean countries where tourism is a vital part of the economy, as millions of jobs depend on it. Although long-haul holidays bring employment to poorer countries, some people are concerned about the effects upon the environment. However, the trend will continue and develop. Places like the Caribbean can guarantee year-round sunshine so people can escape from the dreary British winter to tropical sunshine. Tour operators also like this because it spreads the holiday season over the whole year instead of just the summer months.

7 Entertainment

Exercise 1

a 1 **A** You look tired, Arthur.
    B *I've been working late.*
  2 **A** You look worried, Mary.
    B I've been working out the accounts.
  3 **A** Your flat's in a terrible mess, Jason.
    B We've been having a party.
  4 **A** Peter, your hands are covered in oil.
    B I've been fixing the car.
  5 **A** You look happy, Meg.
    B I've been celebrating my promotion.
  6 **A** You look scared.
    B We've been watching a horror movie.
b 1 *Arthur looks tired because he's been working late.*
  2 Mary looks worried because she's been working out the accounts.
  3 Jason's flat is in a terrible mess because he's been having a party.
  4 Peter's hands are covered in oil because he's been fixing the car.
  5 Meg looks happy because she's been celebrating her promotion.
  6 The girls look scared because they've been watching a horror movie.

Exercise 2

1 I've always *wanted* to play the piano.
2 She's *worked/been working* here for three years.
3 He's *been watching* TV for two hours.
4 I'm tired. I've *been studying* all evening.
5 She's *been decorating* the house, but she hasn't finished yet.
6 Have you ever *won* anything on the lottery?
7 I've *lived/been living* here since last year.
8 Paul McCartney has *written* hundreds of songs.
9 Has Mr Terrill *arrived*? I've *been waiting* for half an hour.
10 Have you *finished* that book?

Exercise 3

A	**B**
I've been to the cinema three times	*in the last week.*
	lately.
I saw him	last month.
	the other day.
	a couple of minutes ago.
She's been waiting for a bus	for ages.
	since 2.00.

Exercise 4

1 He *lived* here until he got married.
2 I *haven't seen* him since Monday.
3 **A** Sorry I'm late. *Have you been waiting* long?
  B No, I *arrived* ten minutes ago.
4 I *didn't see* James yesterday.
5 She *was working* here until 1993.
6 Your hands are filthy! What *have you been doing*?
7 I *haven't been* to the bank recently.

Exercise 5

Reporter Today, West Side Radio, the area's first local radio station, *has been broadcasting* for ten years. I*'ve come* down to the radio station to interview one of the people who *has made* the station a success – DJ, Frank Frankham. How long *have you worked* for West Side Radio?
DJ I*'ve been* with West Side ever since it *started*, but I *haven't been* a DJ all that time. I *was* an assistant producer at first. Then one day about five years ago the normal DJ *didn't come* in, so I *stood in* for him. Well, I obviously *did* a good job, because they *asked* me to be a DJ and I *have presented* my own show ever since.
Reporter Why do you think West Side Radio *is* successful?
DJ Well, I think it's because it*'s become* part of the local community. Last week, for instance, there was a big traffic jam in the city centre and we *reported* that, and I'm sure that *helped* a lot of people. And one of my colleagues *has* just *talked* about a local music festival that's happening next week.
Reporter And you also *have also run* several campaigns about local issues.
DJ Yes, that's right. Earlier this year we *had* a campaign about traffic in the city. Our current campaign is about the plans for the new market. We*'ve been running* it for about two weeks now. People *phone* us with their views and we *pass* these ideas on to the local council.

Exercise 6

music	film
classical	war
folk	comedy
country	western
mainstream pop	adventure
soul	thriller
blues	musical
heavy metal	horror
jazz	crime
rock and roll	romance

Exercise 7

Eric Clapton is one of the most *successful* rock stars of all time. He has sold millions of *copies* of his records and has appeared in live *concerts* all over the world. Many people regard him as the greatest *guitarist* ever.

Clapton was *born* in 1945 in a small town near London. When he was only two *years* old his mother left him. She went abroad and Eric was *brought up* by his grandparents. Until he was nine he *believed* that they were his parents and it was a terrible shock when he *found out* that they weren't. In the 1980s he told his biographer: 'It explains a lot of my *behaviour* throughout my life. Because I still don't *know* who I am.'

But his grandparents *treated* him well. In fact they probably *spoilt* him. When he was a *teenager* they bought him his first guitar and when he left school they paid for him to go to *art* college. But Eric had already become interested in *music* and he started playing the guitar in pubs and *clubs* in London. At that time groups like the Rolling Stones were starting to play blues, which up to then had only been played by *black* musicians in the United States.

Clapton first became *famous* when he started a group called Cream, with Jack Bruce on *bass* guitar and Ginger Baker on *drums*, in 1966. The group only lasted two years but they had a *huge* impact on rock music. They changed rock and roll from just *entertainment* into serious music.

After Cream *broke up*, Clapton formed a new group called Derek and the Dominoes. He had several *hits*, most notably *Layla* and *I Shot the Sheriff*. Clapton showed that he could not only play the guitar and sing but could also *write* excellent songs. But while on *stage* he was the brilliant guitar-playing *superstar*, his private life was falling apart. He became addicted to drugs and *alcohol*. At one point he was spending over £1,500 a day on *drugs*. Then in 1991 his four-year-old son, Conor, died *when* he fell from the window of a New York *skyscraper*.

Eric Clapton has *certainly* had his problems, but he has survived. He finally *defeated* his addiction and has continued to *develop* as an artist. Perhaps he has finally found out who he is.

Exercise 8

1 She wants him to post some letters.
2 He doesn't want her to put her drink on the computer.
3 He wants her to give him a lift to the station.
4 She doesn't want him to park there/on yellow lines.
5 She wants her to send a fax.
6 He wants her to switch the television off.

7   He wants him to turn his Walkman down.
8   She wants him to leave his dog outside.

Exercise 9

Possible answers
a   1   *I don't think violence on TV affects children.*
    2   In my opinion people should be able to watch what they like.
    3   I don't believe animals should be used for experiments.
    4   I maintain that drugs should be legalized.
    5   I would say it's wrong to eat meat.

Exercise 10

looked	*1*
wanted	2
ideal	2
station	2
create	2
dream	1
neglected	3
violence	3
society	4
believed	2
diet	2
died	1
million	3
everything	3
unnecessary	5
studio	3

Exercise 11

1   Local playwright Hanna Godber has given her home town a chance to see her most successful play, *The Letter*, at the Lexford Playhouse.
2   The story is set in the 1930s.
3   John Barlow, who has been out of work for several months, is offered a job by a large engineering firm.
4   He writes a letter to the company accepting the job and he gives it to his son, Bobby, to post.
5   Bobby isn't too pleased, because he'd rather play football with his friends, but he sets off on the long walk to the post office.
6   On the way he meets two older boys who offer to post the letter for him.
7   Unaware of its importance, Bobby gives them the letter and runs off happily to play football.
8   If you want to know what happens next, you'll have to go and see the play for yourself, but believe me, you won't regret it.
9   The play is excellent, and the lighting, scenery, and sound effects are all very good. The cast perform it brilliantly.
10 My award goes to young Justin Time, who plays Bobby.
11 *The Letter* is on for just one more week, so don't miss it.

8   Time out

Exercise 1

1   *Where has David gone?*
2   Did you see the news last night?
3   Were Simon and Mary at the party?
4   Can you play the piano?
5   Are you doing anything this evening?
6   What does Kelly do?
7   Would you like a drink?
8   Where was the woman sitting?
9   How long had he lived there?
10 What have you been doing?
11 When will you be back?
12 Did you use to go out with Clara?

Exercise 2

1   *She doesn't know what time it is.*
2   He doesn't know whether Carl has passed his driving test yet.
3   She has no idea where Peter lives.
4   He doesn't know what the capital of Peru is.
5   She is not sure whether she can make it to the rehearsal tonight.
6   He can't remember where he parked the car.
7   She doesn't know whether they will be there by 10.00.
8   He has no idea what happened in the meeting.

Exercise 3

1   *I'd like to know what the pigeon's name is.*
2   I wonder how many miles it flew.
3   I'd like to know how many hours it took.
4   We don't know where the bird was released.
5   We don't know what time it was released on Wednesday morning.
6   I'd like to know how many other pigeons were released at the same time.
7   I wonder what the weather was like.
8   I'd like to know what the winner's average speed was.
9   We don't know how old the pigeon's owner is.
10 I wonder what the pigeon's owner said.

Exercise 4

football	*a goal, a pitch, a net*
tennis	a racquet, a net, a court
golf	clubs, a course
athletics	a race, a track
rugby	a goal, poles, a pitch
basketball	a court
badminton	a racquet, a net, a shuttlecock, a court
skiing	poles, a piste
motor racing	a race, a track
cycling	a race, a track
volleyball	a goal, a net, a court
hockey	a goal, a stick, a pitch
ice skating	skates, a rink

Exercise 6

A	B
score	*a goal*
hit	a ball
	an opponent
win	a ball
	a game
	a match
	a race
beat	an opponent
	the other team

Exercise 7

1   *a kitchen knife*
2   a toy shop
3   computer games
4   an exercise bike
5   a fitness expert
6   a radio presenter
7   a pizza restaurant
8   a car magazine
9   a fish and chip shop
10 tennis shoes

Exercise 8

Possible answers
1   *Can you tell us if you will increase taxes again?*
2   I'd like to know what your policy on education is.
3   I want to know why you have cut spending on hospitals.
4   I'd like to know how long we have to wait for a new road.
5   Do you know whether the government intends to cut unemployment benefit?
6   Can you tell us whether the government is going to do anything about youth crime?
7   I want to know whether you agree with capital punishment.
8   Do you know what you will do for old people?

Exercise 9

1   Excuse me. Can you tell me if the flight from Paris is late?
    Yes, I'm afraid there is a two-hour delay.
2   Could you please tell me where I can change some money?
    Yes, over there near passport control.
3   Excuse me. Could you tell me how much this watch is, please?
    Yes, it's £159.
4   Excuse me. Could you tell me how I get to the train station?
    Yes, go down this escalator and turn left.
5   Could I possibly change my ticket for a flight tomorrow?
    Yes, certainly, could I see your ticket, please?
6   Excuse me. Could you tell me how much hand baggage I am allowed?
    Yes, you're allowed one piece.
7   Could you tell me where I can send a fax?
    Yes, go to the business lounge upstairs.

Exercise 10

1   *a fifty-thousand-dollar car*
2   a forty-minute delay
3   a forty-five-minute lesson
4   a twenty-four-hour flight
5   a four-kilometre-long swim
6   a six-man team

Exercise 11

It's 5.30 am, and while the *rest* of us are still snoring in our beds Susan Wates is putting on her *trainers* and getting ready for her morning *jog* around the streets of East London. Two hours later she's back home and while she's *preparing* breakfast for her family she's already looking *forward* to the evening and another two hours of *exercise*.

Every day, *whatever* the weather, she exercises for four hours. Once a week she also does an hour of running and *weightlifting* at the local *health* club. That's followed by a long swim. On Sundays – just for *fun* – she goes for an extra ten-*mile* run or cycle ride. Susan doesn't smoke, drink, or eat *meat*, and she's very careful about her *diet*. She very rarely eats *sweets*, chocolate, or ice cream.

Just reading about Susan's *gruelling* schedule makes most people feel *tired*, so why does she do it? 'Well, you probably won't believe it but I used to be a real *couch potato* – overweight and *unfit*. I hated myself. Then one day I said to myself, "You've got to get off your *backside* and do something with your *life*." So I went to a *gym*, and started training, and well, I just felt so *great*. I found that the more I trained the more *energy* I had.'

Now Susan is in *serious* training. She is going to enter the selection *heats* for the *Ironman* triathlon in Hawaii. The *event* consists of a four-kilometre swim, a 42-kilometre run, and a 180-kilometre *cycle* race *back* to back, so you've got to be very *dedicated*. 'I know I won't *win*,' says Susan, 'but just to be a *participant* will be terrific.' And in case you think Susan is unusual, the triathlon is one of the *fastest* growing sports in the world, and the *Ironman* race has thousands of *entrants* every year.

Exercise 12

16 St John's Walk
London SE13 6GH

2 August

The Reservations Manager
Hotel Belmont
The Parade
Birmingham
B4 7JB

Dear Sir or Madam

I wish to reserve a double room for the nights of 3–5 September. Could you please tell me whether you have a room available for those nights and what the rate will be?

Thank you for your attention.

Yours faithfully

John Clarke

Grammar check 3

Exercise 1

1 **A** What time's the next bus?
   B It's at 12.00. If you *hurry* you *'ll get* it.
2 I'm bored with revising. If I *didn't have* an exam tomorrow, I*'d go* out.
3 If I *were* the prime minister, I*'d ban* all exams.
4 I'm going to the post office. If you *give* me those letters, I*'ll post* them.
5 I*'d be* careful if I *were* you.
6 **A** I can't get my car started.
   B I*'ll give* you a lift if you *want*.

Exercise 2

1 *We'll start as soon as Ken arrives.*
2 I'll have a drink before we go.
3 I'll wait until it stops/has stopped raining.
4 I'll do it when I've got/have time.
5 We'll book the restaurant after Jack phones/has phoned.
6 We'll lock up the house as soon as the taxi comes.

Exercise 3

1 *Who won the tennis match?*
2 When does the film start?
3 Why did they do it?
4 What are you looking at?
5 Can you swim?

Exercise 4

1 **A** I*'ve lost* my glasses. I can't find them anywhere. I've *been looking for* them for hours.
   B Don't worry. I *did* the same thing the other week, but I *found* them a few days later.
2 We're too late. The train *has gone*. Why *did* you *take* so long to get ready?
3 **A** Where *have* you *been*?
   B We*'ve been playing* tennis.
4 The newspaper *hasn't arrived* yet. It's the second time this week it*'s been* late. It *came* late on Tuesday, too.

Exercise 5

1 *They've been jogging.*
2 He's been reading.
3 She's been swimming.
4 They've been watching a film.

Exercise 6

1 Do you know *where the computer's gone*?
2 Could you tell me *whether you've got a fax machine*?
3 I'd like to know *what time the museum opens*.
4 Do you know *if anyone phoned yesterday*?

9 All in the mind?

Exercise 1

1 There's a witch cooking something horrible.
2 There's a ghost walking through a wall.
3 There are skeletons playing cards.
4 There's a spider crawling on the table.
5 There's a mad professor playing the organ.
6 There's a monster watching TV.
7 There's a face looking through the window.

Exercise 2

1 They can see a ghost walking through a wall.
2 They can see a spider crawling over the table.
3 They can smell the candles burning.
4 They can smell the witch's cooking.
5 They can hear the mad professor playing the organ.
6 They can hear a wolf howling at the moon.

Exercise 3

1 **A** I've stopped *smoking*.
   B Lucky you. I've tried *to stop* several times, but I've never managed *to give up* yet.
   A Oh, if you really want *to stop*, you can.
2 **A** Did you remember *to lock* the door before we left?
   B I think so, but I can't remember *doing* it.
3 We had forgotten *to buy* a newspaper, so we stopped *to get* one.
4 **A** Are you good at *keeping* in touch with people?
   B Not really. I don't mind *telephoning*, but I can't stand *writing* letters.
5 **A** Have you finished *writing* that report?
   B Yes, but I didn't really enjoy *doing* it.
   A Never mind, it's done now, so do you fancy *going out* somewhere this evening?
   B That would be nice. What do you feel like *doing*?
   A Would you like *to try* that new club in the square?
   B OK. Let's start *getting/to get* ready.
6 **A** Could you stop *making* all that noise, please?
   B But I like *playing* the drums.
   A Well if you carry on *playing* that loudly, there's going *to be* trouble.

Exercise 4

One day in August 1971 an old woman and her young grandchild were *sitting* in the kitchen of their house in the village of Belmez, in southern Spain. Suddenly the child started *shouting* and *pointing* at the floor. When the old woman looked down at the tiles, she was *amazed* at what she saw. There was a human face *staring* at her. The face was terribly sad. *Scrubbing* the floor couldn't remove the face. In fact its eyes only started *opening* wider. The *frightening* tiles were *replaced* by the owner of the house, but three weeks later the family saw another face *appearing* in the new concrete floor.

Experts were *called in*. After *digging up* the floor they found a medieval cemetery under the house. The faces continued *coming*, so microphones were *placed* in the house. When people listened to the recordings they heard voices *speaking* in strange languages. There were other voices *groaning* in terrible pain. The kitchen was *locked up*, but four more faces appeared in different parts of the house. Then, as suddenly as it had started, the house stopped *producing* faces. The mystery has never been *explained*. The experts could only suggest that some *terrifying* incident, such as *burning* witches, had happened there long ago.

Exercise 5

1, 3, 4, 5, and 7 should be ticked.

Exercise 6

After seeing the face, the old woman tried to scrub it away.
Before calling in the experts, the owner replaced the tiles.
While listening to the voices, the people felt very frightened.
After closing the kitchen, the family thought they would see no more faces.
After digging up the floor, they found a medieval cemetery.

Exercise 7

Base	Strong
tired	*exhausted*
ugly	hideous
frightened	terrified
cold	freezing
surprising	amazing
big	huge
interesting	fascinating
difficult	impossible
bad	awful
good	brilliant

Exercise 8

1 The town was *fascinating*, and the view from our hotel window was *absolutely* magnificent.
2 **A** The film was *very* interesting, wasn't it?
 B Well, the special effects were absolutely *amazing*, but the acting wasn't *very good*.
3 **A** You look absolutely *exhausted*.
 B I am. I just want to go to bed.
4 **A** Was the exam *very* difficult?
 B It was worse than difficult – it was *absolutely impossible*.
5 That dress is *absolutely* hideous.

Exercise 9

a 1, 2, 3, and 4 should be ticked.
b 1 *Putting on his jacket, Jason set off home.*
 2 Thinking that it was his phone number, she dialled it.
 3 Sitting in a café on holiday I saw my neighbour.
 4 Sailing from England to New York, the *Titanic* sank.

Exercise 10

1 **A** Guess who I *bumped into* the other day. Ken Smart.
 B Really! It's a small world.
 A Yes, he *turned up* at a party I was at. Anyway, we got talking and it *turned out* that he works just round the corner from you.
 B Wow! That's a coincidence. Did you *find out* exactly where he works?
 A Yes, at Simpsons.
 B How strange. I must *walk past* there at least twice a day and I've never seen him. I'll have to *call* him *up* sometime.
2 **A** My car *broke down* last week.
 B Oh dear. What did you do?
 A Well I *looked at* the engine, but I couldn't see anything wrong, so I *set off* to find a garage.
 B And did you find one?
 A Yes, but there was a notice *pinned up* on the door saying 'Closed for two weeks'.
 B That's bad luck.
 A Well, yes, but then this really smart sports car *pulled up* and the driver asked me if I needed any help.
 A What did you say?
 B Well, I said yes, so he *called up* another garage on his mobile phone.

Exercise 11

1 *Neither can I.*
2 So have I.
3 So do I.
4 So can I.
5 Nor/Neither do I.
6 Nor/Neither have I.
7 So did I.
8 Nor/Neither was I.

Exercise 12

1 *Oh, I didn't.*
2 Oh, I don't.
3 Oh, I didn't.
4 Oh, I had.
5 Oh, I did.
6 Oh, I will.
7 Oh, I'm not.
8 Oh, I wouldn't.

Exercise 13

won	come
mother	brother
son	done
ago	so
boy	noise
four	short
goes	toes
among	some
move	prove
front	once
our	sour
short	score

Exercise 14

In the 1880s Lord Dufferin was staying with friends in Ireland. One night he woke up suddenly because he heard someone calling his name. He got out of bed and went to window where he could see a dark shape moving across the lawn. He went outside and saw a man carrying a coffin. He called out and as the man turned round Lord Dufferin could see that he had a very ugly face. Suddenly, he disappeared, and Lord Dufferin felt the man walk through him. Several years later he was staying in a hotel in Paris. Lord Dufferin was waiting for the lift. When the lift arrived, Lord Dufferin saw that the lift operator was the ugly man he had seen all those years ago. Lord Dufferin was absolutely horrified and refused to get into the lift. Then, as the lift was going up to the fifth floor, the cable snapped and the lift crashed down the shaft, and everyone inside was killed.

10 Your health

Exercise 1

1 We *should* do something to reduce air pollution in cities.
2 When it's hot some people *can't* breathe properly, because the pollution is so bad.
3 People *shouldn't* use their cars so much.
4 Public transport *must* be improved, so that people *can* leave their cars at home.
5 If nothing is done soon, it *may* be too late.
6 Thousands of people *might* die if we get a very hot summer.

Exercise 2

1 We ought *to* leave soon.
3 Do you want to go *to* the party?
5 You aren't allowed *to* drive till you're seventeen.
6 There's someone at the door. I'll have *to* call you back.
7 The shops were so crowded I wasn't able *to* get what I wanted.
10 I need *to* go to the shops.
12 What would you like *to* do today?

Exercise 3

A	**B**
She must come.	*She has no choice.*
She may come.	I don't know for certain.
She should come.	I think she'd enjoy it.
She can't come.	She hasn't got the time.
She doesn't have to come.	It's not necessary.
He might leave.	But I don't think he will.
He shouldn't leave.	We need help with this work.
He mustn't leave.	He'll be in trouble if he does.
He ought to leave.	It would be better for him if he does.
He can leave.	It's all right if he does.

Exercise 5

1 *a bandage*
2 eye drops
3 plasters
4 ointment
5 a cut
6 tablets
7 an injection
8 an X-ray
9 a thermometer
10 a splinter

Exercise 6

1 I've got a *sore* throat and *a* temperature.
2 There have been 6,000 *cases* of flu this winter.
3 Have we got any *painkillers/aspirin*? I've got *a* headache.
4 My father has high blood pressure.
5 The doctor wrote me a *prescription* for *some* antibiotics.
6 You've got *high* cholesterol. I'm going to put you on a low-fat diet.
7 You might have *a* fracture – you should have *an X-ray* to make sure.
8 I've got *a* pain in my side here. I think it's indigestion.
9 I've got *a* cold, but my sister's got flu.
10 She's got *a* nasty cough. She needs *some* cough *medicine*.

Exercise 7

1 *Someone might break into the house.*
2 The plane might crash.
3 I may become ill.
4 You could lose all your money.
5 We might have an accident.
6 We could be mugged in the street.
7 The flight may be delayed because of bad weather.
8 We may have terrible weather while we're away.

Exercise 8

In the early 1950s an American *researcher*, Professor Ancel Keys, first noted a *connection* between diet and heart disease. *Research into* the diets of men in seven countries *showed* that people eating a Mediterranean diet, such as those in Italy and Spain, *were less likely to die* from heart disease than people in the USA or Northern Europe. At first the research team thought *it likely* that fat in the diet *might* be causing the difference. However, *the study revealed that* the difference did not *seem* to be *connected* to the amount of fat. The *findings* of the study *appeared* to indicate that it was the type of fat that made the difference. The Mediterranean diet is rich in monounsaturated fats, such as olive oil, which it is *thought* to reduce levels of cholesterol in the blood. More recent studies have *supported* these findings.

Exercise 9

1 **Patient** *Good morning, doctor.*
 Doctor *Good morning. What seems to be the problem?*
2 **Patient** I've got a rash under my arm.
 Doctor I see. Just slip your shirt off. How long have you had the rash?

3 **Patient** About two weeks.
   Doctor Hmm, yes. Does it itch?
   Patient Yes, it does.
4 **Doctor** Well, you've got a bit of an infection there.
5 **Doctor** I'll give you a prescription for some ointment. Put it on twice a day.
6 **Doctor** Continue the treatment for a week after the rash has disappeared.
   Patient Thank you, doctor. Goodbye.
   Doctor Goodbye.

Exercise 10

1 You *mustn't* leave disks in the disk drive.
2 You *must* keep disks in their files.
3 You *needn't* use your own disks.
4 You *mustn't* put drinks near the computer.
5 You *needn't* switch the computer off.
6 You *must* lock the door when you leave.

Exercise 11

miss	*kiss*
pill	fill
mile	while
nice	price
hi-fi	sci-fi
think	drink
item	high
third	birthday

Exercise 12

The *case* of Child B has raised the difficult *question* of which patients should get *priority* when the amount of money available to *health* authorities is limited. Of course, it *would* be good if anyone could receive any *treatment* that they need, but unfortunately this is not possible. So what *should* we spend money on – old people or *children*, people who do important jobs or the *unemployed*, people with conditions that are not *life-threatening* or only on emergencies? What should we do about people who *injure* themselves in some way, such as people *who* smoke, eat too much or take *drugs*, people with dangerous hobbies such as rock climbing or *skiing*? And what about the treatment? Should we *refuse* to pay for anything that *costs* more than, say, £10,000, or should we only *provide* treatment when the *chances* of survival are good?

Doctors will always have to make *choices* about what treatment any *patient* should receive. Health *spending* already takes a huge share of *taxes*. And the problem will only get *worse*, as new kinds of treatment are *developed*. Many countries also have the problem of an *ageing* population. There will be more *old* people and they will live *longer*. Who is going to provide the *money* that will be needed to look *after* them?

Exercise 13

                                                    88 *Green* Lane
                                                          Oxford
                                                        OX5 9PL

                                                        23 *May*

Dear *Tim* and Yolande,

I'm very *sorry* we weren't *able* to come to your *party* on Saturday. I'm *afraid* Tania fell *downstairs* and hurt her arm, so she *had* to go to the hospital *for* an X-ray. *Fortunately*, she hasn't broken *it*, but it's still very painful.

Anyway, I hope the party went *well*. I'll be in *touch* again soon.

All the *best*,

Roger

11 Priorities

Exercise 1

1 *She got her husband to take their son to school.*
2 She *let* the teacher leave early.
3 She *got* the Chief Education Officer to increase the school's budget.
4 She *made* Kate wait outside her office.
5 She *made* John write his essay again.
6 She *got* Arthur to organize a play.
7 She *let* her son go and play football.

Exercise 3

1 *Mr Oldcorn has had his computer repaired.*
2 Mrs Jones has had her carpets cleaned.
3 Mr White has had his house repainted.
4 Ms Hardy has had her bathroom decorated.
5 Ms Riley has had a tyre replaced on her car.
6 Mr Ridge has had a new garage built.
7 Mr Downham has had a new engine fitted into his car.
8 Mr Fleming has had a gas fire installed.

Exercise 4

1 Fatma has had her films developed at the chemist's shop.
2 Mrs Peck planted some flowers in her garden.
3 Mr Nye will have his front door painted.
4 Brenda has dyed her hair.
5 Colin has had his suit cleaned at the dry cleaner's.

Exercise 5

Verb	Noun
create	*creation*
survive	survival
decide	decision
agree	agreement
protect	protection
destroy	destruction
examine	examination
injure	injury
suggest	suggestion
produce	production
introduce	introduction
imagine	imagination

Exercise 6

Across
1 reduce
4 smuggle
10 adolescent
12 release
14 loo
15 to
16 opera
17 so
19 did
21 pain
22 on
23 intelligent
27 can
28 flush
31 ape
32 rapidly
33 baby

Down
2 developed
3 cut
5 meet
6 extraordinary
7 made
8 doorbell
9 agreement
11 cross
13 abandon
18 cage
20 used
24 let
25 get
26 nappy
29 had
30 him
31 all

Exercise 7

1 *Excuse me, I've dropped my knife on the floor. Could you get me a clean one, please?*
2 Excuse me, I've locked my key in my room. Do you have another key?
3 Hello. I bought this radio last week but one of the switches is broken. Could I have a new one, please?
4 Excuse me, I don't like sitting next to the window. Would it be possible for me to have an aisle seat, please?
5 May I stop the meeting for a moment, please? I think I may have left my car unlocked. Would you mind if I go and check?
6 Excuse me, this glass is dirty. Could I have a clean one, please?
7 Excuse me, may I speak to the manager, please? I'm not at all satisfied with the service here.
8 Hello, is that the box office? I was at your cinema last night and I think I may have left my umbrella. Has it been handed in to you by any chance?

Exercise 8

1 *His eyes need testing.*
2 The test papers need marking.
3 The TV needs repairing.
4 The lawn/grass needs cutting.
5 His hair needs combing.
6 The dog needs washing.

Exercise 9

head	*bread*
easy	leave
real	read
early	heard
week	clean
dead	leather
seal	seat
bean	clean
death	breath
beneath	east

Exercise 10

1 **A** Hello. *Sorry to disturb you*, but I was just wondering how our new advertising manager is getting on.

   B Well, *she's still learning the ropes* at the moment, but she seems to be doing fine.

   A Good. *We don't want a repeat* of the problems we had with the *chap* who was doing it before.

   B I don't think that's very likely. Sonja *has got a good name* in her field.

2 **A** Has Charlie done that survey yet? *It's holding everything up*. We'll never meet *the deadline* if he doesn't get it done soon.

   B Yes, I know. I spoke to him yesterday. He says *he can't find the time for it*.

   A What? Oh *this is the limit*. This is the second time *he's let us down* on something important.

   B Well, he says his *workload* is too heavy.

   A Oh, that's just an excuse for *putting things off*.

   B I'm not so sure. He's threatened to resign again and *I think he means it* this time.

   A Well, I don't believe it. *I should have known better* than to get him to do it *in the first place*.

Exercise 11

1 'We've released more than fifty apes,' said Dr Willie Smits. 'But there's another two hundred at the Wanariset Centre.'

2 'What's the time?' said Sally, sleepily. 'Is it five o'clock yet? I'm hungry.'

3 'Is that Ken's girlfriend?' asked Fiona.
   'Yes, it is,' said Alison. 'She's French, you know.'

4 'Sandra's parents went to Italy in June,' said Larissa.

5 'On the left you can see the Houses of Parliament,' said the guide. 'And on your right's Westminster Abbey.'

6 'I'd like to know,' he whispered, 'what you've done with the children's money.'

7 'How often have you been here before?' demanded the customs officer.

Grammar check 4

Exercise 1

I had a strange dream the other night. I was in a room. There were two women *sitting* on chairs. I saw one of the women *point* to two doors and I heard her *say*: 'Choose.' I opened one of the doors and I found myself *standing* on top of a tower. There was a strong wind *blowing*. I could hear people *laughing* and there was someone *shouting* very loudly: 'Wrong door. Wrong door.' Then I felt myself *falling*. When I woke up I was *lying* on the floor.

Exercise 2

1 *Liam almost fell asleep while driving.*
2 After stopping he opened his window.
3 He had a rest before continuing his journey.
4 But after almost falling asleep again, he checked into a hotel.
5 Before going to bed he phoned his wife.

Exercise 3

1 Would you like *to leave* now?
2 Oh no. I've forgotten *to switch off* the computer.
3 Do you remember *playing* here when you were younger?
4 How do you fancy *going* out?
5 You ought *to take* a break.
6 You must *look* after yourself.
7 She made them *wait* for hours.
8 The photocopier's stopped *working*.
9 I'll get the mechanic *to fix* the car.
10 The windows need *cleaning*.

Exercise 4

1 *So do I.*
2 Nor/Neither can I.
3 So will I.
4 So did I.
5 Nor/Neither have I.

Exercise 5

1 *Oh, I have.*
2 Oh, I didn't.
3 Oh, I would.
4 Oh, I'm not.
5 Oh, I will.

Exercise 6

1 *I'll have to go.*
2 Neil won't be able to make it.
3 We won't need to take the exam.
4 I'll see you next week.

Exercise 7

1 She *needn't bring* her passport.
2 She *mustn't forget* her ticket.
3 She *must be at the airport by 6.00.*
4 She *needn't bring any cash.*

Exercise 8

1 He *had* his coat *cleaned*.
2 She had a new key cut.
3 They had their photographs taken.
4 She had her eyes tested.

12 News

Exercise 1

1 **A** Andrea said *that she had passed her driving test.*
   B That's good news.
   A And she said *she was going to buy a car when she can afford it.*
   B What's she doing to do till then?
   A She said *she'd use her parents'.*

2 **A** Is Tim coming to the cinema?
   B No, he said *he was playing tennis this evening.*
   A I thought he played on Mondays.
   B Yes, that's right, but he said *that he hadn't played/didn't play this Monday because John had broken his racquet.*

3 **A** I saw Pauline the other day. She didn't look very happy. She said *she'd like to get a new job.*
   B Oh, why's that?
   A She said *she just didn't enjoy what she was doing in her present job.*

Exercise 2

1 *Helena asked her dad whether he had seen her keys.*
2 Fred asked Peter whether/if he had ever been to Australia before his recent trip.
3 Sandra asked Ken where he was going.
4 The police officer asked Mrs Cassidy how long she would be away.
5 Mr Hoyle asked Roberta where she'd put the disks.
6 The receptionist asked Mrs Carlucci if/whether she would prefer a double or a single room.
7 The Managing Director asked Mr Walsh why he had left his last job.
8 Helen asked Dean whether he liked living in London.

Exercise 3

1 **Sam** *Hello, Frank. Have you heard? Lena and I are getting married.*
   Frank When will the big day be?
   Sam We haven't fixed the date yet, but you'll be the first to know.

2 **Jane** I've got a new job. I'm working at the Clyde bank now.
   Betty Why did you leave your old job?
   Jane Well, I applied for promotion, but I didn't get it, so I decided to leave.

3 **Sandra** Peter's had an accident.
   Sanjit Is he all right?
   Sandra Well, he's broken his leg and he can't walk.
   Sanjit How did it happen?
   Sandra I don't know.

Exercise 4

1 She *put* on her coat and *went* out, but it was raining, so she *came* back and *picked* up her umbrella.

2 **A** Can you *turn* the TV off, please?
   B But it's the football match and they're just *kicking* off.
   A *Turn* it down then. It's too loud.

3 **A** Oh, there isn't anywhere to park.
   B Just *pull* in a minute. I'll *get* out and *look* for a parking space.
   A It's all right. That car's *coming* out. I think I'll be able to *get* in there.

4 I *grew* up in a small town and I got very bored. I decided to *run* away. I *headed* for the city, but I soon *turned* back, because my money *ran* out.

Exercise 5

1   **A** Have you fixed that shelf yet?
     B No, but don't worry. I'll *get round to* it.
2   I forgot our wedding anniversary, so I had to book a holiday to *make up for* it.
3   Children *grow out of* shoes so quickly.
4   You have to *stand up for* your rights. If people try to push you around, don't let them *get away with* it.
5   The flight's at 12.40, so what time should we *set off for* the airport?
6   I tried to *get out of* going to the meeting, but I still had to go.
7   I can't afford a new computer, so I'll just have to *put up with* my old one for now.
8   Well, it was nice to talk to you, but I suppose I'd better *get back to* work.

Exercise 6

1   The teacher asked *Paul to close the window.*
2   Sally's father told her not to leave her jacket on the floor.
3   The painter asked Lady Barnham not to move her hands.
4   The driving instructor told Miss Handy to stop at the next traffic lights.
5   The flight attendant asked the passenger not to smoke.
6   She told them not to touch the sandwiches.
7   Tom's grandfather asked him to take the dog for a walk.
8   The dentist told the boy to brush his teeth twice a day.

Exercise 7

1   *His sister begged him not to join the army.*
2   The sergeant ordered him to collect all his equipment.
3   William Ross begged him not to shoot.
4   His father advised him to forget about William Ross.
5   His father warned him not to try to talk to Ross's wife.
6   His mother advised him to send the diary back.
7   Mrs Ross begged him to give her the diary.
8   The boy ordered him to put his hands up.

Exercise 8

1   John *said* he was going out.
2   I *told* you to leave me alone.
3   Have I *told* you what happened yesterday?
4   The manager *said* we could all go home.
5   Has Isobel *said* anything to you about the party?
6   The police officer *told* the boys to go home.
7   Sally *told* a very funny joke yesterday.
8   Frank *said* he'd finished the job.
9   My father *told* me a story.
10   You should have *told* the truth.

Exercise 9

Here is the news. There has been a serious earthquake in San Francisco. A scientist said that *the earthquake had happened at 4.13 in the morning.* She said that it *had measured 6.5 on the Richter scale.* The earthquake has caused major problems for the emergency services. The city's fire chief said that *fires had broken out all over the city.* Transport has been badly hit. A spokesman for the police department said *that most of the major roads were damaged.* He asked people *to stay at home if possible* and he advised *them not to drive unless they had to.* Local hospitals are full. A doctor said *that hundreds of patients were waiting for treatment.* As the city tries to deal with the damage the Mayor said that they *would do everything they could to get the city back to normal.*

Exercise 10

silent *c*	silent *h*	silent *k*
scientist	school	knife
	chemistry	knee
	what	
	where	
	hour	
	ghost	

silent *l*	silent *w*	silent *b*
talk	who	comb
calm		bomb
walk		doubt
half		climb
		debt

Exercise 11

1   *high-heeled shoes*
2   a long-sleeved shirt
3   a bearded man
4   a short-tailed dog
5   a five-bedroomed house
6   lined paper
7   a long-eared bat
8   a stamped addressed envelope

Exercise 12

That	£153,000
then	in 1961
it	the money
She	Viv Nicholson
that	to 'spend, spend, spend'
her	Viv Nicholson's
They	Viv and her husband
this	living a life of luxury
the whole lot	the money
The big winner	Viv Nicholson
he	her husband
it	the sports car

Exercise 13

Mukhtar and Sayeeda Mohidin couldn't believe it. *Their* dream had come true. *They* had won the £18 million jackpot in the National Lottery. *The Asian factory worker* gave up *his* £240 a week job and *the family* bought a new and expensive house near London.

Today, less than six months later, *Mr and Mrs Mohidin* are suing *each other*. *Both* Mukhtar and Sayeeda have accused *the other* of giving too much money to *their* relatives. Now Sayeeda has gone to court to claim that half the money should be *hers*. *Her* husband maintains that *all of it* is *his* since *he* bought the ticket with *his* own money.

A friend said *the money* had changed everything, but yesterday *Mrs Mohidin* claimed that there was no problem. 'I am living happily with *my* husband and family,' *she* said.

13   Regrets

Exercise 1

1   *I'm going to be late for my appointment.*
2   I hope the car will be all right there on the double yellow lines.
3   Oh, they're towing that guy's car away.
4   Excuse me. Your car's been towed away, I'm afraid.
5   It's my lunch break. Can I give you a lift to the pound?
6   Thanks very much, Clara. Look. Are you doing anything this evening?
7   Will you marry me?

Exercise 2

1   If Ben *hadn't overslept*, he *wouldn't have been* late for his appointment.
2   If he *hadn't been* late for his appointment, he *would have had* time to find a parking space.
3   He *wouldn't have left* the car on double yellow lines if he *had found* a parking space.
4   The car *wouldn't have been* towed away if he *hadn't left* it on double yellow lines.
5   But if the car *hadn't been* towed away, he *wouldn't have met* Clara.
6   And if he *hadn't met* Clara, she *wouldn't have given* him a lift to the pound.
7   Ben *wouldn't have asked* Clara out if she *hadn't given* him a lift to the pound.
8   And they *wouldn't have started* going out together if Ben *hadn't asked* her out.
9   So Ben and Clara *wouldn't have got* married if Ben *hadn't overslept* one morning.

Exercise 3

mammals	birds	fish	insects	reptiles/amphibians	others
lion	pigeon	shark	*fly*	snake	octopus
dog	duck	tuna	bee	lizard	worm
dolphin	parrot	salmon	ant	frog	spider
cow	ostrich	trout	mosquito	crocodile	
elephant	eagle		wasp	tortoise	
horse	owl		butterfly		
pig	chicken				
tiger					
sheep					
bat					
monkey					
bear					
cat					
whale					

Exercise 4

1   *Carol shouldn't have left her bag in the car.*
2   The footballer shouldn't have kicked the goalkeeper.
3   Mr Warren should have looked before he crossed the road.
4   Nina shouldn't have shouted at her little brother.
5   John should have had the car serviced.
6   Mr and Mrs Jarvis should have paid the phone bill.
7   Mary shouldn't have left her books at school.
8   Alan should have bought a ticket.

Exercise 5

It was a small town *like thousands of others* and life had hardly changed there *for centuries*. The people weren't poor. They did their *daily work* and in the evenings they sat *in the town square* and talked. But Jasna *dreamed of* being rich and famous. She wanted to be a fashion model like the ones she had seen *in the magazines*, and she decided to leave the small town. Her boyfriend, Miro, and her parents *tried to get her* to stay, but she wouldn't listen to them. She wanted to have a life of her own. So one day she said goodbye to her family and to Miro and went *to the big city*. Jasna was an attractive young woman and she soon got some small modelling jobs. At a fashion show *a couple of years later* she met Hans Becker. He became her manager and soon Jasna had a big house and lots of new friends. *It seemed as if* she had everything. *All she had to do* was be photographed wearing beautiful clothes. It seemed like *money for nothing*.

But one day it came *to a sudden end*. Jasna and Becker were involved in a car crash. Jasna was badly injured and Becker died. Then Jasna discovered that Becker had gambled away all her money. There was *no money left*. She had nothing but debts and her modelling career was over. And perhaps *it was just her imagination*, but she didn't seem to have so many friends any more. She was alone. *She finally realized* that her only true friends were back in her home town, but she felt so ashamed that she couldn't go back.

Exercise 8

A I crashed my car the other day and broke all the lights on the back.
B *That's a bit rough.*
A Yes, and when the garage told me how much it was going to cost, *I was stunned.*
B Did it cost *quite a bit?*
A *You're telling me.* It cost me *an arm and a leg.* The lights were over £50 each.
B *You're joking.*
A I'm not. I phoned the insurance company, but they weren't *much help*, because it was my fault.
B Oh well, *that's the way it goes* sometimes.
A Yes, *I suppose so.* Anyway, I think *it's my round.* Do you want the same again?

Exercise 9

A Hi. *I haven't seen you around for a while.*
B Well, *we've been away* for a couple of weeks, in Jamaica.
A Oh, very nice. *Did you have a good time?*
B Well, *we did in the end.*
A Why? What was the problem?
B The flight was delayed, so *we were hanging around at the airport* for ages.
A *Oh dear.* How long did you have to wait?
B About seven and a half hours. *I wasn't in too good a mood* by the time we took off. *Nor was my husband.* We won't be travelling with that company again, *I can tell you.*
A Well, *I hope it didn't spoil your holiday too much.*
B No, it was OK *when we finally got there.*
A *Something similar happened* to my sister's family last year. They were going to Jamaica, too, *funnily enough.*
B Oh really, what happened?

Exercise 10

Possible answers
1 *Are you? Where are you moving to?*
2 *Has he? Is he all right?*
3 *Did you? How is he?*
4 *Would he? Where would he go?*
5 *Does she? When did she start?*
6 *Have they? When did that happen?*
7 *Is it? How much do they want?*

Exercise 11

A	B
tell	lies
knit	a jumper
change	a wheel
offer	a reward
cook	a meal
claim	compensation
deceive	people
win	a match
fire	a gun
burst	into tears

Exercise 12

1 *unhappy*
2 dishonest
3 impolite
4 careless
5 incorrect
6 unnatural
7 useless
8 unlucky
9 inexpensive
10 impatient

11 unimportant
12 unreliable
13 inefficient
14 unusual
15 insensitive
16 dissatisfied
17 inconvenient
18 intolerant
19 independent
20 unhealthy

Exercise 13

I am writing to complain about the insurance cover on our recent skiing holiday in the USA. *While we were on holiday* my daughter decided to try snowboarding *and unfortunately* broke her arm. After taking her to hospital *I was amazed* to find that our travel insurance did not cover us for snowboarding. The treatment, *as a result*, cost us over $2,000.

I appreciate that I should have read the insurance cover first. *However*, many people these days go snowboarding and *I feel that* ski insurance should cover people for it. *I would be grateful if* you would explain to me why snowboarding is not covered in the policy.

14 Success

Exercise 1

One summer the Grant family – David, Kate, and their three children – *decided* to follow their dream and travel round the world. They *sold* their house in Scotland, bought a caravan and a horse, and set *off*. They *thought* that the whole trip *would* take two years. Now, six years later, they *have reached* the west coast of the USA.

Their days *start* very early and they are on the road by six o'clock. After *travelling* for about fifteen miles in the morning, they stop. The children *can't* go to school, so in the afternoons they have lessons from their parents. They *don't* watch television in the evenings. They *usually read* or play games.

They *have had* many adventures on their journey so far. While they *were travelling* through Italy the caravan broke *down*. Fortunately, a man *recognized* the caravan from an article which David *had* written for a magazine. He took the family to his house and repaired the caravan. He also helped them when one of the children became ill and *had* to go to hospital.

In Mongolia someone tried *to steal* their horse and then in China they *were arrested*. The authorities *told* them that they shouldn't have received a visa and *made* them leave the country.

Now they are in California and they *are getting* ready to set off across the USA and Canada. For the last few days they *have been visiting* San Francisco. Eventually, *they will return* to Britain. They *are looking* forward to seeing Britain again, but they *don't know* what life will be like. The trip hasn't been easy, but the Grants *would* do it all again if they *had* the chance.

Exercise 2

1 They had the caravan repaired in Italy.
2 They had photographs taken in Slovenia.
3 They had the horse taken to America by plane.
4 They had money sent out to different places.

Exercise 3

Interviewer Where *were you living* before you started your journey?
Mrs Grant In Scotland.
Interviewer How long *has the journey taken* so far?
Mrs Grant Six years.
Interviewer How far *do you travel* in a day?
Mrs Grant About 15 miles.
Interviewer What *have you been doing* for the last few days?
Mrs Grant Visiting San Francisco.
Interviewer *Are you getting* ready to cross the USA now?
Mrs Grant Yes, we are – and Canada.
Interviewer *Will you return* to Britain after that?
Mrs Grant Yes, eventually.
Interviewer *Are you looking* forward to it?
Mrs Grant Yes, but we don't really know what to expect.
Interviewer *Would you do* it all again?
Mrs Grant Oh yes, we would.

Exercise 4

1 They wonder *if/whether they will feel at home there.*
2 They aren't sure *where they will live.*
3 They have no idea *whether/if the place has changed much.*
4 They aren't sure *if/whether they can sell their story to a newspaper.*
5 They don't know *what other people think of them.*

Exercise 5

1 Joanne had tears *in* her eyes as she said goodbye *to* Eric. She knew that she was *in* love *with* him.
2 I'll be *at* a conference *in* London *at* the weekend.
3 A lot *of* people like to get married *in* church even though they don't go *to* church regularly.
4 I don't live *in* the country these days. I've got a flat *in* town.
5 A How did the boss react *to* the news?
  B I think he was rather pleased *with* me.
6 What are we doing all this work *for*? I can't see the point *of* it. I sometimes feel that life is passing us *by*.
7 Mr Allan was charged *with* assault because he fired a gun *at* two burglars. He had to pay one *of* them £2,000 *in* compensation *for* his injuries.
8 There was no water *in* the village so the women walked *to* the river *with* pots *on* their heads.

Exercise 6

1 *funeral*
2 humdrum
3 a backwater
4 a parish
5 a rectory
6 resolve
7 amazement
8 reflect
9 packed
10 farewell

Exercise 7

A	B
I think that hunting should be banned.	*I'm afraid I have to disagree with you there.*
Ouch! You just hit me in the eye.	Oh, I'm terribly sorry. Are you all right?
Right. Shall we make a start on the cleaning?	Yes, I suppose so.
Did you have a nice Christmas?	No so bad. What about you?
I think I'll be off now.	Well thank you very much for coming. See you again.
Shall I post these letters?	Yes please, if you wouldn't mind.
Well, it's my round. What would you like?	I'll have a gin and tonic, please.
Do you mind if I take some of this paper?	Not at all. Help yourself.
Could I possibly speak to Mr Andrews, please?	Certainly. I'm just putting you through.
I don't feel tired at all.	Me neither.
I think I might have the day off tomorrow.	Lucky you. I wish I could.
Shall we have a night out?	Mmm, that would be nice.

Exercise 8

Possible answers
1 A *Shall we go abroad for a holiday this year?*
  B *Yes, that would be nice. Where would you like to go?*
  A How about Amsterdam?
  B Good idea, I've always wanted to go there.
  A I'll go to the travel agent and find out about it.
  B Great, thanks.
2 A Could I speak to Harry Brown, please?
  B I'm afraid he's not here. Can I take a message?
  A Yes, my name's Margaret. Could Harry call me back?
  B Will you be in all day?
  A Yes, I will.
  B I'll give him the message.
3 A I must go – I've got a job interview.
  B Good luck!
  A Thanks. I'm feeling pretty nervous, actually.
  B Don't worry. You'll be fine.
  A Thanks!

Exercise 9

1 I didn't think we would get that new contract, but *we pulled it off*.
2 Sarah's desk is always so *messy* and she's *rather ill-mannered*.
3 Colin is *very punctual*.
4 I don't like that man. He *was unfair to me* when I first joined the team. He's *a bully*.
5 You'd better leave now, if you *want to avoid* the director.
6 I didn't like this job at first but things are *improving* now.
7 You'll find this job will certainly test *your abilities*.
8 Do you think this colour *suits* me?
9 I need a quiet room. I'm *a light sleeper*.
10 *I'm very tense* today.

Exercise 10

1 Fiona didn't *give* me a chance to explain.
2 I wanted to *see/watch* the late film on TV but I *fell* asleep.
3 Could you *do* me a favour, please?
4 I can't *stand* people who are always late.
5 I *was* very nervous before my interview yesterday.
6 John *turned* down a good job in Hollywood and decided to *settle* for a quiet life in his home town.
7 Don't *take* the boss too seriously. He *gets* angry very easily, but he never *bears* a grudge.

Grammar check 5

Exercise 1

1 *Felicity asked Tim if he was going to lunch.*
2 Mr Clapham asked Molly to phone the travel agency.
3 Samantha said she really enjoyed her holiday.
4 Mrs Usher said she wouldn't be late.
5 Daniel told Bill not to leave the CDs on the floor.
6 Bob asked Kate what she did on Sundays.
7 Jenny asked Rob not to leave.
8 The teacher told the boys to leave their boots outside.

Exercise 2

1 I *told* you to wait outside.
2 Johann *said* he was leaving.
3 Valerie *said* goodbye to her friends.
4 Have I *told* you the joke about the dog?
5 Sally *said* she was OK.

Exercise 3

1 *You shouldn't have left the cage open.*
  If you hadn't left it open the bird wouldn't have escaped.
2 You shouldn't have put your drink on top of the TV.
  If you hadn't put it on there it wouldn't have been knocked over.
3 You shouldn't have eaten so much at the party.
  If you hadn't eaten so much you wouldn't have been sick.
4 You shouldn't have left your bike unlocked.
  If you had locked it up it wouldn't have been stolen.

Exercise 4

I woke up while the flight attendant *was serving* breakfast. The plane *was crossing* the Channel, and when I *looked* out of the window, I *could* see ships far below me. I *was coming* home after a long time abroad. I *had been* away for over twenty years. I *didn't know* what to expect. I *wondered* whether things *had changed* much.

The plane *landed* and the bus *took* us to the terminal building. After I *had collected* my luggage, I *walked* out of the baggage hall. I didn't know whether anyone *would be* there to meet me. But when I *appeared*, I *had* a big surprise. Almost half my family was there. It was wonderful.

'You *won't recognize* the old town,' my sister told me. 'Almost everything *has changed* since you last *saw* it. They*'ve built* a new shopping centre near the park. The old town hall *was destroyed* by a fire about five years ago. They*'re building* a new one at the moment. They*'ve been building* it for the past three years in fact, but they *haven't finished* it yet.'

I*'ve been* back for nearly a month now. And my sister was right. The place looks very different, but strangely enough it still *feels* the same, because the people that I *love* are here. I*'m leaving* again in a few weeks' time, but I know that even if I*'m* away for twenty years again, this *will* always *be* my home.

GOWN

When Erica visited the vast Crosswyn estate in Queensland, she found herself surrounded by unexpected luxury. Yet she wasn't quite happy. She no longer felt sure of urbane, easy-going Jeremy, and as for his brother Matt . . . dark . . . threatening . . . disapproving, she had distrusted him from the first moment she set eyes on him.

With the addition of some difficult female inmates: sleek, predatory Lilyan; disabled and nervous Jenny; and Flo, who was dead but whose presence visibly still influenced the household; plus the echoes of a dying gipsy woman's last mysterious message; it was not surprising that Erica viewed her 'holiday' with some apprehension.

GOWN OF SCARLET

BY

SAMANTHA HARVEY

MILLS & BOON LIMITED
15–16 BROOK'S MEWS
LONDON W1A 1DR

CHAPTER ONE

THERE was no one in the foyer as Erica Fayne passed the open glass doors, crossed the faded carpet, and climbed the narrow stairs to her second floor flat. Yet she could not throw off the absurd feeling that she was not alone, that somebody somewhere was aware of every step she took, and knew just how uneasy she felt. And that of course was quite ridiculous.

As she fumbled in her handbag for her keyring Erica looked down at her fingers in disbelief. Her calm, capable nursing fingers, trained to deal with any emergency, were shaking.

Surely this couldn't be herself—Sister Fayne the unflappable—clutching her keys so awkwardly that she had to draw a deep steadying breath before she selected the right key, put it into the keyhole, and let herself into her flat.

Even then, safely inside, she was astonished to hear her own breathing shallow and irregular as if she might have climbed ten flights of stairs instead of two.

Outside her window the noises of a busy east-coast Australian city hummed. Inside, the early evening shadows made mysteries of her furniture, so that she turned on the light switch quickly, switched on the radio and poured herself a drink, appalled to see her fingers still unsteady.

She sat down, looking at the telephone wistfully.

If only Jeremy would ring and calm her down. She could imagine his amusement if the telephone rang and he was there, and she confessed, 'I'm sitting here praying for you to call and talk to me, because today I let my imagination run away with me.'

A tall, slender girl, with long and perfect legs and a heart-shaped face topped by short coppery curls, Erica had the delicate complexion of the redhead, creamy and fragile. As she sipped her drink she glanced into the wall mirror beside her and discovered that her face was paler than usual, the dark lashes around her green eyes contrasting with the whiteness of her cheeks.

She should have guessed today would be disastrous, from the moment she reported for duty at the hospital to find the rosters had been changed and she was directed to Flip Jennings' ward. Flip had waited for her in the corridor.

Flip was her friend and a splendid nurse with an insatiable curiosity about her patients, but nothing ever went calmly when she was around. Flip liked to dramatise, and today she had been agog with excitement.

'Take a special look at the patient in Three East,' she had hissed. 'She's a gipsy, and she's dying, poor woman. That's her family standing around the door. They won't go away.'

Erica had glanced towards the dark-skinned people hovering in the corridor. They stared back at her with sombre, inward-looking eyes, totally involved in an experience that did not include her. Erica doubted if they even noticed her as she walked away from Flip and began her rounds.

Inside Three East, she had glanced towards a bed by the window where a swarthy middle-aged man sat beside a silent woman. Sunlight beaming in through the glass dropped flecks of brightness onto his grey hair, but his face was shadowed and dark. He leaned forward in the chair, arms hanging limply between his knees, seeming unaware of anything around him.

Yet as Erica approached he stood slowly and quietly, allowing her to pull the screening curtain around the bed. He did not speak as he moved away. His silence had not been rude, only detached, as if his world began and ended with the woman lying in the bed.

As Erica glanced professionally at the unconscious form she saw a powerful face, with strong features, skin the colour of light oak now tinged with pallor. Although no longer young she was a striking woman. Her closed eyelids made deep hollows above gaunt cheekbones and her hair, although silver-streaked, had a sheen of blackness that showed stark against the white pillows.

Compassionately Erica had curved her fingers around the brown wrist, checking the fluttering pulse, when suddenly the eyelids flickered open. Dark brown eyes stared into Erica's.

'You have kind hands.'

'Thank you.'

Erica had a special confidence-smile for those who needed it. She had smiled at the half-conscious gipsy reassuringly, but there was no answering gleam in those fantastic eyes.

The frail head moved against the pillows. 'Helping hands.' Her breath came in a long fluttering sigh. 'But are they strong enough to lift the trap-door?'

The failing mind wandered, of course; but some-thing about the whispered question had shaken Erica. Many times she had listened to the discon-nected murmurings of patients as they drifted through the twilight world that was neither waking nor sleeping. She had given none of them a second thought until today, and there was really no reason why today should have been any different. Yet the whispered words stayed with her.

Erica imagined that her patient had slipped back into unconsciousness as she arranged pillows and settled the head comfortably, but when she finished all she had to do and began to move away, the eyes had flickered open again.

The woman struggled to raise herself, and Erica eased her back gently.

'Run!' The voice sounded faint and far away, but clear. 'Run for the trees . . .'

Those fathomless eyes pleaded with her, and Erica nodded. The eyelids fluttered down and the woman sank back limply onto the pillows. Erica pulled back the curtain, and the man came back to resume his vigil.

There was no way the dark man could possibly have overheard those faltering words, yet as she attended to other patients in the ward Erica felt his gaze follow her, silent and thoughtful, and it seemed to her that his eyes had become strangely intent, as if he might have picked up some vibration that disturbed him. Perhaps that had unsettled her most of all—the knowledge in the swarthy man's eyes.

Later, she had walked out of the ward to find Flip waiting: Flip had taken one look at her face and blinked.

'You look terrible.'

'Perhaps I'm tired.'

So perhaps she was tired . . . She shivered slightly now, clasping both hands around the glass she held. If only Jeremy would call and drive these imaginings away.

She was probably tired from an overdose of excitement, because tomorrow was her last day at the hospital before her leave came due, and a few days ago she had made one of the most important decisions of her life.

She had agreed to spend her holidays with Jeremy at his brother's property in central Queensland. They both knew what that meant—a deepening of the relationship between them, which up to now had been fairly casual.

This could well be the beginning of an affair with the quietly confident Jeremy. It could lead to marriage. She certainly hoped so. Jeremy was the first man who had even vaguely interested Erica in this kind of arrangement.

The decision had not been easy. Erica's lips curved in a wry smile at the thought of what her mother might say if she heard about her daughter's rashness. But both her parents were at home in England, and Erica had no one to dissuade her. She had said Yes, finally, and tried to ignore the smoke from burning bridges or at least not to let it daunt her.

She was twenty-three and she had a life to live. Nobody wanted to go on nursing other people's broken bones forever, then coming home to an empty flat. That was what Jeremy had told her, and it sounded reasonable.

Erica sighed. Perhaps she needed this holiday with Jeremy more than she realised. Certainly her imagination had never played this sort of trick on her before. She was a level-headed, well-trained nurse who took a great deal of pride in her work, and to be thrown off balance by a patient's wanderings was something new to her.

All she wanted right now was a telephone call, bringing a dose of Jeremy's common sense, and she would be all right . . .

Yet when the telephone rang she started, and if the glass in her hand had been fuller she might have spilled its contents over her precious carpet.

She picked up the receiver and said, 'This is Erica Fayne' and held her breath until the caller spoke— it was Jeremy.

'Ric! Where have you been? I called an hour ago. You're late.'

'I know.'

She had stopped to do some shopping on the way home, then driven slowly and carefully through the traffic because of this haunted feeling. Now she was surprised to find herself babbling.

'I've been on a buying spree, I thought I'd get something for the holiday. I've bought a new dress . . . it's jade green and very fetching, I hope you'll like it. Oh Jeremy, I'm so glad it's you. I was hoping—'

'Who else were you expecting?'

She didn't miss the irony in his voice. Jeremy would stay cool and detached if the sky fell on him, but he must have been pleased by some need or warmth he heard in her voice, because he added more softly, 'You can welcome me like that any time, sweetie. It's nice to know you're needing me.'

Jeremy always sounded boyish, although he was in reality a remarkably astute and mature operator. A talented man forging his way to the top of his profession, journalism, the naive approach was something he cultivated because he found it useful in his contact with people. It put them off guard, opening doors that might have stayed shut to a more aggressive man. He had confided this one night in an expansive mood, and Erica understood and admired him for his clearsightedness.

He went on now, 'If you're so pleased to hear my voice, let's hope you'll be even more delighted to welcome me in person, because I'm coming to see you.'

Her heart leaped in relief.

'Now?'

'About an hour and a half, perhaps a little more. Big brother Matt is coming down from Queensland, I'm to pick him up at Sydney airport. I decided as we're spending our holidays with him I'd better bring him along and introduce you two to each other. Think you could whip up supper for two hungry men?'

'Of course.'

Mascot airport in Sydney was more than a hundred kilometres away; there was plenty of time to prepare. Then, just as she expected him to hang up the phone, Jeremy added with a careful casualness that made her fingers tighten on the receiver, 'By the way, Ric, I rang your friend Flip Jennings, trying to get in touch with you. She says you met an interesting patient today—a gipsy. Swears you went in to look at her and came out white around the gills. What happened?'

'Nothing.'

She knew her voice didn't sound convincing, and Jeremy wasn't deceived.

He said, 'Oh?' and Erica felt the chill. Whatever Flip Jennings had told him must have made an impression. He let a small silence grow before he added coolly, 'Well, you might do a man a favour. Keep your eyes and ears open. There could be a story in it. Gipsies aren't all that plentiful in our neck of the woods.'

'The woman is unconscious. She's had a cerebral haemorrhage—'

'All right. Stay cool. I'll see you soon. We'll talk about it then.'

'Jeremy—Yes, all right.' Erica put the receiver down and sat staring at it, forgetting her drink, forgetting how desperately she had needed Jeremy to call her.

He hadn't banished her fears at all. He had thrown her into worse confusion, because she knew she was not going to tell him what had happened today.

Jeremy had his newspaperman's nose pointed in her direction, not his friendship, and instinct warned her not to talk to him. It wasn't worth repeating anyway, just the meanderings of a semi-conscious woman. To make a newspaper story out of it would be absurd.

Gipsy warnings were a joke. Nobody took them seriously, she upbraided herself. It was unfortunate that Flip had aroused Jeremy's curiosity, but it wasn't fatal. She would have to fend him off with casual answers, doing her best to treat it lightly.

Erica sighed. It had been an unsettling day and it was not finished yet.

She walked into her small kitchen, making a quick check of cupboards and refrigerator. She would have no trouble supplying supper.

There was a quiche lorraine in the freezer, rye bread and cold cooked chicken for sandwiches, a selection of cheeses and plenty of cracker biscuits, even a carrot cake she had made yesterday from one of Flip's health food recipes.

Erica checked to make sure there were enough drinks, putting out a bottle of white wine to go with the chicken sandwiches, and her precious Tia Maria. They would finish supper with coffee and liqueurs, not because she wanted to make an impression on her visitor but because the evening called for something special to bring it back to normal.

She wondered idly whether Jeremy's brother would look like Jeremy. It was difficult to imagine Jeremy on the land in outback Queensland or anywhere else. He was city-smooth, neat and urbane, not tall but somehow impressive because he wore a permanent air of self-confidence and determination. Always well-groomed, his cap of thick brown hair shining and well-shaped, with a soft wave dipping over his forehead, he could have made the pages of any glossy magazine showing what the well-dressed man ought to wear and what he should look like.

Erica showered quickly, pampering herself with

fragrance until she felt refreshed, confidence restored. She selected a short frock threaded with lurex in shimmering blue. It made her look frivolous, but she intended it that way. This was an evening for gaiety, for driving away depressing spirits.

She brushed her short red-gold curls, tied a silver band across her forehead, then skipped a few cheeky Charleston steps around the kitchen before she covered the shimmering frock with an apron and began preparing supper.

She must be grateful to Jeremy for providing company on this evening that could have been haunted. Soon, she promised herself happily, Jeremy would bring his calm, reasoning mind to reassure her, and the whole disturbing day would be forgotten . . .

Later, when Jeremy's three sharp raps sounded on her door, Erica almost danced to open it. Here was Jeremy, bringing instant sanity.

She flung open the door, face uplifted in bright welcome. Jeremy whistled once at her sparkling appearance, then bent and kissed her lightly before he said, 'Ric, meet my brother, Matthew', and stepped aside, leaving the man behind him blocking her doorway.

And Erica saw with a cold shock that hit her like icy fingers of premonition and disappointment, that Jeremy's brother Matthew was not at all like Jeremy.

He was a big man, but it was not size that made the impact. It was his overwhelming darkness and something else—an aura of immense and controlled power. He stood there solid as rock, staring at

her out of narrowed eyes, summing her up, and
intuition told Erica that Jeremy's brother was not
impressed with what he saw.

He was dressed entirely in black, as if no other
colour had ever been invented. Trousers, silk shirt,
leather jacket, even his hair was the colour of night,
and jet-black eyebrows made pointed arches above
eyes that were grey and cold as arctic ice.

Erica thought at first that he was bearded, but as
he stepped into the room she saw that he was
unshaven, his jaw dark with stubble. His black curls
were clipped short, except at the back where they
clustered on the nape of his neck.

His lips twisted disparagingly as he scanned
Erica's flyaway appearance, and she thought
crossly, 'He should understand, his hair doesn't
look any easier to control than mine,' but she
managed to say chirpily, 'Hi! Come and sit
down', and the visitor came in quietly enough. He
could have been travel-weary. There were shadows
around his eyes, which seemed to grow icier under
the light.

He took off his jacket and draped it over the arm
of a chair, but he did not sit down. Instead, he stood
looking at her, and Jeremy grinned.

'It's all right to shake hands, you two. You're
officially introduced, so you can touch each other.'

He thought that was a joke, but Matthew Crosswyn was not smiling. Erica found her fingers en-
gulfed in an enormous suntanned hand, but Matthew let her go quickly, not prolonging the contact.

So perhaps the evening was not going to provide
the light entertainment Erica had hoped for. If the
room had been haunted before, there was now an

extra dimension of discomfort—Matthew Crosswyn's obvious disapproval. He didn't have to say a
word, his dislike hovered like an extra presence.

Jeremy said, 'Matt wishes to apologise for the
nine o'clock shadow. He planned to drop off at my
town house in Sydney and have a shave, but I didn't
give him a chance. I carried him here direct from
the airport.'

Then he added deliberately, 'If you want to
freshen up, old son, there's an electric razor of
mine in Ric's bedroom', and Matthew raised one
eyebrow without saying a word.

Erica flushed uncomfortably. There was a razor
belonging to Jeremy in her bedroom; he kept it
there for emergencies, for the times he called to see
her between assignments. Now he was deliberately
giving his brother the impression that he had as
good as moved into Erica's flat. She shouldn't have
minded. After all, she was committed to this holiday they both knew would lead to some kind of
deeper involvement . . . but she did mind.

Matthew Crosswyn didn't waste words. 'I shan't
be staying long. I'll shave later, if you don't mind,
when we get back to Sydney,' and Jeremy quipped,
'Then Ric will have to accept your apology for the
rugged look.'

Matthew did not look apologetic. That heavy
growth of dark hair probably meant he had to shave
more often than most men. His face in stronger
light did not lose its look of shuttered darkness,
except that those piercing eyes grew sharper.

Erica saw him glance around the tiny flat that she
loved, one eyebrow quirked ironically as if its
dimensions amused him. He certainly did not fit in

here. Perhaps he was thinking that Jeremy did.

There was none of Jeremy's carefully cultivated candour in Matthew's eyes. They missed nothing. Erica turned away from his inspection, and walked into the kitchen to collect her cheese tray while Jeremy poured drinks. She didn't like the dark man looking into her with those penetrating eyes that were entirely without compassion. Especially this evening, because tonight she had a secret, and she did not want this hostile man stirring it up.

Yet it was Jeremy who finally touched the raw nerve. As he poured a glass of Scotch and placed it beside his brother, he made his move.

'How is the mysterious gipsy lady?' he queried lightly, and the cheese tray tilted in Erica's hands as if he had pushed it.

As she lost control Matthew's arm shot out, steadying the tray by covering her fingers with his own, engulfing them as he had done before, but this time his grasp was even firmer.

When she regained composure Erica glowered at him indignantly.

He released her, saying nothing, his sardonic smile suggesting he might be faintly amused by her indignation, but he wasn't fooled anyway. He knew she had been startled by Jeremy's question.

Hastily, Erica put the tray on the table beside Matthew's drink. She had a stricken feeling that her hand might be shaking, and she didn't want him to see what he had done.

'Aren't you listening to me, Ric?' It was Jeremy, aggrieved, and Erica thankfully turned her back on Matthew.

'Of course I am listening. What were you

saying?' From behind her Matthew's soft voice prompted, 'Jeremy asked about one of your patients. A gipsy, I understand.'

They were both tuned in to her, waiting for her answer. If only she didn't have this defensive urge to pretend she had no idea what they were talking about . . .

She hated deceiving Jeremy. He was entitled to ask questions. That was natural newspaperman's curiosity, Erica understood perfectly, so why did she resent it tonight?

She produced her brightest smile. 'Sorry to disappoint you, gentlemen, but Flip has made a mountain out of a speck of dust. There is nothing to tell you about the gipsy. Nothing at all.'

Jeremy sipped his drink thoughtfully.

'But there *is* a mysterious gipsy woman dying in your hospital?'

'In the hospital where I work, yes.'

'In one of your wards?'

'In one of the wards where I was rostered for duty today along with a lot of other nurses. Including Flip Jennings, who has a runaway imagination.'

'And that's all?'

'I'm afraid so.'

Jeremy put down his glass slowly, deliberately. He didn't believe her, thanks to Flip and her loose tongue. It was a long time since Jeremy had been either naive or easily sidetracked when he scented a story. He said testily, 'Oh come on, Ric . . . 'White as a sheet' . . . I think that was one of the expressions Flip used to describe you, and she is a trained observer. So what happened between you and the gipsy?'

It took all Erica's willpower to lie to Jeremy, but it had to be done. 'How could anything happen? The poor woman's unconscious. She has her family around her, and if she regains consciousness my guess is that she'll talk to one of them, not to a humble nursing sister.'

Jeremy shrugged. 'Okay. I suppose I'll have to be content with that.'

But he knew her too well. He was still alert, he would wait for her to weaken and tell him what he wanted to know.

She mumbled, 'I have to whip some cream,' and retreated to the kitchen. She whipped the cream, ladled some of it into a crystal jug and put it beside the Tia Maria, with three of her liqueur glasses, for later. She was removing an ice tray from the refrigerator, masked by the open door, when Jeremy's low voice asked, 'Well, old boy, what do you think of her?'

She froze. Matthew Crosswyn's answer sounded slightly bored.

'A little less sophisticated than your usual companions, isn't she? But I suppose she knows her job.'

'Of course she does. What do you think—will she do?'

Erica's lips tightened. She clattered the ice tray on to a bench and flounced into the sitting-room.

'Will I do for what?'

Unconsciously, she had lifted one hand onto her hip, head tilted back in challenge, and for the first time Matthew's lips curved in a genuine smile that was nevertheless faintly malicious.

'I'm sure you'd—ah—do for anything.'

Jeremy hurried in quickly, 'Now, sweetie, we weren't talking behind your back. I was fishing for compliments, that's all.'

But he was not comfortable. He flashed his brother a look as if seeking some kind of support before he explained, 'You see, Matt wondered whether while we are at Vandellan—well, he'd like your professional opinion on a girl who's had an accident—'

'I am not a medical adviser.'

'Of course not.'

Jeremy was turning on the boyish charm, soothing her. 'Matt only wants you to try and talk to this girl, maybe gain her confidence, because she's very prickly. She's in a wheelchair, and it could be a permanent injury, but the doctors don't think so. She has a—a kind of psychological shock that makes her back away from people. I—we—thought that with your experience you might know how to reach her. That's all, isn't it, Matt?'

Matt's voice was terse. 'Perhaps Erica would prefer to come to Vandellan some other time.' He turned those powerful grey eyes full on to her as if he were trying to plant an intention in her mind, programming her to say, 'You're right, I don't want to come just now. Maybe some other time.' She could feel it as clearly as if he had spoken the words.

He didn't like her, he didn't want her on his precious property, and because it became suddenly important to thwart him Erica snapped, 'Are you withdrawing your invitation?'

Jeremy shot her a quelling look, and put in, 'Of course he isn't. Don't be so touchy, Ric,' but Matthew said nothing at all.

He sat on one of her favourite antique chairs, making it look ridiculous with his great frame almost blotting it from sight, the delicately carved legs looking disastrously fragile under him. He saw her observing and their glances locked. 'Don't worry,' he said cynically, 'I'm not as awkward as I appear, but I'll move to something more solid if you're afraid your doll's house might collapse around me.'

She retorted crisply, 'My doll's house, Mr Crosswyn, isn't half as fragile as you might think. I assure you, we'll survive.'

The words hung in the air as if they might have had a double meaning. He looked at her hard from under those strangely peaked brows, and she held his gaze because it was important not to let him defeat her.

Jeremy stared from one to the other of them warily, as if he sensed tension between them, and Erica felt suddenly ashamed.

She had snapped that reply without thinking. What had she meant? 'I, Erica Fayne, will not collapse however hard you lean on me . . . I shall not break . . .'

She made herself relax. 'If you're both ready, I'll fetch supper. You must be hungry.'

Jeremy followed her into the kitchen, took in her mutinous expression and whistled again, this time with raised eyebrows.

'What's all this about?' He was being extra charming, so perhaps that scrap of overheard conversation held some importance after all. He tucked an unruly red curl under the headband, stroked the lobe of one ear, teasing lightly:

'Cyclone Erica! Don't get upset, sweetie. I simply told Matt you are a bright girl and I value your opinion, and he said "Good. Maybe Erica will talk to Jenny while she's at Vandellan, because no one else can get near her." So I said I thought you'd help.'

He picked up the quiche lorraine, warm on its serving platter, and took a plate of sandwiches in his other hand.

'You needn't have gone to all this trouble, old girl, but I'm pleased you did. I haven't had a bite since breakfast and poor old Matt had a long wait between flight connections, so your good work is appreciated.'

He pursed his lips in kissing shape, coaxing her to forget what had happened. Erica wished she could. She thought, 'He's lying to me and I lied to him, and this is the first time such a horrid thing has happened. Whom shall I trust if I can't trust Jeremy?'

Matthew did an about-turn and became surprisingly agreeable over supper. He complimented Erica on the food, thanked her for the wine, came back for seconds . . . yet Matthew being polite sent out as many warnings as when he was openly disagreeable.

Erica didn't care for the feeling she was getting. There were undercurrents in her flat as if the two brothers shared a secret. It showed in the exchanged glances, the silences. She was not the only person holding back tonight.

Matthew made one more attempt to put her off the visit to Vandellan in Queensland.

'We're getting into the wet season. As an English

girl, you'll hardly be prepared for our humidity, and the electrical storms can be rather terrifying.'

Erica said sweetly, 'Oh, but Mr Crosswyn, that's exactly what I want to see. I can't tell you how much I'm looking forward to my first cyclone.'

A muscle moved in his jaw. 'If you're coming to Vandellan, you'd better learn to call me Matthew.'

He didn't want her at Vandellan, that was obvious. He wouldn't care if he never saw her again. Since she felt exactly the same way about him she couldn't understand why she perversely found his dislike rather shattering.

It was Jeremy who defused the situation. 'Since we'll only be in Queensland a couple of weeks, I hardly think the Wet will descend on us in full force.' His frown for Matthew held a tinge of warning. 'Erica will think you don't want us, old man.'

Matthew offered only casual politenesses after that. He raised an eyebrow when the Tia Maria was produced after they had eaten, but he appreciated it. He even seemed to relax a little, but Erica was relieved when he announced not long afterwards, 'I hate to eat and drink and run, but I've had a long day. I hope you'll excuse me if I cut out. I'll ring for a taxi, if Erica doesn't mind me using her phone,' he was looking at Jeremy, 'so you won't need to leave yet.'

He was putting on the leather jacket, fitting his long arms into its sleeves, moving his muscular body quickly, easily.

From somewhere Erica managed to produce a radiant smile.

'Of course we'll excuse you. You must be tired.'

She didn't care if he was totally exhausted. She wanted him out of her flat. She had never, she told herself, taken such an instant dislike to anybody. So let him go quickly, and she and Jeremy could talk. She might ask the exact meaning of that cryptic snatch of overheard conversation, she might ask other things . . . .

But Jeremy was not pleased with her tonight. He stood up quickly. 'I'll drive you back, Matt. Don't bother about the taxi. Ric won't mind being left with the dishes.'

That meant he wasn't overlooking her lack of frankness over the gipsy and what had happened at the hospital. His goodnight kiss was fleeting. For a man who planned to whisk her off in a few days' time for the start of something big it was decidedly casual, but Ric forgave him. She had been difficult. She didn't understand her own behaviour at all.

Over Jeremy's shoulder as he dropped that noticeably slight kiss on her cheek Erica became aware of Matthew's scrutiny. Those ice-grey eyes taunted her, letting her know that the chill of that embrace had not gone unobserved.

'Goodnight, Erica.' His voice was bland. 'Thank you for a pleasant evening. We'll see you at Vandellan, unless you change your mind.'

'Never!'

She closed the door on them both, collected cups and glasses, filled the sink with hot water, stacked things away, her annoyance carrying her through the tasks quickly.

Afterwards, dressed for bed in a filmy nightdress of soft peach, Erica studied her reflection in the bedroom mirror. The glass showed a shadowy figure, with large wide eyes that asked questions, as if something might be happening to her security.

There was no doubt about it, the big dark man had added to her uneasiness. She straightened her shoulders, making the girl in the mirror look back at her with more resolution. That was better . . .

Today she had been foolish, for the first time in her career letting herself become too closely involved with a patient. And, worse still, she had involved Jeremy. Tomorrow she must do her best to straighten things out.

CHAPTER TWO

WHEN Erica arrived at the hospital next day she did not find her dark lady. The bed was empty, stripped and airing ready for its next occupant.

'Gone home,' Flip answered Erica's unspoken question. 'Matron says she came out of coma last night and asked to be taken away. Said she didn't want to die here. There wasn't anything else we could do for her, so the ambulance left early this morning.'

Where was home, Erica wondered, and as if she went in for thought-reading Flip added, 'They've set up their vans in a caravan park a few miles along the coast from Sydney.' She gave a short laugh. 'Joe, the ambulance driver, says they have modern vans, like the tourists. No old-fashioned horse-drawns any more for our gipsies.'

Erica carried out her duties with a sense of relief, knowing that today there would be no hauntings, no distractions.

Matron caught her as she finished for the day. In her hand she held a small parcel wrapped in tissue paper.

'For you,' her smile was half amused, half questioning. 'It seems you made an impression on one of our patients.'

'Not—the gipsy—?'

'That's right.' Matron's brows lifted. 'Her husband left this, with instructions that you

26

wear it. He was most emphatic.'

Erica unwrapped the small parcel. Inside, a ring lay on a twist of lavender tissue, a broad band of gold with bars of diamond crystal. Erica stared at it in dismay.

'I can't keep this. I don't even know the man, not even his name.'

Matron shrugged. 'Those are my orders.' Her lips twisted, 'As I told you, the man was most insistent. It's no use giving that trinket back to me, I wouldn't know what to do with it.'

Erica re-wrapped the parcel. 'Sister Jennings says the gipsies have gone to a caravan park. Could you give me the address? I'll return this ring tomorrow.'

'Oh yes, you're going on holiday, aren't you?' Matron's features stayed carefully expressionless. She wasn't giving anything away, but no doubt the hospital grapevine had informed her of Erica's holiday plans.

Erica copied down the address from the hospital records and hurried to the car park. She pushed the ring into her handbag, and when she arrived home she climbed the stairs to her flat without any of the previous evening's forebodings, and she was grateful.

It was kind of the man to think of her, but he must understand she could not keep the jewellery. Jeremy hadn't telephoned today. Perhaps he was still offended. Erica's face sobered. It wasn't the best way to begin what could be the most important holiday of her life. Despite that, she slept well that night and awoke refreshed. She washed and ironed clothing, shampooed her hair, tidied her flat.

It was late afternoon when Erica drove her small car into the caravan park, but she had no trouble locating the gipsies. They were grouped together along one side of the park. In the doorway of a large caravan Erica found the man she was looking for. He did not seem surprised to see her, he might even have been expecting her. Although he did not smile as she approached, his expression was not unfriendly. He looked remote and composed, as if he gazed out from another world.

'I've brought back your ring.' Erica held out the parcel. 'I can't accept such a valuable gift, I'm sure you'll understand.' She pressed the parcel into his unwilling hand. 'I'm sorry to intrude. How is your wife?'

'She died this morning, as she wished among our people. Would you like to see her? It will please her spirit that you came.'

The voice was deep, grief controlled. Erica said helplessly, 'I'm sorry. I wish we could have saved her', and he inclined his head, accepting her compassion, before he led her into the caravan.

The gipsy lay on a large bed with her hands folded peacefully, brown fingers interlaced. She had been dressed in a long red gown lavishly embroidered in gold, with the skirt fanning out so that it covered the bed. Around her neck there were gold chains, hung with coins and medallions, and her hair was hidden by a scarlet scarf. It too glittered with bright embroidery.

Erica whispered softly, 'Your wife must have been a remarkable woman,' and the man nodded.

'Yes. She was a strong woman and very wise. She will lie here for three days with us, while her spirit searches among our people for its new home. At the end of that time we will know that she has chosen. Meanwhile,' he gently placed the parcel back into Erica's hand, 'she was greatly troubled for you. It was her wish that you wear the ring for your protection.'

With sombre eyes he searched Erica's face, as if he might have been reading something there that she could not see.

'Wear the ring,' he murmured, 'It will bring her peace.'

Light was fading when Erica arrived home. Inside her flat Jeremy waited, calmly sipping a cup of black coffee. He could never have known where she had been, because Matron was no garrulous Flip Jennings. Yet Jeremy's glance at her was shrewd, speculative.

'You're late.'

Erica looked around her quickly. Although she could see nobody else in her flat she had the sharp impression of Matthew's presence, a feeling of prickly discomfort.

'Your brother—?'

Jeremy stared at her with disfavour.

'Why so interested, sweetie?'

He peered into his coffee cup. 'Anyway, he's gone back to Vandellan. Completed his business, whatever it was, and flew home. We'll catch up with him some time tomorrow afternoon.'

Jeremy had been drinking something stronger than coffee before he reached Erica's flat. Not too much, just enough to make him mellow. He put down the cup and came closer, sliding his hands around her waist, pulling her towards him.

'Twenty-four hours, sweetheart. I'm not sure I can wait that long.'

Erica lifted her face and kissed him. To her horror she became aware of a flash of reluctance as he moved his hands over her body. She kissed him again, a sisterly embrace, fond but without fire.

He said quickly, 'I'm not tipsy. In case you think I am—'

'Of course not.'

He looked at her ruefully. 'You have a prudish look in your eye.'

'Not prudish. Just tired.' She eased herself away from his grasp. In her present mood Jeremy couldn't stir her. She doubted whether anyone could.

'Never mind.' He released her abruptly. 'How is your gipsy progressing?'

'She died.'

'Oh well, bang goes my story.'

Jeremy would forget the gipsy now. For Erica it would take longer.

She picked up Jeremy's cup. 'I'll give you one more drink, black and strong, then if you want me to pack for tomorrow you'd better leave me to it. Unless you'd like a meal?'

Her smile was shadowy, apologetic, because she didn't need to be told this was not the reception Jeremy expected. But he drank the coffee, declined the offer of a meal, smoothed his hair and straightened his tie, saying, 'All right. See you tomorrow. I'll pick you up here.'

If his smile was crooked, Erica knew he wasn't

too put out by her unexpected coolness. After tomorrow he would have ample time to light any fires he wanted, and he would do that, because hadn't she led him to believe that was what she wanted?

Packing did not take long. The jade green dress she had bought in that turbulent mood two days ago still hung outside her wardrobe and she draped it against her.

It was by far the most elegant gown she had ever owned, not to mention the most expensive. Perhaps there would be a staircase at Vandellan for her to float down, although Jeremy had never mentioned it, and it was not Jeremy she imagined in the background, it was a larger figure. She dropped the dress quickly on top of the suitcase. Perhaps she should leave it at home.

Jeremy had advised casual wear, cotton shirts with long sleeves and jeans for day wear, or light summer dresses.

'You'll fry if you aren't careful,' he had warned her cheerfully. 'Matt was right, you aren't ready for the Australian sun. We'll buy you a sunhat when we get there.'

They would drive to Sydney airport, Jeremy had their airline tickets, he had practically everything under control, because that was his way. The only item not under control threatened to be herself, and Erica decided thankfully that Jeremy was quite capable of dealing with that, too. All her misgivings, all the shadowy apprehensions she couldn't explain, would evaporate when Jeremy worked on them.

On impulse, she folded the jade green dress

carefully and placed it on top of her other clothing, then snapped the suitcase shut.

She put the gipsy ring on her dressing-table beside the bed, and she must have been tense because she slept only fitfully. In the morning the bedclothes were twisted and her head ached, but she managed to be dressed and ready before Jeremy's knock sounded on her door.

While he carried her luggage into the passage she made a quick check of her flat. Everything seemed in order.

At the last moment Erica picked up the gipsy ring, unrolled the tissue paper and slipped the gold band on to the third finger of her right hand. It fitted perfectly.

As she handed her airways bag to Jeremy he looked down at her hand swiftly, and there was an oddness in his eyes and in his voice. 'Something new?'

His gaze lingered on the ring on her finger, so it was no use pretending she didn't know what he was talking about. Erica managed a careless shrug.

'It's rather old, actually.'

'A bit heavy and ugly, isn't it? Why haven't I seen it before?'

Erica closed the door behind them.

'Maybe I have a few things you haven't seen yet.'

It was a suggestive remark, and it brought an appreciative grin to Jeremy's lips. He picked up her case and followed her quietly downstairs, but his eyes stayed watchful. He suspected she was with-holding information and he didn't care for that sort of behaviour. He liked everything out in the open for him to analyse. No secrets, no holding back.

It hit her, then, that Jeremy might become a possessive and demanding lover, and she was depressed by the thought. Jeremy the cool one, always in control, didn't seem a likely candidate for possessiveness, but you never really did know people. They were always turning up surprises. And Jeremy could well have some surprises for her when they reached Vandellan.

Although Erica was a seasoned air traveller she carried a nagging feeling of unease with her all the way to Brisbane in Queensland, and when they changed planes for an inland town the unrest followed her there as well.

From the inland airport they were to transfer to a coach for the final leg of their journey, but as they alighted Jeremy said, 'Well, well. He's here, after all. Dragged himself away from his chores.'

Erica followed his gaze towards a group of waiting people. A tall man leaned over a white painted fence, watching them.

'Your brother Matthew?'

'Who else? Must have flown in to pick us up.'

Erica said politely, 'That's certainly VIP service,' but she didn't share Jeremy's delight. Aware of Matthew's keen eyes watching, she directed a brilliant smile at Jeremy and slipped her arm through his. Matthew stayed unsmiling as they walked towards him.

He looked more like a station hand than a rich and successful grazier, Erica told herself critically. Hip-hugging jeans, rather tattered, green and white checked shirt with sleeves rolled up to the elbows, and an air of hard-faced determination gave him a rough-tough appearance. But as he uncoiled himself from the fence he was leaning over, he swung a cattleman's wide-brimmed hat over his black hair, and Ric conceded reluctantly that even in this gear he looked more impressive than anyone around him.

Obviously, he wasn't prepared to return the compliment. He wasn't impressed by Erica's appearance at all. He stayed with her while Jeremy collected their luggage, and his critical eyes raked her from anklestrap sandals up, taking in the yellow sheath dress showing a length of slender leg, travelling on to the coloured band holding the bright curls across her forehead, narrowing as he glimpsed the gipsy ring on her finger. She saw him hesitate, react, then move on to scan some other part of her appearance, but she was quite certain he had taken note of the heavy gold band.

'My appearance doesn't meet with your approval, Mr Crosswyn?' she questioned sweetly, and his teeth flashed in a broad grin.

'I'm sure you feel the same about me.' he murmured, 'And out here we dispense with formality. Call me Matt.'

Chin tilted, she challenged him. 'I wonder what else you dispense with?'

'Don't hesitate to ask.' His expression turned ice-cold. 'No doubt you'll be asking plenty of questions. You seem to be the kind of girl who likes to know where she's going.'

That was not intended as a compliment, and Erica seethed, but Jeremy came back with their suitcases, and she smothered the sharp retort that trembled on her lips.

When they reached his private plane Matt indi-

cated that Jeremy was to sit beside him at the
controls. To reach her rear seat Erica had to climb
over one wing via a small metal ladder, and there
seemed to be some misunderstanding as to who
would help her.

Jeremy hesitated as if allowing his brother the
honour, but Matthew stepped back deliberately.
He was extending no chivalrous hand, and the
ironic lift of his brows nettled Erica so that she
brushed Jeremy's hand aside and climbed into the
plane without assistance from either of them.

Her petty annoyance amused Matthew. He
shrugged before taking his place at the controls and
switching on the radio. Erica heard his deep, incis-
ive voice communicating with the control tower.

He taxi-ed on to the runway, then suddenly the
increasing roar set the plane vibrating so violently
that Erica almost put her hands over her ears to
shut out the noise. Just in time she prevented
herself giving Matthew Crosswyn that satisfaction.
Yet somehow as they soared into the sky Erica
suspected that the big man sensed her discomfort.
Once or twice he turned his head, pointing out with
what she could only decide was diabolical cheerful-
ness some feature of the scene below.

From somewhere, it seemed, she had acquired
this morning an unreasonable fear of flying. This
plane was too small. It was noisy. It gave her a
weird sense of instability and downright cowardice
as the world dropped away beneath them. She was
grateful later when the plane banked and glided
down towards the airstrip on Vandellan. They
landed smoothly.

Erica had her revenge, a childish revenge, as she

alighted from the plane. Matthew actually prof-
fered a steadying hand as she climbed on to the
wing but she ignored him blithely, feeling for the
metal rung with her foot, only too well aware that
he stood close by, apparently undeterred by her
snub, as if he suspected she could be unsteady after
the flight.

A yellow station wagon swung in beside the
airstrip, and a youth in tartan shirt and brown cords
alighted. In the distance he appeared to be a very
young edition of Matthew, tall and dark with black
curly hair, but as he walked towards them Erica
noticed that his welcoming smile did not quite
reach his eyes. Then he saw her standing behind
Matt and his face brightened.

'Hey! Where did you come from? It's not Christmas for another few weeks yet,' and Matthew said
drily, 'This is Guy, not long out of school.'

Guy must have been eighteen or nineteen, and
seen close up he lost most of the resemblance to
Matthew except for the colouring. He was obviously another brother. His face was soft, his
mouth vulnerable, eyes insecure.

Matthew tossed him one of the suitcases. 'Watch
your tongue, Guy. This is not a Christmas present
for you. This is Erica, Jeremy's—' a short pause as
he sought the appropriate word—'Jeremy's friend.'

'Very pretty. Fantastic. And that's a quaint ring
you're wearing, Erica. I'm glad it's not on the other
hand. If you're not engaged there's hope for me,
isn't there?'

'No, there isn't.' Jeremy spoke without rancour.
Maybe he, too, sensed the boy's lack of assurance.
Erica gave him an encouraging smile. He was

young and he talked too much, but he meant no offence. More, her training showed her the excessive tension behind the quick and cheerful welcome, a suggestion of nerves stretched so tight she guessed the slightest rebuff would dash the smile from his face.

They settled themselves in the station wagon, Matthew driving with Guy alongside him, and that left Erica sitting with Jeremy in the rear seat.

Guy and Jeremy pointed out landmarks as they drove, explaining that Vandellan was one of several large properties on a tableland known as Shandoven Downs. There were places on the edge of the downs, Jeremy told her, where cliffs dropped sheer and impassable to the plains below. 'So we never have to worry about being invaded.'

Jeremy's grin came accompanied by a cheerful wink, and Erica felt she was being reminded that the Crosswyns had never worried about invasion or any other kind of intrusion.

From the self-confidence that was so much a part of them all, showing traces even in the nervous Guy, Erica understood that they had always found themselves among the privileged whose position in life was unassailable, and as she watched the rise and fall of green grass paddocks and fields of chocolate-coloured earth she realised that this was a rich world, unlike any she had ever seen before.

They crossed a level valley where stockyards, stables and men's quarters were spread out, beside an enormous woolshed, then across another rise until they looked down into the next valley, and Erica realised with a shock that the Crosswyns might look like cowboys but they came home to luxury. No wonder that faint air of hauteur hung around Jeremy and his two brothers.

The Vandellan homestead, with gabled roofs and columned verandahs, stood among orchards and spreading gardens on a series of gentle slopes. There were willows bending over a pond coloured with pink and blue waterlilies, on one side an avenue of pepper trees, and groves of citrus. On the other side of the house a thick forest made a patch of green beyond a tennis court and swimming pool.

Jeremy pointed to the gardens, the forest, the swimming pool. He wanted her to be impressed.

'You'll have to come with me and see the rose garden,' he urged. 'You have to see it all, Ric.'

'I see it. It's truly wonderful.'

Once Jeremy had told her, 'I left Vandellan behind me long ago,' but it wasn't true. She saw now that he had never really left. It showed in his pleasure and pride as he pointed out things for her to look at. He touched her arm, drawing her attention to a vivid tree with outspread branches and masses of scarlet flowers.

'Poinciana,' he informed her, 'Looks like a red umbrella, doesn't it?' but Erica averted her eyes. Her imagination had played another trick on her, jolting her mind with a sudden picture, not of a red umbrella, but an outspread skirt of scarlet, and she found imprinted on her memory in startling clarity the picture of the gipsy lying in her caravan. She turned away from the tree, pushing the image out of her mind.

Vandellan homestead was double-storeyed, and between the columns on the downstairs verandah there were white railings festooned with Mandevillea vines laden with crisp white flowers. Everywhere Erica looked she found a mixture of the new world and the old—petunia borders and flame trees, roses and strange orchid shapes.

A breathtaking piece of opulence, she was deciding, when in the driving mirror she caught the cool, appraising eyes of Matt studying her with unbelievable cynicism. He thought she was assessing, congratulating herself on having chosen well in Jeremy. He didn't have to say so, it was all there written clearly in his hard, cold eyes.

He braked, switched off the ignition, and they alighted. As they climbed the wide steps Erica caught sight of a shadowy figure at one end of the verandah. A girl in a wheelchair.

Erica smiled and waved, but the girl backed her chair quickly away. Jeremy turned an enquiring face to his brothers.

'Jenny Land?'

Matthew nodded curtly. 'Yes. That's Jenny.'

Guy's face whitened suddenly under its tan, and he stumbled against the step.

Erica asked curiously, 'Who is Jenny Land?' Nobody answered until Guy straightened himself. He looked as if he wanted to be sick.

'Poor Jenny is the victim of my crime.' He tried to say it naturally but his voice shook. 'Come inside, Erica, and we will tell you all about it. I'm surprised Jeremy hasn't explained it to you already.'

CHAPTER THREE

MATT did not pause in his stride across the verandah. He snapped, 'Don't dramatise', and to Erica's surprise Guy's face lightened with relief. Perhaps he had expected a dressing-down, a long tirade of blame for whatever his 'crime' had been.

He pushed open the huge carved doors, and as they entered the hallway Erica caught her breath, because this area was spacious enough and grand enough to be a ballroom.

She recalled Jeremy once murmuring about 'dancing in the hallway at home', and she had pictured in her mind a small group of people enjoying themselves in a confined space, but there was nothing confined here.

A large and beautiful crystal chandelier hung from the centre of a carved oregon ceiling, and along the panelled walls there were recesses with pedestals holding flowers and antiques. Paintings and family treasures gave an atmosphere of elegance and nobility, an impression of longlasting solidity, as if they might have been there forever.

Two arms of curving staircase led upstairs to a gallery, and Erica remembered her jade dress and was grateful for the whim that had sent her shopping.

There could be an occasion for grandeur sometime on this holiday, she felt sure, and meeting Matthew's discerning glance she flushed. He seemed to take pleasure in making people feel uncomfortable. She wondered whether this secretive man went about reading other people's thoughts as easily as he did hers.

Jeremy put down the suitcase he carried. 'Where's Lilyan?' he demanded. 'Doesn't she live here any more?'

'She'll be along when she feels like it.' Matthew sounded edgy. Perhaps he hadn't intended waiting for any further welcomes.

A frown creased the pointed eyebrows as he called, 'Lilyan . . . Jenny', in a clear sharp voice. There were seconds of uncomfortable silence before a door clicked and light footsteps sounded in the gallery.

The newcomer made a dramatic entrance. She glided downstairs, commanding their attention, sure of herself because there was no detail of her appearance that could be faulted. Sleek blonde hair drawn back from a perfect oval face, she wore a bright pink leisure suit, and the impact was everything she could have desired.

Matthew waited until she reached them. 'Lilyan, Jeremy wants to say hello, and this is Jeremy's friend, Erica. Erica, meet Lilyan.'

He didn't say, meet my wife. He didn't offer any explanation at all, and Erica was too polite to look for a wedding ring among the jewels that sparkled on Lilyan's fingers.

Lilyan could have been surprised to see Erica. Her recording glance skimmed the slender figure with its firm upcurved breasts, the tiny waist, the long shapely column of throat that gave a look of slender fragility to the girl who stood before her.

She said distantly, 'Welcome to Vandellan. I hope you enjoy your holiday.'

With Jeremy, Lilyan allowed herself more animation, planting a graceful kiss on his forehead, and allowing herself to be kissed warmly in return. Jeremy was still embracing her when the girl in the wheelchair appeared in the doorway.

She didn't want to come in. Reluctance showed in the drooping eyelids, the downhanging head. She brought the wheelchair to a stop beside Matt and darted a flickering sideways glance at him.

'You called?'

'Yes.' Shutters closed over Matt's face, over Guy's also, even Jeremy's expression became guarded.

'I'd like you to meet our brother, Jeremy, and his friend, Erica.' Matt's voice sounded emotionless. 'This is Jenny, who is with us for—ah—for a while.'

Poor little scrap. The girl did not look more than seventeen. She would not look directly at any one of them, moving her head in shy furtive movements that gave her a hunted look. Yet they were beautiful eyes.

Once, she directed them towards Erica, flicking the long lashes down quickly, but not before Erica had seen the soft appeal in them. Amber-coloured, flecked with velvet brown, enormous in the small pointed face, they were heart-wrenching in their timidity. Erica wanted to touch her, to hold her, but the shrinking posture conveyed clear warning . . . no friendly gestures, no approaches, would be welcomed.

Lilyan said coolly, 'If you're ready, Jenny, I

think you're due for exercises. Nell is probably wondering where you've got to.'

Submissively, Jenny turned the wheelchair, and she had almost disappeared behind the staircase when Erica caught the expression on Guy's face. There was nothing youthful about it now. Lips clamped whitely together, jaws set as if to hold back overwhelming emotion, he stared after the vanishing girl in the wheelchair, then his body sagged as if an enormous weight pressed him down.

Lilyan's voice recalled them to reality. 'That girl,' she announced pettishly, 'gets more sullen and less co-operative every day. I don't believe she intends to recover if she can help it.'

Guy made a small strangled sound and Matt turned away abruptly.

'Let's get our visitors to their rooms, shall we?'

Jeremy patted Lilyan's cheek with teasing fingers. 'See you later, sweet stepmother.'

Stepmother! Erica was thinking uncomfortably that there was a lot about Vandellan and its occupants that Jeremy had not told her, when Lilyan snapped coldly, 'I am not your stepmother.'

'Almost-stepmother, then.'

Lilyan's eyes sharpened with hostility, but she handled it well, quickly smoothing her face into calmness she didn't really feel, judging by that flash of glinting anger that had shown in her eyes.

'May I remind you, Jeremy, I was engaged to marry your father. Had he lived I would have become your stepmother. As it is I—I do not appreciate that kind of tasteless remark.'

'Sorry, darling.'

Jeremy's grin was unrepentant, Lilyan's reaction

cool, very cool, and as if it were some ritual they had played many times before Jeremy blew her a placating kiss before he turned away. They understood each other, Lilyan and Jeremy. She called after him as he moved away, in a clear persuasive voice, 'Welcome home, Jeremy,' and he bowed mockingly.

'Thank you, my dear.'

Jeremy had mentioned once that his father had died suddenly of a heart attack two years ago. He had said nothing about the attractive younger woman he was to have married.

They were proving a secretive pair, Jeremy and Matthew. She might do well to remember that, but then Jeremy was certainly not obliged to tell her everything.

As they went upstairs the svelte figure in bright pink stayed exactly where they had left her, head upturned to follow their ascent, as if Lilyan might have been disturbed by their presence.

Matthew led them along the gallery and into a connecting passageway. He paused outside a door, putting down Erica's suitcase which he had taken from Jeremy.

'Yours.'

He waved a hand towards the next doorway, raised eyebrows giving him an incredibly cynical expression as he turned to his brother.

'And yours, old son. Suitable?' His meaning could not have been clearer. Adjoining bedrooms, with all the implications. Maybe even a connecting door.

Erica's lips tightened. Yet what could she say? That unbelievably, hideously cynical man, practi-

cally giving his personal approval to the affair she
had committed herself to anyway. Nevertheless the
innuendo, unspoken though it was, set up shock
waves of anger that made her eyes flash as she faced
him, while Jeremy moved on to his room.

'Do these doors have keys?'

'Don't worry.' Matt laughed down at her de-
risively. 'I assure you there will be no unwelcome
intrusions.'

He accented the word 'unwelcome' . . . He
actually dared! Erica stamped into the bedroom,
brushing past him. Guy hesitated, then walked on
to Jeremy's room, but Matt still hovered there.

'Drinks before dinner in the drawing-room
downstairs, but I'm sure Jeremy has explained all
that,' he drawled. He wasn't convinced by her show
of anger and she shouldn't have expected him to be.

After he had gone, Erica hung her clothes in the
wardrobe. She didn't know what to wear for dinner
and she certainly would not go to Jeremy's room to
ask. She chose a deceptively simple-looking frock
in turquoise cotton, with an elasticised frilled neckline, then made it decidedly less simple by pulling
down the elastic edge of the frill to leave her
shoulders bare.

She couldn't explain the impulse that led her to
add that little bit of seduction to a dress that was
really quite conservative, but she knew it had something to do with Matthew's critical appraisal of her
appearance at the airport. He thought she was a
hussy—let him think so!

He gave her one swift glance later, as he poured
her drink in the drawing-room before dinner, then
took no further notice.

Dinner was served by a pleasant, grey-haired woman whom Matthew introduced as Nell.

'Our manager's wife,' he explained after she had left the room. They sat around the long polished table in the dining-room, sipping white wine with chicken. 'We owe a great deal to her. Unfortunately our housekeeper died not long ago, and Nell is filling in for us while her husband is away inspecting one of our other properties, and her sons are at boarding-school.'

Jeremy put down his glass. 'Poor Waters. I can't imagine Vandellan surviving without her around the place.'

He explained to Erica, 'Flo Waters was our governess when we were small children. She stayed on as housekeeper after our mother died.'

Lilyan's laugh was brittle. 'And she remained housekeeper after my arrival,' she added, 'because I am the world's least domesticated woman.' Lilyan made it sound like an achievement, a statement that she was undoubtedly destined for better things than planning menus.

Erica wondered why Jenny, the girl in the wheelchair, was not at dinner, but instinct warned her not to ask too many questions yet.

However, she did ask casually, 'How did Miss Waters die?' and caught an exchange of warning glances between the two older brothers, while Guy stared fixedly at his wineglass.

'Getting on in years and more than a little unsteady on her feet, poor old thing. She had a fall.' Jeremy seemed anxious that Erica should understand there was nothing untoward about the accident that had resulted in Waters' death.

'Touched, if you ask me,' he added. 'She had no need to work at all, silly woman, only she insisted it made her feel useful. She pottered around talking to herself last time I was here.'

Guy put down his glass. 'It helped her think,' he explained. 'Poor old Waters . . . It was a hangover from governessing. She used to tell us, If you want to remember anything you must write it down, and if you can't find pen and paper say it aloud to yourself several times. It works, too.' He grinned at Erica. 'She wasn't nutty, really, just a bit unsteady on her pins and getting a bit rusty. But she got awfully offended if you suggested it was time to take it easy.' His face sobered. 'She was a good old stick. There wasn't a thing went on at Vandellan that Waters didn't know about.'

'Could we discuss something else?' Lilyan didn't like this conversation. Erica silently mused, 'Not long ago Waters died. How long?'

Vandellan must be accident-prone. The girl in the wheelchair, had she fallen also? And when did that happen?

The overheard conversation in her flat came back to Erica with disconcerting clarity. If only she were sure she could trust Jeremy. His brother Matthew she would never trust. She hadn't needed those few murmured words to tell her that. She had known the instant he had looked down at her from her doorway . . . dark . . . threatening . . . disapproving.

He sat now at the head of the table, and asked blandly, 'What would you prefer to discuss, Lilyan? Our dance next weekend, or the prospect of an electrical storm adding a little drama to Erica's visit?'

Erica shot him a sparkling look; he smiled at her disarmingly, but the smile was a mask.

'No doubt you would prefer the weekend entertainment. As I warned you, our storms can be quite terrifying.'

'What I would really prefer,' Erica told herself after dinner, as they relaxed again in the drawing-room, 'is a little honesty around here. I would like to know what happened to Jenny, and I would like to know more about Waters and her unfortunate accident.'

Jeremy interrupted her introspection. 'Penny for them, Ric. Two pennies if necessary.' And Erica realised she had disconnected herself from the conversation around her. She shook away her puzzlement.

'What does Cinderella wear to the ball?'

'How about that new dress you were boasting about? The one you went out and bought after that gipsy woman scared the wits out of you.'

So he hadn't forgotten. Not at all. He had stored away Flip's useful little gossip item in his memory bank for future reference.

Matt was sitting with Lilyan on a small divan across the room. He looked pointedly at the turquoise dress with its provocative dropped shoulder-line and he said drily, 'Anything less like Cinderella, I find it hard to imagine,' giving Erica the ironic twist of his mouth that she hated.

Matthew with his bitter darkness, Jeremy and his curiosity, they would make a pair of devious conspirators. She could almost wish she had never tangled with either of them until Jeremy said gently, 'You must be tired, Ric. How about one dance for your first evening at Vandellan, then away to bed if you're still weary.'

He knew her so well . . . her passion for dancing, her love of music . . . Her doubts dissolved. She must be careful not to let disloyalty trick her into doubting Jeremy. Of course he understood her. Hadn't he always, from the first day they met?

If he wanted to file away information for recall when he needed it—well, that was his profession. She relaxed comfortably in his arms when Matt put a record on the player. Jeremy would make her a fine and loyal lover. How could she have doubted it?

When the music stopped he whispered, 'Bed, Ric, if you're feeling done in—' but he didn't mean the last bit. When the homestead quietened he planned to visit her bedroom. Erica knew it as certainly as if she heard the actual knocking on her door.

He was leading her to the bar for a last drink when Guy called, 'Can I have a dance with the pretty lady?' His grin was cheeky, but he hadn't lost the vulnerable look.

Jeremy tensed. 'Just one. If the—er—pretty lady isn't too tired.'

He removed his arm from Erica's waist, walked across the room and pulled Lilyan to her feet. Erica and Guy were moving into the centre of the room when Matt blocked their path.

'Sorry, Guy. I think the sound needs adjusting, and you're the expert.'

Disappointed, Guy went to attend to the player, but Matt made no move to dance with Erica.

'How about a breath of fresh air?' Erica hesitated, but Jeremy had begun to dance with Lilyan. He did not look her way. Guy appeared to be having difficulty balancing the sound from the speakers, although the music was quite satisfactory for dancing.

As he ushered Erica on to the verandah Matt nodded towards the boy. 'I organised that.'

Erica hesitated in the doorway. 'I thought so. May I ask why?'

He curved the strong fingers of his right hand under her elbow, guiding her across the dark verandah to where the white-flowered creepers sprawled. The rich flowers spilled a heavy fragrance. Heady stuff, Erica thought. A susceptible female would have to watch herself here.

Matt paused beside one of the columns.

'I thought perhaps we should have a talk.'

'About what?'

'About whether you care enough about Jenny to take an interest in her while you're here.'

'What makes you think I might?'

'When she came into the hall this afternoon—' he turned abruptly—'I saw your face. She needs somebody, desperately.'

'Don't tell me you've decided we could trust each other?' she replied bitingly. He might have smiled. It was difficult to tell, because of the shadows.

'We might have to, mightn't we, if you agree to help. I suppose by now you have a head full of questions, and it seemed only fair to offer you some answers, since we're asking for your assistance. So fire ahead—what would you like to know?'

Very perceptive. Erica drew a deep breath.

'Yes. I could do with some explanations. I'd like

to know, how did Waters die? Don't just tell me she fell. I'd like to know where and how. Please believe me, it isn't just idle curiosity. If I'm to try and help Jenny, I'd like to know the background.'

Erica wished she could see Matt's face more clearly, because the question was important and so was his answer.

'Waters did have a fall. She over-reached herself one morning while she was arranging flowers in the upstairs gallery. She overbalanced and fell into the hall.'

'However could she do that? The banisters look substantial enough.'

He made a slight movement of his shoulders in the darkness.

'Nobody knows exactly, but she would persist in playing around with those bowls of flowers, and some of them were perilously near the edge. We assume that's what she was doing, since she had a flower in her hand when she was discovered. We didn't expect her to do much around the home-stead. Nell has shouldered a great deal of the housekeeping for a few years now. Waters wasn't supposed to know. It would have hurt the poor old lady's pride.' His tone was dry. 'Nobody minded, least of all Lilyan, as long as everything was done. We are—we were—all very fond of Waters. Nell wouldn't let us put on extra staff, she said it gave her something to do. I think she likes being here, around the homestead, while her husband and boys are away. That's what she tells us, anyway.'

He picked up a fallen white flower, twirled it in his fingers. 'Unfortunately, Nell wasn't here the morning that it—whatever happened—did occur.

So it was Jenny and Gregg, one of our stockmen, who found Waters lying in the hall. It was too late for help. She had died instantly. Her poor old bones were frail.'

'Do stockmen work around the house?'

He laughed at that, and shook his head. 'No. Gregg is the young bloke who rescued Jenny after the accident that caused her injuries. It must have hit him pretty hard. He asked to be put on yard duties so he could be near her, and actually,' Matt sighed, and ran a hand through his short black curls, 'we must be grateful to Gregg. He's the only person Jenny will let near her, except for Nell. Nell helps her wash, and assists with exercises, now the physiotherapist—' he hesitated noticeably— 'now the person who looked after Jenny is away, so thank heavens for Gregg.' His smile was flinty, fleeting in the darkness. 'Obviously she prefers him to the rest of us.' His face became suddenly almost haggard. Erica discerned the harshening of lines, even in the dimness. 'Not surprising, I admit, when you consider how the accident happened.'

'How did it happen? Am I allowed to know? And what was Guy's so-called crime that he spoke of so bitterly this afternoon? He seems very young to have such a load on his mind.'

'Guy's so-called crime is that he rode his horse carelessly, without looking where he was going.' In a beam of light from the house, Erica saw Matthew's hand clench. 'Guy was out riding one morning when he found Jenny hitchhiking her way to Vandellan to look for work. He's young and impulsive and a little careless. He offered her a ride, put her and her bundle up on the horse behind him. Being

Guy, he had to do some skylarking. He rode low
under some trees alongside the road. He was swept
off the horse by a low branch and the girl with him.
Gregg found them both unconscious, Guy knocked
out with concussion, the girl more seriously injured, as you have seen. After hospital treatment
we brought her here. Naturally, we will look after
her.'

'Are her injuries permanent?'

Matt frowned. 'That's the hard part. According
to every doctor who's examined her, they shouldn't
be. They all say the damage is mainly psychological. The damaged spirit, it seems, has to want
urgently to walk before the legs will obey the
command.' His face was grim. 'Sometimes I wonder.'

Erica's lips parted in surprise. 'You think she
may be faking?'

'Perhaps. No—no, I don't. I really don't know
what I think, but I can't believe the girl is pretending. She seems honest enough. But it appears she
can't take the first steps unless she wants to with all
her will-power, and Waters' death seems to have
put paid to that for the time being. If only she'd
come right out and tell us what she thinks and
feels . . .'

'She was very upset by the poor old lady's death?'

'More than upset.' Matt stared intently over the
garden, screening his face from Erica.

'She was distraught, I'd say. The fall, the fuss,
the drama must have brought back the shock of her
own disaster. She retreated into her shell even
farther than before, and it's as much as she can do
to face any of us without flinching.' He sighed. 'I've

asked her if she would be happier elsewhere. We'd pay, of course. But she burst into tears and begged to stay here.'

'Poor Jenny.'

He turned, his face inscrutable. Erica added softly, 'And poor Guy too. He's suffering a great deal, isn't he?

'Yes. It's preying on his mind, he's becoming imaginative about the accident and what happened afterwards. He swears he remembers seeing Jenny standing on her feet as he became unconscious.'

'Actually walking?'

Matt shrugged again. 'Well—he's a little hazy about that. His description is half-walking or half-floating . . . but he's convinced himself she was actually erect. Guy was dazed, of course, suffering from severe concussion.' In the dimness Erica saw the arched eyebrows lowered into slight frowning. 'Perhaps he dreamed it or perhaps it's what he wants to believe.'

Erica nodded. 'I can understand that. To want to undo something that's happened so desperately that you convince yourself it wasn't true. What a dreadful time that boy must have had.'

Matthew moved suddenly, turning himself into a dark shape between Erica and the star-spangled sky behind him.

'Careful, Sister Fayne. I'm beginning to wonder whether you have a soft heart under that frivolous exterior.'

'You think so?'

He mimicked her. 'Poor Jenny. Poor Guy. The only person you haven't showered with your sympathy is myself.'

Erica laughed. 'I can't imagine you in need of sympathy.'

'You're right about that, Erica. It wouldn't be sympathy I'd require from you.'

His voice dropped to velvet softness, the broad shoulders, lithe figure, outlined like a dramatic cardboard cut-out against the sky and the fragrant flowers. He looked so unreal that it shook her when he moved, stepping towards her so that his figure took shape and dimension, rounded, powerful, commanding. He towered over her.

'You're a bright young woman. You've a level head under that curly wig. I'm sure you'd think carefully before giving away anything more important than sympathy.'

Was he implying something about Jeremy and those two adjacent bedrooms?

Erica murmured shakily, 'It's not a wig,' and he threw back his head and actually laughed.

'I know that. Why don't you let it grow, Erica? Let it float around that flower-face. Just think of the attention you'd attract.'

'No, thank you.'

'Get in the way of your nurse's cap, would it?'

Erica said frostily, 'My nurse's cap, Mr Crosswyn, is not a joke, even if you do think so.'

She stepped towards the doorway, but once again the quick-moving Matt was too fast for her.

'Sorry.' He managed to sound faintly regretful. 'I didn't mean that comment quite the way it came across to you.'

'Which way did you mean it?'

She tilted her chin at him and in the half-light she sensed the chuckle that curved his mouth.

'Don't go looking for a fight with me, love. I'm too much of a heavyweight for anything your size.'

'I'm sure you are.'

She flounced into the room ahead of him, wondering guiltily if Jeremy resented her absence. To her surprise she found him engrossed in his dance with Lilyan. It was a tango, and they danced it with abandon, gliding and twirling with dramatic gestures. Only Guy, standing dolefully beside the record player, looked at Erica with reproachful eyes.

He mouthed 'My dance' and she walked across the room to join him, but when the dance finished she found herself suddenly bone-weary.

She was relieved when Jeremy rescued her, but after they had said goodnight and were walking upstairs, she found herself dreading the moment when they would reach her room.

She knew what he expected. A tender love scene, an invitation to share her bed. And she couldn't do it . . . not tonight.

As she expected, Jeremy paused at her doorway. 'I think I can remember the number.' There was no number on the door, but Erica knew what he meant. He was promising to present himself after he had showered. She pleaded swiftly, 'Jeremy, I'm exhausted,' and his reaction was immediate disbelief.

'Oh come! You've dined, you've danced, you should be rejuvenated.'

'Yes, I ought to be.' How could she explain this feeling of heaviness? 'I'm sorry, Jeremy. Truly, I am.'

'I could revive you.' His mouth was sulky.

'If anybody could, it would be you, but not tonight.'

He put his hands on her shoulders and pulled her towards him. 'If you say so, but you won't fob me off every night, Ric.'

'Of course not.'

His goodnight kiss was sweet and coaxing. She should have responded. Any other time, she told herself helplessly, watching the clouds gather on his face, she would have been persuaded.

He slid the fingers of one hand around the neckline of her bright frock.

'That's a mighty provocative dress you're wearing, for a girl who's too tired to play games.'

'Is that what you had in mind, playing games?'

'You know darned well what I had in mind.' There was a cutting edge to Jeremy's voice. He thrust her against the door before he turned on his heel and walked to his own room. Erica gazed after him guiltily.

Whatever could have happened to her serene assurance that Jeremy was the one, the only man she knew she could trust with her body, her emotions, her loving?

She had been so certain she was making the right decision. Now her emotions wavered like crazy things, out of control, dissolving into doubts while she tried to read them.

Erica thought she knew the best way to deal with that kind of problem—sleep on it. She soaked under a warm shower, relishing the slow easing of tension, and when she was ready for bed she switched off the lights in her room and walked to the window.

The curtains waved in a light breeze as Erica

looked out across the upstairs balcony and down on to the gardens. Below her the valley dipped.

A group of several jacaranda trees waved lacy leaves in a slight breeze, and beyond them she glimpsed the shape of the tennis court and the sheen of water on the swimming pool. Very handy, she thought wryly. The affluent Crosswyns might play a set of tennis, then follow it with a plunge in the pool. Everything here was designed for luxury and pleasure.

Erica was turning away from the window when a splashing broke the surface of the pool. Somebody was swimming at this late hour.

Curiously she watched as a broad-shouldered figure, naked except for the briefest of briefs, climbed from the water and walked to a low diving-board.

Moonlight shone on wet footprints, clinging with a kind of lingering mystery on the powerful shape of the man as he plunged back into the water . . . Matthew Crosswyn.

So Matt was cooling off in the night. Erica watched him swim again towards the side of the pool with powerful strokes before he pulled himself up once more to dry land. Mesmerised, she followed his strides to the diving-board again, but this time he did not launch himself into the water.

Through patchy shadows around the jacaranda trees she saw him tense and look up, head thrown back as if he scanned the window where she stood. He could not know she was there. Yet her heart began beating like a crazy drum, her whole body alert as if something momentous was about to happen.

She stepped back from the window and crept into bed as furtively as if she had been discovered in some kind of misdemeanour.

Even in bed she remained uneasy, in some weird way feeling Matt's attention still focused on her. Nothing would have drawn her back to the window, so she had no way of knowing whether he still swam alone while the rest of the household slept.

Let him drown, Erica told herself crossly, trying to blot out of her mind the image of the man standing there, his wet skin gleaming in the moonlight. Let him drown if he likes. He means nothing to me. Nothing at all.

CHAPTER FOUR

TWICE during the night Erica woke to a distant rumble of thunder, but next morning except for a line of scudding clouds along the horizon there was no sign of storm.

'We missed it,' Guy explained cheerfully at breakfast. 'Thought we might have shown you a real black storm with lightning and thunder and all the trimmings, but it wore itself out before it reached us.'

'Others weren't so lucky.' Matt had glanced up with a cool 'Good morning' as Erica came in. He added, 'They copped it at Carisma,' and Guy's face sobered.

'Oh, poor Hilarie—'

Jeremy arrived not long after Erica. 'Hi, sweetie.' He kissed her cheek, a lingering caress. 'Sleep well?' He was putting on an act for his two brothers. His voice was suggestive, even to Erica's ears, and she flushed uncomfortably because Matt looked straight at her, and those grey eyes were cold and contemptuous.

But she did owe Jeremy her loyalty. She had sent him away last night; at least this morning she could help him bolster his pride.

She managed a radiant smile, 'Yes, thank you, best sleep I've had for ages,' before she lifted covers from the dishes on the enormous sideboard and ladled herself a not-too-substantial breakfast.

She avoided Matt's scrutiny as she sat down. He could think what he liked.

Matt ignored her, waiting for Jeremy to join them at the table. His own breakfast was finished, except for the cup of tea he poured himself. He was dressed again in working clothes, the lean-hipped trousers and checked shirt, and his manner was preoccupied and distant. He spoke to Jeremy without smiling.

'They copped a deluge at Carisma in the night. Their creeks are running bankers. Hilarie Carrison's husband is in hospital with a grumbling appendix. How about lending a hand, Jeremy?'

'Don't they have any men?'

'Some of their cattle were spooked by the storm, and the stockmen are out rounding them up again. There'll be some sandbagging needed around the homestead if the creeks burst their banks. I told Hilarie you might offer your services.'

Jeremy poked at his breakfast. 'Can Ric come with me?'

Matt's voice was level. 'If you want to take somebody I'd prefer you take Lilyan. She and Hilarie can do some organising for our weekend party. It might help take Hilarie's mind off her troubles. I'll see Lilyan.'

'Why can't Guy go?'

Matthew didn't appreciate obstruction. His jaw hardened. 'I have work for Guy to do here.'

That ended Jeremy's mutiny. 'All right. If you say so. But Ric's going to be lonely.' He gave her another secret smile, and Matt announced calmly, 'Two day at the most. I imagine Erica can last that long without you. Then you'll have the rest of your holiday to show her Vandellan.'

Almost as an afterthought he added, 'Perhaps Erica wouldn't mind spending some time with Jenny while you're away. It could be a good opportunity. That is,' he looked at her across the table with raised eyebrows, politely asking her, 'if Erica doesn't mind her good nature being imposed on.'

When he put it that way, how could she refuse? Jeremy offered no more protests and Matt's dark face remained carefully unrevealing, so why was she so positive that he had just manoeuvred them both to fit in with some plan of his own?

You're getting paranoid, my girl, she admonished herself. Certainly, Matt could not have organised the storm nor the overflowing creeks on the other property. But he was quite capable of arranging events to suit his convenience, she suspected. Perhaps, as he had suggested himself, he merely wanted Jeremy out of the way for a short while so that Erica might concentrate on breaking through the barriers the girl in the wheelchair had erected around herself. Perhaps . . .

Erica did feel a fleeting wonder about Lilyan's reaction at being whisked away with Jeremy, but apparently nobody argued with Matt. The plane took off less than an hour later with Jeremy and Lilyan as passengers, and in due course Matt returned alone. He did not appear at the homestead for lunch, nor did Guy, and Erica seized the opportunity to eat in the kitchen with Nell and Jenny.

The pleasant grey-haired woman seemed pleased to have her company, and although Jenny hesitated and flushed she made no objection, and

Erica quietly made herself salad sandwiches and sat down. This could be a chance to get to know the girl, to feel her way carefully around that reticence in case there was some way of breaking through.

She wasn't doing it for the autocratic Matthew, nor even for Jeremy, but because she honestly wanted to help.

Her efforts didn't look like being a great success. Jenny ate silently, leaving Erica and Nell to talk to each other. She ate sparingly. Too sparingly, Erica decided. She was far too thin. This morning she had been out in the garden, but the fresh air had not put colour in her cheeks nor had it brightened her eyes. She drooped, as she always seemed to droop.

Earlier that morning, Erica had discovered the wheelchair not far from the homestead, a young lean-hipped man in attendance. This must be Gregg, the stockman. She had studied him curiously from a distance. He wore his wide-brimmed hat jammed down hard over his forehead, obscuring most of his face, his only prominent feature a hard, square, out-thrust jaw. He sauntered beside the chair, yellow and black shirt flapping at the waist, his jeans faded with ragged pockets, but he had an air of distinction, a suggestion of arrogant strength and youth.

Erica had not been sure she approved of the way he strolled carelessly through the rose garden, leaving a trail of scattered petals behind him.

She had watched only a few minutes, knowing how prolonged surveillance sometimes prickles the skin, how quickly the watched became conscious of being observed, and she did not intend disturbing the pair of them.

Now, as she handed Jenny the sugar bowl, she said, 'I saw you in the garden this morning with Gregg, but I didn't interrupt. I thought you might prefer not to be disturbed.'

Jenny drew a swift, sharp breath, pressing her lips together as if to hide their quivering. She dropped her spoon, tried to retrieve it and missed. It clattered on to the floor.

Quietly Erica reached for a clean one, carefully ignoring Jenny's agitation, saying casually to Nell, 'That's quite a rose garden, isn't it? Who planted it?' so that Nell collected herself quickly.

She launched into the story of Matthew's great-grandmother, Marion Crosswyn, who had lived in the Australian sunshine but never stopped dreaming of her home in England.

'The rose garden was one of the first things she planted. And that bit of rain forest behind the tennis court, that's Marion's Wilderness,' Nell explained. 'She insisted it be preserved. I guess she was a conservationist ahead of her time.'

'She must have been a very creative woman. It's quite a fascinating mixture, isn't it?' Erica flashed a quick sideways look at Jenny, noting her gradual relaxation. 'An English rose garden and a tropical rain forest, living side by side.'

'Yes.' Nell, too, covertly watched Jenny regain composure. She added to Erica, 'You must visit the rose garden, but I don't recommend an excursion into Marion's Wilderness. There are enough vines in there to tangle the feet of a centipede. But it's nice to know it's there, a little bit of rain forest just as it was when the first Crosswyns arrived, and probably a few million years before that. The

Wilderness and the rose garden are two of Vandellan's traditions. Matt won't have either changed.' She smiled warmly at Erica. 'You must ask Matt to show you around the gardens some time.'

That was something she would most certainly avoid doing, Erica promised herself. She would take herself anywhere she wanted to go, not call on the master of Vandellan to escort her.

She helped herself to Nell's delicious fruit salad. 'I'll give you a hand with the dishes after lunch, then I might take a look around by myself if there isn't anything you want me to do here. We must be putting you to a lot of extra work, it doesn't seem fair.'

Nell laughed. 'If you only knew how grateful I am to have something to keep me occupied while Robert and the boys are away!'

'How old are your sons?'

'Twelve and fourteen. They're both like my husband, quiet thoughtful types, beautifully good-natured and so easy to get along with. Anyway, they'll all be home in a few weeks, so if you stay around long enough you'll meet them.'

Something about the careful way Nell spoke set a small alarm buzzing in the back of Erica's mind. She said clearly, 'Nell, you do know I'm only here for a short visit?' and Nell said hastily, 'Of course— yes, of course—' before she changed the subject.

'Don't worry about me being too busy, will you? I love it.'

'I could help with dinner if you like. I'm no gourmet cook, but I can cope.' Erica hid her disquiet.

'No worries.' Nell waved a casual hand. 'Dishes

go into the dishwasher. Dinner is already under control. Like I said, I'm a workaholic, I can't bear sitting still. So please relax and enjoy yourself.'

Casually, carefully, Erica risked an invitation to the girl in the wheelchair.

'How about showing me around, if you're not too tired?'

Jenny flushed, hesitated, then shook her head. 'No. I don't think so.' She darted a flickering glance at Erica. 'I really am a little tired. I ought to rest. I hope you'll excuse me. Thanks for lunch, Nell.'

She wheeled herself away without looking back. Nell pursed her lips sympathetically.

'If you're trying to make friends with that one, you've an uphill job.'

'Yet she trusts *you*.'

'Does she?' Nell poured herself another cup of tea. 'Sometimes I wonder. I think she puts up with my company because she has to roost somewhere once in a while.'

She sipped her drink. 'She doesn't confide in me. I know no more about Jenny now than what I learned the day we met. She's eighteen, she came inland from one of the northern coastal towns looking for work. Her private life is certainly not the proverbial open book.'

'You're taking care of her?'

Nell nodded. 'I'm doing my best since—since the physio departed. I learned the exercises, and I help her in the bathroom. I've moved up here until Robert comes back, so I'm in the room next to hers. Of course, I can't offer professional care, but I do the best I can.'

'Good for you! Matthew was saying Jenny was very fond of the old lady who died.'

'She was certainly shaken up after the accident. Who can blame her, poor kid, coming so soon after her own tumble? But I don't know that she was friendly with Waters. She never talked to any of us very much, except that stockman who's taken her under his wing. Young Gregg.'

Nell laughed. 'Now, there's an unexpected development. If ever there was a loner, young Gregg was it. Fancied himself a real macho-man, planned to save his money and take himself off on the rodeo circuit. He's certainly a fancy rider. He took time off to do some competing once and I understand did very well. Now he's taken a fancy to Jenny, and had himself put on yard duties to be near her. That's a bit of soft-heartedness nobody expected.'

'He sounds a very kind young man.'

'Yes.' Nell began gathering dishes from the table. 'I don't know whether it's a romantic interest, or merely sympathy. It must have given him a jolt, finding her helpless on the road. Anyway, it's a good thing to have happened. She'd be a poor little lost soul without him. He's very attentive.'

'I noticed that.'

Nell made no more comments about Gregg's character, and Erica asked no more questions. She was on delicate ground, a stranger feeling her way among people she scarcely knew. It would be easy to give offence.

After lunch she explored the grounds. She spent time in the delightful rose garden, revelling in its colours and perfumes, carefully avoiding the poinciana tree with its tantalising reminder of the gipsy's scarlet gown.

For a while she stayed dreaming beside a pool of waterlilies, their pink and blue flowers cool and beautiful under a hanging willow tree that dropped green reflections around them. Then she wandered down to the swimming pool, until the heat reminded her that this was not her kind of climate. She had not yet obtained a shady hat, and the humidity sent her looking for shade. She reached the clump of jacaranda trees with gusts of hot wind puffing at her heels, and she stood near a tree-trunk, sheltered by lacy leaves.

The erratic wind shook the flowers, sending down a shower of small purple trumpets. Erica was brushing lavender petals from her shoulders when a cool voice drawled, 'Lady in a purple snowstorm. Very fetching.' The voice was Matt's. He stood beside her, and before she could twist away he had reached out to untangle more flowers from her hair. She froze until he took his hand away. Then she asked pertly, 'Your day's work done already?'

'No.' His lips twitched. 'I came to see how you were faring without company. Does that embarrass you?'

She met his ironic gaze without flinching.

'Not at all. Should it?'

'No. But it's just as well I came. I'd say another half hour out here and you'd be nicely baked, ready to serve.'

'Oh!' Erica's hands flew to her flushed face. Tendrils of hair streaked her damp forehead. She brushed them back impatiently.

'I don't feel burned.'

'Just lightly cooked at the moment. Rare . . . very rare. I'd recommend a cold shower or a swim. Either should fix you up nicely.'

Her head throbbed faintly. She touched her hot cheeks. 'I don't think I'll have a swim. A shower perhaps and a couple of aspirin.'

Matt took the wide-brimmed hat off his own black curls and tilted it rakishly over her hair.

'Now you look like a jillaroo. No—' he grabbed her arm as she raised it to give back the hat. 'Keep it. You may not fancy a piece of dusty gear that's been out in the hot sun for a few hours, but you'll have to put up with it. We can't have you laid up with heatstroke when your lover comes back.'

The way he said 'lover' she knew he was looking for an argument, trying to stir up another confrontation, but she wouldn't oblige him. You needed to be at your coolest to joust with Matt.

Erica walked quietly beside him until they had almost reached the homestead, when she said abruptly, 'If you're wondering how I got on with Jenny, I don't have much to report. She's very withdrawn, isn't she?'

'Yes. I suppose it's too soon to ask what you think of her?'

'Does she have parents, family?'

'No one, according to her, and I see no reason to disbelieve her. Any girl in her condition would be only too eager to see her family if she had one. So—' he gave a long deep sigh and Erica looked at him curiously, because just for a moment his face had looked strangely sad, even haunted.

'We'll have to be her family, if she'll let us. We

owe her that much since it was Guy—' He left the
sentence unfinished. 'We're involved.'

Erica hardly liked to ask her next question.

'What will you do if Jenny doesn't walk? If she
doesn't make the breakthrough, who will help
her?'

'We will. We have to.' His face was bleak. No
doubt he knew that Jenny's presence was a con-
tinual cruel reminder to Guy of his own guilt and
carelessness. For the first time Erica felt a stirring
of sympathy for this man who must already have
many responsibilities and now was forced to add
this extra one to his commitments.

As they entered the courtyard at the rear of the
homestead Matt threw away his mood of gravity.
He reached for his hat, removing it deftly from
Erica's red curls.

'You don't need it here. You're in the shade.'

'Thank you for lending it to me.'

A grin uptilted his wide, strong mouth.

'Think nothing of it. I'm sure my headgear has
never looked so good.'

Erica wasn't sure whether he was teasing her, but
she preferred him in this lighter mood. Although
they walked in shade the grey eyes had a suspicion
of sun-glitter in them, as if the ice had suddenly melted, and his face lost some of the shuttered look. Matthew was taking pains to show
her a pleasanter self than usual. She wondered
why.

He put a brown finger under her chin and tilted
her face.

'Dimpled chin, devil within,' he quoted, his voice
low and husky and seductive. 'What bedevils you,

Erica? Is it me, or is it the absence of your young man?'

'Don't be ridiculous.'

He opened the back door and motioned her ahead of him. 'About Jenny—' She wheeled to face him, and found his expression sober again. 'Thanks for trying,' he said wryly. 'I can't say I expected any startling success, but you know the proverb. Nothing ventured—'

She smiled at him spontaneously.

'Don't give up. I might surprise you yet.'

'I'm sure you will.' Sparks danced in his eyes again; he was showing her a depth and charm that startled her.

The doorway opened into a square area, paved like the courtyard outside. Erica saw a flight of narrow stairs leading to the upper storey. She looked around her curiously. This must be an uncommonly large homestead.

'Would you care to select the wines for dinner?'

Erica shook her head. 'I'm sure your taste is impeccable.'

'Yes, it is,' he agreed calmly, daring her to contradict. 'All right, I'll choose, and trust my selection meets with your approval.'

He stepped towards a secluded area under the staircase, and Erica stared in fascinated horror as he bent down, curled his fingers around a heavy ring set in the floor and slowly, carefully, lifted an immense trapdoor. It must have been heavy, since he used both hands to raise it.

Involuntarily, Erica closed her eyes, trying to shut herself off from the shock. She opened them to find Matt watching her intently.

'Head aching?' His voice sounded puzzled, eyes keenly searching her face. Her heart beat wildly, incredulously.

'A little.'

Erica shook herself. Of course there was a trapdoor. There had to be. People kept their wines in cellars, didn't they? Yet she could not drag her eyes away from the massive timber square that Matt had lifted. On dragging feet she walked towards it. A sharp descent down a narrow wooden ladder led to vaulted cellars. Erica caught a glimpse of heavy wooden casks, racks of bottles, a domed ceiling, and dimness. Matt clicked on a switch and a pale light flickered.

Erica struggled to keep her voice casual. 'I didn't know Vandellan had a trapdoor.'

'Where did you think we stored our wines, in an attic?'

He was watching her face, as if alerted by something he saw there. Then he added more seriously, 'Matter of fact, there's a real labyrinth of tunnels down there, mostly unused or blocked up. Some of the early settlers in these regions treated the aboriginal people very harshly. They stirred up a lot of hostilities, so the first Crosswyns put a maze of tunnels below the trapdoor, in case the homestead was attacked. Women and children would have been able to hide down there. I don't know whether the tunnels were ever used, or how often, but there are a few overgrown entrances and ventilation points dotted about the grounds. You can come down and have a look around, if you like.'

'No, thanks.'

Erica watched him descend, the dark head disappearing, the thump as he dropped from the steps on to the floor beneath. He looked up at her, raising ironic eyebrows.

'Don't wait,' he drawled, 'unless you've decided to supervise.'

Erica drew back hurriedly. Whatever must the man think of her, hovering around as if she could not let him out of her sight? He had made her uneasy from the beginning. Now it was a thousand times worse. She found herself urgently wanting to run, up the stairs, along the gallery, putting herself as far away from him as she could. But this was no time to panic.

In that soft mood underneath the jacaranda trees, Matt had weakened her defences. Now she would have to put them up again. He could be an enemy—

She forced herself to climb the stairway calmly, and when Matt emerged from the cellars she had only just reached the top of the staircase, because her traitorous knees were shaking and she had to feel for every step of the way.

She leaned over the banister, and as if she had summoned him Matt turned his head and stared up at her, his mouth twisting.

'Don't jump.' He was being sardonic. 'I don't have a spare arm to catch you just now.'

'Why should I jump?'

Some of her panic must have shown in her voice. He stood astride, gazing up at her.

'Damned if I know. You're mighty touchy this afternoon.'

The bottles shone dully, as if they might have been down in those cellars a long long time, so perhaps he had chosen of his best. Maybe he planned a celebration. It would be a fizzer if there were only herself and Matt and Guy to celebrate. Nell would no doubt be busy with Jenny, as she had been the previous evening. How could you celebrate with a confusing, threatening person like Matthew Crosswyn beside you?

He was frowning up at her now, in a very odd way that made her skin creep. She wanted to back away, but he would not let her move. It was as simple as that . . . as if he called on some extraordinary inward power to hold her there, and so dominant was his presence that the space between them diminished and she felt as if he stood beside her, exercising his will to make her stand immobile when all she wanted to do was get away from him.

He was studying her face and figure intently, as if they were unfamiliar territory that he intended to remember. Erica had met forceful people before, but never a man like this. He knew he was intimidating her, she felt sure of it. The pleasant beguiling Matthew who strolled beside her in the hot sun had done a turnabout, changing himself back into the dark stranger who had so disturbed her at their first meeting.

'I have no plans to jump,' she was astonished at the belligerence in her own voice, 'and I shan't allow myself to be pushed, either.'

'Now there's a declaration of independence,' he drawled. His gaze slid over her flushed face, the too-bright sparkle of her green eyes, the tendrils of damp hair over her forehead.

'Go and have a shower, idiot girl.' His voice became curt, as if he was tired of sparring with her, or perhaps he did not understand her. As suddenly and as effectively as he had switched on the power that stopped her moving, he broke the contact between them, the strong features becoming austere, remote. He had detached himself from her, even before he turned and disappeared behind a door on the side of the paved square.

But Erica did not release herself immediately. She remained frozen beside the banister, like a slave in thrall. With the tip of her tongue she licked dry lips. Whatever had the man done to her?

The shock of seeing the trapdoor, here where she least expected it, followed by Matt Crosswyn's little exercise in persuasion—or was it domination?—had shaken her beyond belief.

She stumbled along the passage to her room, making her legs move carefully, slowly although a voice somewhere in the back of her mind was urging, 'Run . . . run . . .'

CHAPTER FIVE

MATT had been right about her need for a shower. Erica came out feeling cooler, saner. Wrapped in a daffodil-coloured towel she paused before the mirror, holding the towel with one hand, brushing her wet curls with the other.

That odious man should see her as she was this minute, the flush faded, her eyes reasonably clear and calm, her whole body refreshed. She moved uneasily. No, he shouldn't see her now. What on earth was planting these demented ideas in her head?

She couldn't bear to think of those self-contained, secret eyes assessing her as she looked now. She was, she knew, at her most vulnerable, with Nursing Sister Fayne packed away in storage and this troubled girl with the wide emerald eyes ready to take alarm at the slightest hint of anything unexpected.

All because this afternoon Matthew had shown her something she did not wish to see. A trapdoor.

Matt's special selection of wines had suggested a celebration, so Erica dressed carefully if not elaborately in a cream silk skirt bordered with pale flowers, and a tiny cream top, adding a fine gold chain with one tear-shaped pearl gleaming against the skin of her throat.

Guy was impressed. With youthful enthusiasm he broke into a stream of compliments when she came downstairs, but Matthew poured wine, lifting his glass politely in an unspoken toast, without much warmth in his eyes. He had become wary and distant.

Guy kept up his lighthearted commentary all through the meal that followed, and despite the tension between herself and Matt, Erica found herself laughing and responding. Once, after a particularly outrageous suggestion from Guy, Erica caught Matt's appraisal, and the grey eyes actually glinted in appreciation. So he did have a sense of humour lurking somewhere under that rather frigid exterior.

After dinner, Guy played records in the drawing-room, but as soon as it seemed polite Erica made her excuses.

'I thought I might call and see Jenny. I know she retires to her room early, and if there's any chance she'll talk to me, I'd like to try.'

Matt leaned back indolently in a comfortable leather chair. He wore the dark tailored trousers, this time with a vivid peacock-blue shirt clinging to his broad chest as he stretched his arms negligently across the broad arms of the chair. A powerful beast . . . the description flashed into Erica's head, then Matt spoilt the whole effect by looking up at her, his lips curving in a smile of such seductive warmth that Erica almost blushed like a schoolgirl. His voice was soft.

'Thank you very much. We are grateful.'

'You may not have anything to thank me for.'

'In that case, we thank you for trying.'

She looked at him suspiciously. The beguiling tone bore no resemblance to the clipped voice he often used, nor to the mocking drawl that irritated her so much at other times. You had to hand it to Matthew, he could be any kind of person he chose. He studied her now, eyes still warm, and all at once Erica became intensely aware of her own appearance.

She wished she had chosen a less revealing outfit. Guy's extravagant admiration had not embarrassed her, she had let his compliments slide over her without being in the least rattled. But Matt, sitting there in that relaxed pose, made her experience another desperate impulse to run and cover up, to shield herself from his penetrating assessment.

Spellbound, she watched his lips move. 'Another glass of wine before you go?'

'No, thanks.' She felt supercharged, extra sensitive, alive and aware as she had never been before. Dangerous sensations evoked by a dangerous man.

Guy broke the spell. 'Come back and join us if Jenny doesn't welcome you. She might send you away, you know. She—she doesn't like talking.'

He was so vulnerable, her heart ached for him. Although he pretended desperately not to be concerned, Erica knew her visit to Jenny was of great importance to him. His eyes beseeched her.

'Good luck, Erica. Would you like me to come with you?'

'No,' she refused gently. 'Thanks for the offer, Guy, but I'll go alone.'

Jenny occupied a small suite of rooms on the ground floor towards the rear of the homestead, with wide doors opening on to the verandah so that she could wheel herself out to enjoy the garden whenever she felt like it.

Erica knocked on the door she knew was Jenny's, and Nell opened it, smiling a welcome.

'How nice! Come and join us.'

Jenny lay in bed, propped against pillows with a book in her hand. There was no welcoming smile on her face and her eyes were wary. Erica settled herself casually on the end of the bed.

'Forgive the interruption. I thought I'd come and say hello. I wondered if I could do anything for you. I'm a nurse, and I'm available.' She offered Jenny her warmest smile. 'Can I help?'

As usual, Jenny's eyes flickered away from her. 'Nell looks after me. That is—until they get me someone else.'

'Someone else? I thought your physiotherapist was away on holiday.'

A faint flush of resentment crept into Jenny's pale cheeks. 'No.' Her voice lost some of its timidity. 'He sent her away.'

'Who?'

'Matthew.'

Nell looked uncomfortable. 'He must have had his reasons, Jenny. Perhaps he thought her incompetent.'

'He lost his temper.' Nervously, the girl's fingers rustled the pages of the book she held. 'He was awfully rude, and very angry.' She darted another surreptitious glance at Erica.

'He—he didn't ask whether I wanted her to stay He just—just snapped out that she was discharged.'

'She will be replaced, Jenny,' Nell reminded the girl gently. 'Matt promised. It's taking him a little time to find somebody suitable who's willing to come so far away from the cities.'

Erica listened, suddenly alert. So there was no new attendant for Jenny in view as yet. Surely Matthew and Jeremy weren't hoping to persuade her to stay and take care of the girl. For one thing, she was a nursing sister, not a physiotherapist. For another, she had her position at the hospital to go back to. She wasn't in the least interested in staying here under the critical, watchful eyes of the master of Vandellan any longer than she had to.

That strange fragment of overheard conversation in her flat came back to her. 'Will she do?' . . . Will I do for what?

Jenny burrowed her head into the pillows, letting the book drop from her fingers. Erica leaned forward and picked it up.

'Oh—music! Do you play, Jenny? You have some of my favourite folk songs here.'

'No.'

Nell shot Jenny a quick, considering look.

'You had a guitar with you,' she reminded her carefully. 'Don't you remember, Jenny? It was broken in the accident.'

Erica handed back the book. 'That must have been an odd sight, a guitar on horseback. How did you manage it?'

At first it seemed Jenny was not going to answer. She shrank back even farther into the pillows, and looked everywhere except at Erica. Then she answered sullenly, 'I carried it on my back in a case, and it got smashed.' A bitter smile twisted her thin lips. 'So did I,' she added.

'Yes, I know, and I'm sorry. I don't know anything about guitars, but I'm not bad at doing what nurses have to do, so if you need help washing and dressing when Nell is busy—'

'Nell takes care of me. I'll wait for her.'

Erica caught Nell's sympathetic gaze from the other side of the room where she was hanging Jenny's clothes in a wardrobe. Erica made a last effort.

'If I can get hold of a guitar, do you think you might play? I love music.'

'No.'

It was not only ungracious, it sounded final. Nell closed the wardrobe door quickly.

'Matthew and Guy offered to buy Jenny another guitar, but she doesn't feel like trying to play just yet.'

'Oh, I see.' Erica pushed the book closer to Jenny's unresponsive hand. 'Well, maybe later on.' To press any further would antagonise the frightened girl, nervous as a young kitten. Erica asked lightly, 'How long does it take to get acclimatised to the sun out here?'

'Oh—ages.' Nell walked across the room, and touched Erica's cheek lightly. 'I was wondering whether that becoming flush was a sign of sunburn or excitement. Now I know. You're quite warm. I think you'll have a little more colour than usual on your skin tomorrow.'

'Yes.' Erica pulled a small face. 'I got into trouble from Matthew this afternoon for not wearing a hat.'

Jenny's mouth made a small 'o', her eyes widened. 'Was he very angry?'

Erica laughed. She said airily, 'Nothing I couldn't handle'. She sounded braver than she felt, and Jenny giggled nervously.

To be fair to Matt, Erica went on to explain how he had loaned his hat to keep off the sun, and Jenny looked doubtful, as if she might have liked to imagine an ulterior motive. Erica found herself wondering if Jenny found some kind of fascination in being so afraid of Matthew.

A few moments later she took her leave. 'I'd better go now, and let you finish your reading.' She offered her most cheerful smile. 'Goodnight, Nell. Sleep well, Jenny.'

Jenny did not say goodnight. Golden eyes wide, she lay studying Erica with a kind of wistful intensity. Finally she picked up the book, looking over it with huge doleful eyes, and her voice when she finally spoke quivered with feeling.

'I bet you think I'm a coward.'

'Why?'

'Because I—I won't try and play the guitar. But—but I know I can't. I just know. I don't feel like it.'

Erica patted the tensed fingers curled around the book.

'I can't see anything cowardly about that. It sounds reasonable to me. Everything takes its own time and that's a pretty important move, isn't it—starting to play again.'

The tense fingers relaxed, Jenny's quivering lips moved in the faintest, most fleeting, of smiles.

That was enough for tonight, Erica knew—that the girl had tried to smile. It was only the slightest of cracks in the wall she had built up around herself, but it was important.

'Time for me to leave.' she managed a faint

yawn. 'I'm planning an early night.'

Nell laughed. 'Catching up with you, is it, the change from city smog to country fresh air?'

'Are you going upstairs?' Jenny's tense voice arrested Erica halfway to the door.

'Yes.'

'Be careful up there.' Her face tightened with anguish. 'Don't go near the edge.'

Erica heard Nell's faint, shocked gasp, but she did not look away from Jenny. Whatever terrors the girl had in her mind, they must be exorcised She produced a smile of confidence.

'Don't worry about me. I bounce.'

She raised one hand, waved and smiled, and some of the anguish left Jenny's features.

'I'll come with you, Erica.' Nell turned out the ceiling light, leaving a bedside lamp glowing, and pushed a small brass bell where Jenny could reach it. 'Ring if you need me, love. I'll hear.'

Jenny nodded silently. Outside in the passage Nell said softly, 'She's a strange one, that girl. I wouldn't take too much notice of some of the things she says, not until she's better and a lot more rational.'

'Of course.' Nell was trying to be kind, and Nell had to be loyal to Matt. She was caught in a complex situation, just like the rest of them, and Erica found herself wondering uncomfortably how much was honest in the behaviour of Vandellan's residents and how much that was inexplicable was going on beneath the surface.

Later, she drifted to sleep thinking about Jenny. She knew she must not be over-confident because the girl had smiled at her. Tomorrow, some slight nervous reaction could send her retreating into isolation again.

Why had Matthew sent the physiotherapist away? Because he was angry, Jenny had announced, and Erica could not help feeling slightly sorry for the physiotherapist. It would have been a powerful anger, scorching and strong. Erica wound the sheet around her throat and shoulders as if she, too, might need protection from the force of the dark man's anger.

It must have been after midnight when she awoke, finding herself suddenly alert. She knew something had disturbed her, although she could not remember what it was. She sat upright, straining to listen, giving herself time to tune in to whatever had interrupted her sleep.

Somewhere in the night there had been a sound that ought not to have occurred. All her nurse's instincts told her she would have to find out what it was before she would be able to sleep again.

Without waiting to cover up with a dressing-gown she walked to her door, opened it, and looked along the passageway in both directions. Faint gleams from a narrow skylight filtered onto the floor. Erica glanced down at her flimsy attire, hesitating. The soft material floated around her like a cloud.

If there was somebody moving around out there she might scare them. She would make a ghostly sight in the dimness. She listened again but nothing moved. All around her the homestead was silent.

She crept to the gallery, looking around her carefully, feeling like an intruder waiting to be discovered, yet knowing she would not sleep again until she assured herself everything was right. The gallery was streaked with bars of light and shadow because of an odd arrangement of windows. The whole atmosphere, with the faces in those portraits staring silently down, was eerie, unreal. She crept to the banisters and looked down.

In the hallway, glitters of red and yellow and green danced on the carpet, reflected by moonlight beaming through leadlight panels over the doors. A strong white band of light glowed through an open door on one side of the hall. She wondered about that door. Should it be open? Should she go downstairs and close it? But though she continued watching for several minutes there was no sign of anybody moving.

It seemed that this time her instincts had misled her. There was nobody around who ought not to be there. She was turning to go back to bed when a dark figure detached itself from a patch of shadow, and Erica gasped.

Even when the figure moved closer and she saw by the shape and stance that it was Matthew, her heart pounded.

'Looking for me?' He was speaking in that drawl again, the voice that always nettled her.

'Don't be ridiculous. Of course I'm not looking for you.'

She had clutched the wooden railing by instinct when she first became aware there was somebody in the gallery. As Matthew advanced towards her she found herself desperately loosening her grip and straightening her fingers, and that desperate reaction to have her hands free shocked Erica into instant sanity. Wht did she have to be afraid of?

Guy must be sleeping not too far away and Nell was downstairs. They would hear if she called. Yet she stood half-mesmerised while Matt closed the gap between them.

'Positive you aren't looking for me? That's very disapppointing.'

'Of course I'm not.'

Matt wore a mulberry-coloured silk robe and he must have donned it hurriedly because it hung open, and Erica thought 'Oh lord, the man sleeps naked, wouldn't you know?' before she remembered her own state of undress and clutched the floating white flimsiness around her. She saw the suggestive glint of his smiling as he fastened the girdle around his own robe.

She said tremulously, 'I heard a noise', and his eyebrows rose in immediate disbelief.

'Sure you weren't lonely?' The voice dropped to an insulting drawl. 'No lover to keep you company. I was hoping perhaps you might be seeking a little diversion.'

Erica took one pace backwards, feeling the carved wooden railing push against her spine.

'No, I'm not looking for a diversion, and if I were you'd be the last person I'd choose for it.'

'Tut, tut. That's not very complimentary.'

'I assure you it's the truth.'

Matt's voice was mild, yet the very mildness was as menacing to her composure as the thunder of approaching storm. Now she could hear his breathing. Her heightened senses picked up the faint rustle of the silken robe, the aroma of whatever he used after showering still clung to his body, and she received it as clearly as if he were trasmitting some special message to her, making potent contact with sensuality that set her composure rocking, her heart thudding a warning.

She flinched as he put out his hand and with astonishing gentleness brushed the coppery curls over her forehead.

'I shan't return your insult. On the contrary, I cannot imagine a more enchanting dalliance. In that gear you make a truly seductive nymph.' His voice came almost a whisper, husky and teasing, like a caress.

'You're enough to threaten any man's controls, young lady, standing there looking so innocent.'

In an attempt to take him by surprise Erica slid sideways, pushing herself between the banister and Matt's body. She should have known it was doomed to failure. Without any effort at all, he halted her by curling an arm around her waist, holding her close, turning his own body sideways so that she was pressed against him. She heard his heartbeats, slow and steady. No crazy fluttering, like hers. He touched her ear with his lips.

'Just how innocent are you, Erica? Do you lead brother Jeremy on like this, wandering around in the early morning hours? What brought you out here?'

She protested desperately, 'I told you. I heard a noise. I came to see what it was.'

'Really?' He sounded unconvinced.

'I *did* hear something.'

Erica twisted herself out of his arms and looked around her frantically. Some object or creature must have created the sound that alarmed her and brought her creeping barefoot from her bed. But nothing showed. Only Matthew Crosswyn, laughing at her with that disbelieving expression. She almost began to doubt herself.

Then she found it. A small metal ashtray had rolled from a drum table in a recess and now lay close to his heel. The shadow cast by his foot had concealed it from both of them. Erica pointed to it with one quivering finger.

'You must have m-mice.'

Her laugh was shaky and he looked down at her quickly, his mouth softening unbelievably into gentleness.

They stared at each other, heightened awareness blotting out the gallery, the fallen ashtray, everything except the two of them. He took the fingers of her right hand in the palm of his own. The gipsy ring glinted.

'So you wear that bauble to bed. I wonder why. Is it some kind of talisman?'

She pulled her hand away. 'If you like.'

She must move now, before his nearness overwhelmed her. Already his expression was changing, the gentleness intensifying into something more powerful, much more dangerous. The heat of his body assailed her, coaxing her into languor, drugging her will-power.

She turned to run, but once again he was too quick for her. With a swift movement he imprisoned her in his arms. She heard his breathing, ragged and rasping, as he moved his lips against her forehead.

'Damn you!' They weren't exactly words of love but they were fraught with passion, and a wave of fear set Erica's body trembling. This was heady stuff, outside the range of her experience.

She gasped 'I'll scream,' and he gave one short, harsh laugh, before he increased the pressure of the arm that held her, forcing her even harder against the hard strength of his own body.

Whatever the force that drove Matt at this moment, it was too potent for her to repel on her own. And she *was* on her own. The quiet gallery offered no refuge, even if she found strength to break away.

The screams she had threatened died in her throat, as Matt skilfully aroused in her a passion answering to his own. Her head swam, so that she clung to him for support. Soon she would be entirely out of control, carried away by a wild upspringing of desire that was too hot and strong for her to curb.

Unconsciously, she relaxed in his arms, letting her body go limp in a movement of surrender that reacted like a signal to Matt. His arms slackened their grip, his hands began moving in gentle exploration over the curves of her body, bringing her to even greater life, stirring raptures.

He muttered thickly, 'Anything you want, Erica. If it's Vandellan, I can give it to you. Jeremy can't.'

He would have established his hold then, one hand untying the ribbons on her fragile gown, sliding her shoulders free, but Erica made a last desperate effort, frantically twisting herself out of his hands.

'I want—I want a guitar!'

'What!' His face went blank. He knew she was making a bid for escape, but the unexpectedness of her request shook him, and he stood there staring at her incredulously.

'You want *what*?'

'I want a guitar.'

She backed off nervously, her voice breathy, apprehensive. 'It's for Jenny. I talked to her, and she plays guitar.' Now she was talking too fast, gabbling away desperately, but she could not stop. 'Folk songs, I mean. That's what Jenny sings. And her—her instrument was broken in the accident, you see.'

Matt's lips tightened. 'Yes, I do see. I know all about it. I've already offered Jenny a new guitar and she won't accept it. And what the hell does Jenny's guitar have to do with what's going on here?'

His forehead shone with beads of perspiration, the hands that reached for her, sliding open-palmed around her waist, were hot. Damn you, he had muttered. And damn you too . . . Erica called up the last shred of her faltering resistance.

She backed away, talking fast. 'It's worth a chance, for Guy's sake, isn't it? You wanted me to do something and I'm trying. All you have to do is buy a guitar for Jenny.'

She was fending him off with words, the only weapons she had. 'You could buy a guitar and leave it in her room. That's what I think. Even if she doesn't touch it now it'll be there, tempting her—'

'Talking about temptation—' he ran a shaky hand through his tumbled hair. 'You know how to torment a man, don't you? I'd say you were expert.'

Her eyes filled with tears. Mortified, she tried

blinking them away, but to her horror moisture trickled down her cheeks.

'I didn't set out to tempt you. I'm sorry if I did that.' She glanced down apologetically at her diaphanous attire. 'I can see—you think—but I did hear something that startled me, even if you don't believe me.'

Dejectedly Erica tried to screen her slender body with the floating material of her nightgown. It was a pathetic effort. There was no way she could cover herself from this man's piercing inspection.

In an abrupt change of mood he took his hand away from her waist, cupped her tear-stained face in his warm fingers, holding it immobile while he searched her expression intently. A faint smile curved his lips.

'All right, young lady. You've made your point. I grant it—you heard a noise. We have the ashtray to prove it. And you shall have your guitar tomorrow if there's one in the nearest town. That's a promise.'

A slight, ironic smile flitted across his face. 'May I claim a slight reward?' He bent lower.

Feeling Erica tense he shook his head, and the long, strong, brown fingers curved even more possessively around her jawline. 'Don't panic. A slight reward only.'

His lips touched hers in the softest of caresses, surprisingly gentle, yet arousing in her enough response to make her instantly wary. He kept his lips against her own, brushing them softly, gently, until she relaxed. Then he gave a soft laugh as he put her away from him.

'You don't know how lucky you are, Erica. Next

time the mice play games with our ornaments I suggest you let them go about their business. Pull the sheets over your ears and don't go roaming around. Unless, of course, the homestead is on fire. In that case I'd be too busy to notice how seductive you look on your midnight prowling.'

He gave her a gentle push. 'Off you go now, while you're in luck.'

As she retreated thankfully, his soft voice called after her, 'It *was* the mice, of course.'

What did that mean, and what an extraordinary man! In the sanctuary of her own room, Erica pondered the suggestion behind those final words.

If he had rolled the ashtray himself, then she should be angry. Very angry. Surely he wouldn't bother to do that, yet even as she denied the possibility, Erica recalled the urgency of those possessive hands, the sheer vitality he had directed towards her.

Matthew Crosswyn had stirred her senses to a kind of burning rapture she had never experienced before. He didn't even like her, so how could he do that? Erica recalled the night Jeremy had brought his brother to her flat and introduced them to each other, she remembered his antagonism, his instant ill-concealed dislike. Perhaps Jeremy was the key to Matt's inexplicable behaviour. He might have decided to separate them.

If his plans for Jenny included sending her physiotherapist away, then could there be a plan in his dark mind for Erica that did not include a close relationship with his brother Jeremy?

Although the night was warm Erica shivered. At least, if Matt hoped to cause a rift between her and

Jeremy by retailing the details of some ghastly seduction scene in the gallery, then he had failed. There was nothing to tell . . . if he stuck to the truth.

She moved restlessly in bed, unable to settle. The gold band glinted on her finger. How strange that Matt should be so strongly aware of her gipsy token. He seemed to have sensed from the beginning that it was not just another piece of jewellery. Perhaps it did have some magic charm that might protect her. That was fantasy, of course, but she had certainly needed protection tonight.

And just in case there was something to be said for gipsies and charms and magic that had no proper explanation, perhaps it would not hurt to keep the ring on her finger. 'Wear it always', the gipsy man had urged, and there had been something in his eyes that made it difficult to believe that he was mistaken in the things he knew.

Erica curled her fingers lightly, feeling her fingertips touching the palms of her hands. It felt better that way—safer—because if ever she needed a talisman it was now, while she was at Vandellan.

CHAPTER SIX

WHEN Erica came down to breakfast next morning, Matthew and Guy had already left for the nearest town.

'They've taken my shopping list,' Nell told her, 'and they had some business of their own to attend to.'

So Matthew had not mentioned the guitar. Erica thanked him silently for that. The gift would be a complete surprise, and Jenny would have no chance to build up resistance.

Jenny looked better this morning, some colour in her cheeks. Although the furtive glance she offered Erica when she entered the kitchen was as timid as ever, at least she did not back away.

'Is Gregg taking you outside this morning?' Erica was careful to make the enquiry casually. She did not want to stir up any more storms. This time Jenny remained calm at the mention of Gregg's name.

'Yes. He wants to show me the new stallion, the one they're so proud of. But I'm scared of horses. They spook me.'

'I expect they would make you feel nervous after the accident.' Erica helped herself to breakfast. 'Were you always nervous around horses, before you had the fall, I mean?'

'Yes. No. I don't know,' Jenny fumbled.

'Well, you were jolly brave, hopping up behind Guy when he offered a lift.'

94

As usual Jenny began to hedge when conversation became personal. She ducked her head, turning so that neither Nell nor Erica could see her expression clearly.

'There was nothing else around, and I had to get to Vandellan. You see, I was going to apply for work here, and then when—when—nobody met me—'

'Did they know you were coming?' Nell's eyes widened in surprise. 'I understood you were headed here on the off chance.'

'Oh yes, of course. That was it.' Jenny's face reddened, then turned pale. Her voice sank to a mumble. 'And I thought, maybe somebody will come along and offer me a lift, but nobody did. Then Guy came and said—that he would take me—' Her eyes glittered feverishly, 'I don't want to talk about it.'

'Of course you don't.' Erica patted her arm sympathetically. 'I shouldn't ask so many questions. Sorry if I sound inquisitive. It's just that I'm concerned.'

After breakfast, when Jenny had retreated to her own room, Nell said reflectively, 'That's the first I've heard about Jenny expecting to be met. I'm certain nobody here knew she was coming.'

'She's probably confused. She's a very tense young lady.'

That could be so. Jenny hadn't stated flatly that she had expected to be met by somebody from Vandellan, but Erica knew that another small doubt had taken root in her mind.

This homestead with its trapdoor and its complicated people was making her distrustful. Nobody

behaved as she expected. The conduct of Matthew
in making that pass at her in the gallery last night,
Jenny's desperate refusal to talk about her accident, and her own behaviour, so unlike her—

Why had she sent Jeremy away from her room on
their first night at Vandellan when she knew full
well that she had led him to expect something
different?

Nell folded the tablecloth. 'Why so pensive?'

'I don't know. I'm finding it difficult to get my
bearings here. I don't live surrounded by crystal
chandeliers at home, so perhaps that is what's
putting me off.'

Nell chuckled. 'You'll get used to it.'

Erica doubted that. She couldn't understand herself any more, so how could she expect to understand Vandellan?

Later she stood on the verandah, staring out over
the gardens. They should have pleased her, with
their colour and beauty. Instead, they added to her
disquiet. There seemed an atmosphere out there,
under the vibrant, vivid splashes of yellow and
lavender, red and orange, mixed up with all the
perfumes and strange exotic shapes, a teasing suggestion of something hidden.

She didn't trust the poinciana tree, her eyes
veered away from it, because it had been translated
by her overworked imagination into a whirling
gipsy skirt. The oleanders . . . she knew about
those. Poison trees, for all their beauty. The white
sap they carried in their branches could make man
or beast vilely ill. They waved their splashy heads of
rose-pink, or white, or smudges of apricot against
the clear blue sky. Exciting but dangerous.

Even the roses of Vandellan, Erica mused, brandished their old-fashioned thorns like weapons.

She decided on a swim to shake herself out of this morbid mood. Since nobody was around to see her she chose her skimpiest bikini, a shoestring concoction of black nylon, and after collecting a book, a tube of sunblock cream and a towel, she took herself to the poolside to relax.

After a long cool swim she found a shady place and lay reading until the heat made her pleasantly drowsy and she dropped the book and closed her eyes. She had not intended to sleep, but it wasn't long before she drifted into blissful slumber.

When she awoke the sun gleamed almost overhead.

'Oh darn!' Whatever would Nell think of her? She had planned to help with lunch, now she had frittered the morning away while she slept.

Erica picked up her book and towel and ran for the house, but as she passed the jacaranda trees Vandellan's yellow station wagon swung along the drive.

'Damn!'

There was no chance of Matt and Guy not seeing her. They pulled up with a jerk and Erica became suddenly selfconscious, aware of her near-nakedness.

She would only make herself look coy if she grabbed for her towel. It was easy to imagine what Matt would make of such a cover-up. So she continued walking towards them, inwardly embarrassed but outwardly—thank goodness—preserving her dignity by appearing unruffled. She even managed a carefree smile.

Matt and Guy climbed out of the vehicle. Neither
man took trouble to disguise his interest as she
approached.

'Cover-girl material.' Guy's dancing eyes took
the sting from his comment. He looked her over,
unabashed, from sandalled feet to tumbled red-
gold curls, but his inspection lingered longest on
the slender but shapely figure almost fully revealed
by the tantalising bikini, before he placed one hand
melodramatically over his heart.

'I pant for you.'

'It's the heat, not my appearance, that makes you
short of breath.' Erica could not find it in her heart
to be angry with Guy. The vulnerable look of youth
and immaturity, with its underlying strain, touched
a chord of sympathy. Guy was paying dearly for an
act of youthful carelessness, she need not add to his
misery by becoming offended.

But Matt was another proposition. From him she
suffered a blatant inspection that set sparks glittering in her eyes, but when she compressed her lips
and offered him her iciest look he relaxed as if he
might have been amused by her reaction.

Guy spoke impetuously, eagerly. He was so
desperately anxious to hope. He announced, 'We
found a guitar in the music shop. It looks like the
one Jenny had with her when she—when we—
had the accident.' He flushed uncomfortably.
'Near as I can remember, anyhow,' he added awkwardly.

He turned away and reached into the vehicle for
a large parcel, obviously a guitar-case, but Matt
stood his ground, not taking his eyes from her, and
Erica's expression grew frostier.

'Don't tell me you haven't seen a bikini before.'

Surprisingly, the tough face softened. 'I must apologise. Yes, I've seen a bikini before, but never one that looked better. I really must mend my manners. I don't know why I'm forever needling you. Perhaps if you weren't such a firebrand—'

Erica gave him her most dulcet smile. 'Possibly you haven't grown up yet', she said sweetly, and his lips twitched.

'You certainly bring out the tiger in me. I'll make an effort to curb my baser impulses in future. And don't hesitate to wear that outfit next time you swim.' His eyes skipped lightly over her appearance. 'I thoroughly approve, and I'm sure Jeremy will, or has he seen it already?'

Surprised by the peace gesture, Erica replied without thinking. 'No, he hasn't.' She glanced suspiciously at Matt but his expression remained unrevealing. He glanced down at his wristwatch. 'Did you have a long swim?'

'No, I—I fell asleep. I didn't mean to.'

'Ah!' He surveyed her blandly, but his lips curved in amusement. 'You should try getting more sleep at night, perhaps.'

He dared, he actually dared! Reminding her that she had been out in the gallery last night, instead of sleeping. She was choking on a suitably cutting reply when Guy handed her the parcel.

'There you are, Ric. One guitar, as requested.'

Erica took it doubtfully.

'Will Jenny be able to handle this? It looks rather large and awkward.'

'So much more of a challenge.' Matt's voice was crisp. He reached into the station wagon and came towards her with a white stetson, which he placed on her head, tilting it down over her face.

'There! Now do you want a lift to the back of the house?'

Erica shook her head, and they left her holding the parcel as they drove around to unload near the kitchen. The hat firmly settled on her head, Erica wrapped her towel around the guitar and took it into the kitchen, where Nell was finishing lunch preparations.

'Welcome. I'd just decided Jenny and I would have to eat all this ourselves when Matt and Guy arrived at one door and here you are at the other.' She studied Erica's flushed face. 'Have a good swim?'

Erica nodded.

'Fall asleep, or were you resting?'

'I fell asleep,' Erica admitted. 'Sorry, Nell. I meant to help with lunch.'

Matt had disappeared, but Guy leaned against the doorway, nibbling a stolen sandwich. Nell put another near his hand.

'Don't worry,' she told Erica. 'Like I told you, I don't need any assistance while my sons are away. When they come back it'll be another matter. They keep me running off my feet. Maybe you can help then, that is, if you're still here—'

There it was again, the innuendo, the veiled suggestion that she might stay longer at Vandellan than she had planned.

Nell said quickly, 'Soon we'll have a new house-keeper, and what will I do then, anyway?'

'You'll be obsolete,' Guy teased, ducking as Nell pretended to hurl a saucer at him. He disappeared, and Nell went quietly back to her sandwich cutting.

'What's the bulky-looking object you're carrying in that towel? Not a bomb, I hope.'

'It's a guitar for Jenny. Guy and Matthew bought it in town. What do you think I should do with it, leave it here for Jenny to find or take it to her room?'

'Take it around to her, unless you want to change into something more comfortable first.' Nell's eyes twinkled. 'You look remarkably eye-catching. How did the boys react?'

'Guy was very complimentary. He said I took his breath away.'

'And Matthew?'

Nell leaned over the table, slicing bread, carefully looking away, but Erica was not deceived. She knew a loaded question when she heard it.

'Why Matthew?' she asked bluntly, and Nell put down the knife.

'I'm sorry. I shouldn't have asked. But there's been something different about Matt since you came. I know you're Jeremy's friend. But there's a—a crackling in the air—' she pushed the platter of bread away from her. 'Tell me to mind my own business if you feel like it.'

'It's all right. The crackling is merely a sharpening of swords. Matt and I make natural-born antagonists. Jeremy brought him to my flat one evening before we came to Vandellan, and he wasn't impressed.'

'I see.' Nell's lips widened into an understanding smile. 'He can be very dampening, our Matt. I don't usually stick my neck out interfering in other people's lives, but Lilyan doesn't take kindly to females looking Matt's way. I thought I should warn you. There've been a few and she got rid of them very swiftly. She carries a sharp little hatchet, our Lilyan. No matter how innocent your intentions, she'll pounce if Matt shows any interest in you.'

'Oh, I see. I wondered—'

'Lilyan's very defensive about her position here. She loses Vandellan if Matt marries anybody else, and she won't let that happen without a fight to the death. Figuratively speaking, of course. I'm sure she wouldn't attack you physically, but she'd go as close as she dared if she thought Matt was seriously interested in you.'

'Lilyan doesn't have to worry about me.' Erica picked up the guitar. 'I'll go and call on Jenny. Lunch any minute?'

Nell nodded. 'I'm setting a table on the verandah. Go and help yourself when you've freshened up. And forgive my presumption talking to you this way. You're far too nice a person to get hurt by Vandellan's politics.'

Erica said lightly, 'I'll remember your warning, although it isn't necessary. Matthew Crosswyn finds me about as attractive as a plague of foot and mouth disease.'

She walked thoughtfully around to Jenny's rooms. A crackling in the air, Nell had said. Could Nell have any inkling of what had happened in the gallery last night? Perhaps she too had been awakened by the rolling ashtray, and from the hallway below had glimpsed their two figures and misunderstood what was happening.

Matt had only been looking for a little dalliance,

an outlet for sexual appetite, but Nell could have misread their actions and taken it for a love scene.

Erica sighed as she knocked on the door of Jenny's rooms and eased her way in carefully, with the guitar in her hands.

'What do you want?' Jenny didn't sound welcoming. She sat in her wheelchair reading, and when she saw the shape Erica carried her face whitened.

'Don't leave that here. I told you—'

'—that you don't fancy trying to play again just yet. Yes, I know you told me, but I can't see any harm in having the instrument around in case you change your mind.'

'Well, I won't have it.' Jenny's voice rose to piercing shrillness. She covered her mouth with her hands, as if the sound had shocked her, and when she uncurled her fingers her lips quivered.

'I said—' her voice a mere whisper, 'not to bring that thing here.'

'So you did.' Erica kept her voice light and easy as she pushed the guitar underneath the bright hanging curtains beside Jenny's windows. 'It doesn't matter if you don't use it. I—we—thought it would be a splendid idea to have it here, in case you feel like experimenting some time later on.'

The way she was looking now, with that wildness growing in her eyes, Jenny could well decide to crush the guitar against the wall with her wheelchair, and Erica thought compassionately that she was likely to do even more damage to herself, she was so resentful and defensive. She pulled the curtains across the guitar, standing between it and the wheelchair, making herself smile as if she hadn't a doubt that what she had done was quite the most natural thing in the world.

She touched her damp bikini. 'I've been swimming. Nell tells me you exercise in the pool sometimes. Care to join me one morning?'

'No.'

'Did you get to see the stallion?'

'Yes.'

'I don't suppose they'll let me anywhere near him.' Erica shook her head. 'My fiery hair would probably incite him to all sorts of dangerous antics.'

Jenny gave a reluctant laugh. 'He's not that bad. His name is Kerellah, and he looks handsome really, sort of proud and distinguished. It's only when someone tries to ride him that he acts up.' She studied Erica consideringly. 'Gregg says only Matthew has ridden him so far, but he reckons he could do it.'

'They tell me he's quite a horseman, your Gregg.' Jenny gave a small gasp. She muttered through white lips, 'He's not—not my Gregg. He takes me out because he feels sorry for me. That's all.'

Erica knelt beside the wheelchair. 'Hey! I didn't mean to upset you.' She slipped her fingers around Jenny's wrist, noting the fast pulse, hearing the shallow agitated breathing, then waiting until the girl calmed. She did her best to sound unperturbed.

'You must be hungry, Jenny. I know I am. So I'm off upstairs to cover myself, then I think I'll eat. Does that interest you? I know Nell's ready.'

'I'll—I'll see Nell, then.' As though Nell and the kitchen were a refuge, Jenny steered towards the door.

Erica went thoughtfully upstairs, changed quickly, and joined Matt and Guy on the verandah, where Nell had set up everything in the shade.

Later, Nell wheeled a traymobile out with tea, coffee and cool drinks. She remarked that Jenny had had enough of her company and retired to her room after a snack.

'She's a prickly creature at most times, poor little soul,' Nell leaned back, savouring the coffee, 'but she seems extra touchy today.'

'I'm afraid I did that,' Erica confessed. 'I haven't been much help at all. The guitar might not have been such a smart idea, the reaction wasn't good when I took it in. Then I made an unfortunate remark about Gregg being her stockman, and that really upset her.'

Matt frowned, his clear grey eyes suddenly alert. 'How come?'

'I don't know, I didn't understand why she should become so upset. I'm wondering whether she finds herself attracted to him. In a boy-girl way, I mean. Man-woman, that is.' Matt was looking rather cynical, and she flushed. 'Well, that could complicate things, couldn't it? Poor girl, she has enough to cope with, she certainly wouldn't want to find herself emotionally involved with a man who only feels sympathy for her.'

Matt's cynicism deepened. 'You women!' He swallowed the last of his coffee and set down the cup. 'Always ready to go overboard for romance. A young fellow feels sorry for an injured girl and you've got her into a love affair before the poor chap has time to say "Good morning". The unfortunate girl was probably protecting her privacy

against what she might have seen as interference.
I'm not criticising—' oh yes, he was—'I'm merely
pointing out—' he waved a dismissive hand in
Erica's direction— 'that you may not always make
the correct decisions, professional or otherwise.'

Erica went into battle. 'Neither might you, but I
bet that doesn't stop you making decisions. Anyway, it was worth a try.'

'Point conceded.' He stood up abruptly. 'Now I
must leave you, if I'm to collect your young man
before dinner.'

Her young man . . . Erica had not expected
Jeremy back until tomorrow. She said, 'I thought
you sent him away for two days.'

His brows rose. 'I did not send him away, I asked
him for some help.' Then he relented and explained, 'I've been in touch with Hilarie at Carisma. She says everybody's done a great job,
the creek level is dropping, there's no more flood
danger. So I'll pick up Lilyan and Jeremy today.'

Erica walked to the traymobile to refill her cup.
As Matt passed he leaned down, speaking softly.

'That is what you want, I presume? To have
Jeremy back as soon as it can be arranged.'

His expression was quizzical, challenging. The impertinence of the man. Did he imagine he'd made
such an impact on his midnight excursion that she
was ready to forget Jeremy and fly into his arms?

She eyed him coolly. 'Of course it's what I want.'

Strange how relieved she felt when Matt and Guy
left the verandah, and she and Nell were left to
relax in peace. Nell settled back in a lounger with a
sigh.

'I suppose Lilyan will arrive with a host of instructions for the dance and our weekend of entertainment.' She chuckled. 'A great planner, our Lilyan, and very good at delegating. Watch out you don't cop too many orders.'

'I don't mind.'

Dreamily Erica watched the filtered sunlight splashing the verandah floor. 'I prefer to be busy,' she confessed. 'The prospect of a houseful of strangers, however pleasant and friendly, scares me a bit. So don't hesitate to do a bit of delegating yourself. Your husband won't be too happy if he comes back and finds you being worked to death looking after us, and Jenny too.'

Nell brightened. 'Robert will be back on Friday, the day before the dance. He knows I like to keep busy. Matt tells me the new housekeeper arrives next Tuesday, when the weekend festivities are over. He made some enquiries while he was shopping for the guitar, and this time he's found someone suitable.' She chuckled.

'Matt has booked caterers for the weekend. He didn't like to break in a new housekeeper with such a heavy workload, in case she thought we did it all the time. And about that delegating we spoke of,' her smile was cheerful, 'how are you on sorting sheets and pillowslips, making up beds, or polishing crystal?'

'If you mean chandeliers and the like, I don't have much experience, but I can learn.'

'There won't be all that much to do.' Nell uncurled herself from the lounger and began loading the traymobile. Erica stood up to help clear the table. 'We'll have no food to prepare and the wine cellar is well stocked.'

The wine cellar . . . Erica had forgotten the trapdoor. She had locked it away in a blind corner of her mind where it could not disturb her. Now it came back to trouble her. 'Oh lord', she groaned inwardly, 'surely I'm not going on a worry-binge like a nervous patient.'

Undoubtedly, some of the security had gone from the pleasant lazy afternoon, and later as she stepped into the shower after a busy few hours with Nell, Erica heard the buzzing of Matt's plane over-head, and felt even less secure. Because Jeremy was in that plane and he would no doubt be looking forward to taking up their relationship where he had left off. The sound of the plane shocked Erica into awareness that she was no longer sure what she wanted or how she would handle the reunion.

She towelled herself vigorously, sprinkling fragrance over her lightly tanned body. Vandellan had already wrought its changes. Her session at the pool had altered the colour of her skin, and there could be other changes too. Maybe Vandellan had begun altering the colour of her life.

She took her time about dressing and going down to the drawing-room. Lilyan and Jeremy would take a while to freshen up and change, and she did not want to sit making conversation with Matt for too long.

She chose a light dress in pale blue cotton to wear for dinner, a simple frock not designed to make impact. Even so, Lilyan reacted frostily. She had taken considerable trouble with her own appearance. Her blonde hair shone like silk, her make-up was impeccable, and her long white gown could have graced a fashion page. She did not look like a woman who had laboured in a disaster area, and her first words after the cool 'Hello' dispelled any illusions anybody might have had about Lilyan wielding a shovel on the embankments.

'I've been terribly busy organising this weekend.' She flourished several pages of notes. 'I hope you don't mind taking on a few small tasks, Erica. We won't expect too much of you. I realise you aren't used to entertaining on this scale.'

Erica accepted the drink Guy handed her.

'I don't mind helping. I'll do what I can.'

Lilyan consulted her list. 'I thought tomorrow morning you might check and air the bedrooms and linen, and get them ready.'

'Mission accomplished!' Erica sipped her sherry, smiling a thank-you at Guy.

'Really?' Lilyan raised beautifully shaped eyebrows while her thin lips hardened.

'Nell and I did all that this afternoon.'

'Oh, I see.' Lilyan gave a short, artificial laugh. 'You have been energetic, haven't you? You're way ahead of me. I'll see you about a few other things later.'

Lilyan sounded a little put out, and Erica wished uncomfortably that she had kept quiet about the work she and Nell had done today. It might sound a little like a takeover bid, perhaps, to Lilyan's suspicious mind.

She smiled apologetically at Lilyan. 'Any time that suits you, I'm available. I've nothing important to do.'

Jeremy's entrance created a diversion. He had earned his keep at the neighbouring property. His face was lined, eyes heavy-lidded, as if he had not slept. Gratefully he accepted the drink Matthew offered, and made himself comfortable on a settee.

'If anybody shows me another bag of sand. or one more hunk of rock, I'll hit him with a shovel,' he groaned.

'You did well.' Matt's quiet approval lightened his glum expression. 'Hilarie tells me she worked you into the ground.'

Jeremy grimaced. 'Best exercise I've had in years,' he admitted. 'We erected miles of stone wall, and sandbags by the billion, I think. And I'll be a fit man by the time I get back to the big smoke. At the moment,' he gave an exaggerated moan, 'I'm suffering. You'd better sacrifice a bottle of your best Scotch and let me relax with my lady tonight.'

His grin at Erica was intimate and suggestive, yet somehow appealing. Jeremy wearing that exhausted air made her feel protective. Dear Jeremy, how could she have pushed him out of her thoughts these past twenty-four hours?

Yet when Lilyan crossed the room to join him he stood up, offering her the same warm intimate smile he had given Erica. Some kind of personality contact had occurred between them during their stay at Carisma. Jeremy murmured something softly, and Lilyan's laughter came like the sweet, clear laughter of an amused child. She linked her arm through Jeremy's, lifted her face, its expression persuasive, and Jeremy responded by giving her his whole attention.

Erica had not noticed Matt move. His voice startled her.

'Gin and tonic, or another sherry?'

'No, thank you.'

'So you and Nell have been busy this afternoon?' He sounded mildly amused. He knew of course exactly what was going on between Lilyan and Jeremy, but he was pretending not to notice.

'Not busy,' Erica offered him a cool smile over the rim of her glass, 'just usefully employed.'

His lips twitched.

'I'm pleased to hear it. We can't have you bored while you're with us.' As Matthew always did, he changed moods quickly. 'You're disappointed because Jenny failed to show any interest in the guitar?'

'Yes, I am.' It was no use trying to screen things from Matt. 'As it turned out you were right, it wasn't such a brilliant idea.'

Matthew became surprisingly amiable. 'Isn't it a little soon to decide? Surely you weren't expecting an instant miracle?'

Erica looked at him doubtfully. Matt in this seemingly approachable mood confused her. Impulsively, she asked, 'That stockman—the one you call Gregg—how much do you know about him?'

'Very little. He does his work. That's all I care about. He's spending a fair slice of his time with Jenny at present, but it seems to be helping her, and with the wet season coming there won't be all that much to do. We can spare him at present.' He looked at her mockingly. 'Why so interested in Gregg?'

'I don't know.' Erica shrugged helplessly. 'It's just that Jenny got so upset when I mentioned him.'

'Perhaps she thinks you have designs on her only friend.'

He mocked her now, but pleasantly, gently, and Erica answered in the same tone.

'Perhaps so, but she doesn't need to worry. I don't even know what the man looks like.'

When Matthew moved away Jeremy disentangled himself from Lilyan and crossed the room to Erica's side.

'You haven't welcomed me.'

She laughed and kissed him.

'That's better.' His smile was complacent. 'I was thinking perhaps you'd forsaken me.'

'Of course not.'

'I missed you, Ric.'

He trailed his fingers lightly along her arm. The contact was not meant to be arousing, just a pleasant friendly gesture reminding her that she was committed, reminding Matt and Guy too, if they cared to notice.

As she turned away to place her empty glass on a side table, Erica caught Matt's scrutiny. The pleasant understanding mood was gone. Once again, Matt had done an about-turn. His jaw was set hard, his eyes glacial. He looked not at her but through her, as though she did not exist. He could have been carved out of granite.

Nell came to remind them dinner was served. As they moved towards the dining-room Erica stayed close to Jeremy's side. She did not want to see the look that Matt wore now. Surely he hadn't intended it for her!

If he did, then they were antagonists again, for it was the face of an enemy, cold, implacable, unforgiving, with no trace of friendliness in it at all.

CHAPTER SEVEN

MATTHEW was too good a host to allow discomfort at his table. Whatever had caused his displeasure, he veiled it skilfully, and afterwards as they relaxed again in the drawing-room, discussing with Nell the final plans for the weekend, he showed no sign of the anger that had hardened his features so suddenly. Erica almost persuaded herself that she had been mistaken.

Guy was playing records. He wanted to dance, but he was outvoted and put to work instead, planning tennis matches for Saturday morning.

'I don't know why you're so hooked on all this organising,' he complained. 'You've done it all before dozens of times.'

'Every time is different,' Nell warned, 'and don't think you'll escape more chores tomorrow. There's a marquee to be erected on the lawn near the barbecue, and we'll need garden lights strung up.'

'I did that last time and seven times before that. That's nothing different,' Guy retorted, and Matt's cool voice offered tersely, 'Perhaps something else will turn out to be different this time. Don't give up hope.'

Matt was taking the part of observer. He had arranged for caterers and musicians, the rest he was apparently willing to leave to Lilyan. He sat back and listened lazily while Lilyan and Nell put things into place.

They didn't seem to need Erica. As soon as she could politely do so she said her goodnights.

'I ought to go and talk to Jenny. What do you think, Nell?'

'By all means, if you can spare the time.' Nell's expression was rueful. 'I tried to coax her out, but you know Jenny—'

'Are you coming back?' Guy's voice arrested Erica in the doorway.

'No, I don't think so. I've decided on an early night, these hot days are making me lazy.'

It was only the tightening of Matt's lips that told Erica she had made a mistake. He didn't believe she planned an early night. His face went blank, but his peaked brows were raised in that ironic way she hated. It hit her like a thunderbolt! Matt believed she was going early to her room, setting herself up for a visit from Jeremy, and so, she realised with sinking heart, so did everyone else in the room.

She mumbled an awkward 'Goodnight, everybody' before she fled into the hall, furious with herself for the embarrassment. She had made a harmless mistake, but nobody was going to believe that. Thanks to Matthew and that cynical expression, they believed she was enticing Jeremy to follow her.

Why did she allow Matt to demolish her confidence so easily? A look, a gesture, a swift change of expression on that unyielding face did it every time. He must know what he was doing to her.

Of course she had blundered terribly. Jeremy would knock on her door as soon as he eased himself away from the pleasant company in the

drawing-room. She had unwittingly issued him a
barefaced invitation.

Furious with herself and with Matt too, Erica
crossed the hall. It was not long after ten o'clock,
and light gleamed under Jenny's door. Erica
knocked softly and opened the door.

'Is there anything I can bring you, Jenny? Tea or
coffee, or a snack before you sleep?'

'No thanks. Nell promised to call in later.' Pretending not to notice the guitar still propped under
the curtains where she had left it, Erica smiled
warmly.

'It's a lovely night. We've all been sitting around
planning the weekend dance and the other activi-
ties. It all seems a bit overwhelming.'

Jenny eyed her consideringly. 'It's in your
honour. Nell says so.'

'Oh.' Of course it was. She should have guessed.
Outback hospitality. Thank heaven for the jade
dress hanging in her wardrobe.

Jenny appeared a little less strained tonight,
perhaps she had been feeling lonely, so Erica took a
risk.

'I hope you're coming to watch the dancing and
listen to the music. And the tennis and swimming.
Do you have anything special to wear?'

When Jenny failed to respond, she added, 'I've a
fantastic blouse that would look smashing on you.
It's rose pink, just the right colour for your shiny
brown hair. How do you feel about frilly necklines
and balloon sleeves with tight cuffs?'

'How do I—?' Jenny stared at Erica. Interest
flickered in her eyes, then disappeared. 'I expect
they look very nice on you.'

The prim voice held no warmth at all. Erica settled herself in the chair beside Jenny's bed.

'I'll get Nell to bring it when she's helping with your exercises tomorrow. If not, I'll bring it down myself. You don't have to wear it, but you might care to look it over.'

'I don't think so.' Her voice wavered slightly, the first sign of emotion Jenny had allowed herself.

'Well, you might change your mind tomorrow.' It wasn't easy, making conversation with a girl whose answers came so slowly, reluctantly, yet something—a need, a yearning, deep in those lustrous golden eyes belied her determined rejection.

Erica said lightly, 'I like your flowers.' It wouldn't have been the young stockman, surely, who arranged the half-opened rosebuds so generously in crystal vases around the room. They looked like a feminine touch. 'Did Nell bring them in?'

Jenny nodded. 'Yes. They're changed every day. Last week we had frangipani flowers, and fuchsias. It must be nice, being rich.'

'I suppose so, but you don't have to be rich to grow roses.' Perhaps Jenny was thinking about the swimming pool and the horses and the tennis court, as well as the flowers. She veiled her eyes with drooping lashes, studying Erica covertly.

'Are you rich?'

'No. Not many nurses make fortunes.'

'Oh.' Jenny digested this thoughtfully, before she said slyly, 'But Jeremy will have lots of money, won't he?'

Erica stiffened. 'If you mean what I think you

mean, Jenny, that's not a very nice remark,' and Jenny flushed and blinked.

'No, it isn't.' She played with the bedspread, drawing patterns on it with one finger. 'I knew it wasn't. I'm sorry, really I am.' Limpid golden eyes begging forgiveness, Jenny said abjectly, 'Sometimes I get so bored just lying here, or tied to a silly chair, then I get mad and want to throw things. And so—so I turn spiteful. I—I guess I can't help lashing out—I really didn't mean that.'

She swallowed unhappily, and Erica answered, 'I can't say I blame you. If it does any good—well, go ahead. I guess I can take a few insults if it makes you feel better.'

'No, it doesn't. It makes me feel ashamed and miserable.' Jenny raised her head, and for the first time her eyes met Erica's in a long, level, woman-look that changed her subtly, wiping away the impression of a frightened child, revealing an intelligent young woman.

'I don't know what gets into me,' she apologised. 'I suppose it's frustration, or something like that. And fear. I feel so cowardly, sometimes, wondering what's going to happen to me, what sort of future I'll have.'

'That's understandable. But try not to worry too much. You're in good hands . . .'

'I'm sorry I made that nasty suggestion that you're marrying Jeremy for his money. It would serve me right if nobody talked to me at all. I get so muddled—things get difficult.'

'Of course they do, Jenny.' Erica bent and kissed her lightly on the forehead. 'Don't give it a thought. I'll say goodnight and let you get some sleep. Are you certain about that bedtime drink? I like lemon and honey myself.'

Again, Jenny shook her head. As Erica turned to leave, she said suddenly, as if the words pushed their way out through a wall of reticence, 'I suppose they told you—they're saying I can walk if I really want to.'

Erica paused. 'They haven't told me very much at all.'

'Well, I can't, you know. Do they think I haven't tried? But she said—the physiotherapist said—that sometimes you have to accept—' Enlightenment flooded Erica's mind. Was that why Jenny's previous attendant had been dismissed so abruptly? Because she was defeatist, because she did not trouble to hide her disbelief in what the doctors promised?

'They say I don't want to walk. I do, you know.' The passionate truth in Jenny's tear-filled eyes was convincing.

Erica put her arms around the girl's shaking shoulders, holding her tightly.

'Of course they don't feel that way, my dear. The doctors say you have to get over the shock. It isn't easy, and it might be slow. You've got to force yourself over the barrier that's holding you back. It'll come, in its own good time. I've seen it happen.'

'You have?'

'It's called hysterical reaction, along with a few technical-sounding phrases. It just means there is a nervous block somewhere. That's over-simplifying, of course, but everybody believes you'll eventually walk, just as you did before.'

'They say I could do it now, if I wanted.' Golden eyes, enormous in the pale face, appealed to Erica. 'If they only knew—'

'And you will.'

Gently, Erica stroked Jenny's hair, talking calmly, then holding her hand until she settled back on the pillows and fell into exhausted sleep.

Erica checked that the bell was within reach before she tiptoed quietly out of the room, up the stairs.

Now she could feel grudging sympathy for Matthew. No wonder the tactless physiotherapist had felt the rough edge of his tongue. No doubt he considered that those few careless words could have undone all the good work the doctors had accomplished.

The accidental death of the elderly woman Waters, following so closely after Jenny's injuries, and the fact that Guy had ridden so carelessly, could well account for the grim face Matt often turned to the world.

Yet as she pushed open the door to her own room and switched on the light, Erica told herself she need not waste sympathy on Matthew Crosswyn. He was quite capable of dealing in his own ruthless way with any problems fate served up to him. And he might not always bother about being ethical. That was a chilling possibility.

Dominant men like Matt did sometimes resort to devious means to get their own way, their very strength sometimes giving them a contempt for the scruples that restricted others.

Now Erica had a problem of her own to face. She must decide whether to get ready for bed or to wait

as she was until Jeremy knocked. She sat in her
bedside chair with a magazine, and she had hardly
turned more than a few pages when Jeremy arrived.

'I called before. Where've you been?'

'Talking to Jenny.'

'Oh, I see.' That diverted him. 'Did you make
any progress?'

Jenny was entitled to her privacy. Erica said
lightly, 'I never get far with Jenny at all.' That was
the truth, if evasive. 'She doesn't confide in anybody.'

'Oh well,' he settled himself comfortably on her
bed, 'it's early days yet. Maybe you'll have better
luck tomorrow.'

He patted the bed. 'Come and join me.' He was
so sure she would do just that. He had brought two
bottles with him, and two glasses. One of the
bottles was the Scotch he had threatened to take
from Matt.

'If you'd rather something not so strong I daresay
it could be arranged.' He studied her quizzically,
watching her expression, then suddenly laughed.

'Don't worry, Ric. I remembered your conservative tastes. The soda water is for you.'

But he poured a generous supply of the strong
spirit into both glasses before adding the soda water
to hers and pushing it towards her.

She said apologetically, 'I'm sorry, Jeremy. I
honestly don't know why I feel so edgy. It must be
the change of climate. I feel as if I can't relax.'

'Don't you like it here?'

'Not always. It's magnificent and I'm very impressed, but there are things here—atmospheres—

a feeling of conflict—that makes me uneasy.' She added without conviction, 'Perhaps it's the heat.'

'Oh, for heaven's sake—' Disgustedly he levered himself to a sitting position, swinging his legs over the side of the bed.

'You haven't been yourself since we arrived, Ric. What's got into you? I can't stand temperamental females. They're not my line at all.'

No, they wouldn't be. That wasn't Jeremy's way. Keep everything cool and calm . . . cool, cool, and under control. No scenes.

But she couldn't help thinking there was a disturbing suggestion of something not so cool about Jeremy at this moment. Hair ruffled, shirt open, the appearance a little tousled, not quite so smooth as the Jeremy Crosswyn, natty reporter, that she knew.

He poured himself another drink, and it went down swiftly.

Then he slid off the bed, pulled her from the chair towards him. His mouth, moist on hers, did not touch the turbulent emotions she now knew herself capable of feeling. She put her arms around his shoulders, trying to answer his kissing with her kissing, but it didn't work. After a while he raised his head.

'Ric!'

'Yes?'

He said softly, 'I don't think you're ready for me,' and Erica felt the tears sting her eyes.

'I don't believe I'm ready for anybody,' she confessed.

'Well, I'm damned if I'm going to spend the evening persuading a reluctant damsel.' He stretched an arm and grimaced. 'I ache all over. So much for manual labour.'

'I've cheated you.' Her shoulders drooped.

'Serves me right,' his crooked grin made her feel even worse, 'for tangling with a redhead.' He gave her an oblique look. 'You've been edgy ever since you got here, Ric. Before that, even. We'll take it slowly.'

It was unlike Jeremy to make such generous allowances. She held his hand against her cheek, grateful but not stirred.

'I feel as if I came here under false pretences, but it wasn't intentional.'

His mouth twisted. 'A man can take a friend on a holiday.' Teasingly, he cupped her face in his hands and dropped a chaste kiss on her forehead. 'You may not be ready yet, but you'll keep.'

Then he headed for the door, smiling faintly. Thank goodness she hadn't damaged his pride. He opened the door jauntily, clutching his precious bottle of whisky, waving it cheerfully. 'For a more grateful recipient, I hope.'

Where was he going?—to Lilyan? No, of course not. Perhaps he and Matt and Guy would sit on the verandah and talk the night away.

In the hustle of preparations next day Erica luckily had little chance to worry about what had happened between her and Jeremy. They had time for only a few passing words as he headed for the garden to help Guy with the marquee and the barbecue.

'Sorry, old girl, I came on a bit strong last night. I'll give you more time to acclimatise.'

His grin was cheeky, his kiss brotherly, undemanding. 'Don't worry, Ric, we'll sort ourselves out. Meanwhile, on with the show.'

He was not harbouring grudges, and she was grateful. The 'show' as Jeremy called it, was rapidly building up to a full weekend's entertainment, with swimming, tennis, riding, and the Saturday barbecue. Nell's husband Robert returned, the caterers arrived and took over the kitchen, while the musicians drove up in two panel vans decorated with psychedelic patterns.

Even Matt became more relaxed. At lunch time he announced, 'I could be onto a capable physiotherapist for Jenny. It's not certain—'

He avoided looking at Erica when he told Nell this. Perhaps he considered her a failure as far as Jenny was concerned. So much for her pride in her profession. She had failed to communicate with somebody who desperately needed her support . . . at least, Matt obviously thought so.

Ric had told nobody of her experience last night when Jenny wept out her shock and her terrors. It hadn't really achieved anything. All through the preparations Jenny sheltered in her room, except for a brief visit to the kitchen for lunch, and her excursions with Gregg. Nothing had changed.

Late that afternoon as Erica emerged from the pavilion alongside the tennis court, where she had been checking the supply of equipment on Guy's instructions, she glimpsed Jenny in her wheelchair standing on the edge of Marion's Wilderness. She hurried over.

'Are you all right?'

'Yes.'

'Where's your escort?'

'He went after a snake.'

Erica stepped back hastily. 'Shouldn't you move away?'

Jenny offered a thin ghost of a smile. 'It's okay. The snake slithered off—that way.'

She pointed to a track straggling between over-hanging trees. 'Gregg's probably killed it by now.'

'How do you know he hasn't been bitten?'

'What, Gregg! He's a bushman. He knows how to deal with snakes. Don't worry, he'll be back in a minute.'

Erica wavered. 'I think I ought to go and look for him.'

'No, you needn't.' Jenny's eyes glittered, her cheeks flushed. 'He's safe, I told you.'

'I'll check a little way. Don't worry, I'll look out for snakes.'

One of Jenny's hands moved convulsively, as if she might have reached out to hold Erica back.

'Don't go too far, and don't leave the track. It's nasty in there. Gregg says so.'

Erica stepped warily into the green world of the rain forest. The canopy of leaves overhead cast a greenish tinge over everything, even the air had a filmy look, while the smell of dampness and de-caying leaves added an eeriness that occasional bird-voices failed to brighten. In fact they sounded ghostly, an effect heightened by the way they darted like swift silent shapes through the dimness after each call. There were only occasional flicker-ings of sunlight, the whole area seemed like a huge hothouse where vines and creepers hung in grotesque shapes from the trees or sprawled on the ground.

There was no sign of Gregg. Erica was about to turn back when she heard a faint rustling. It came from the other side of an enormous fallen tree-trunk. There were dead branches jutting into the air, and from them a tangle of creepers hung.

Carefully Erica pushed aside greenery until she could see over the tree-trunk. A man's broad-brimmed hat lay on the ground, and as Erica pushed her way towards it she saw a sudden drop in the earth, like a narrow shaft, and while she watched brown fingers scrabbled at the earth and rotting leaves around it, and a man's head appeared. A pair of startled eyes gazed at Erica.

'What the—?'

He didn't look all that pleased to see her. This was the first time Erica had seen Gregg's face clearly. A daring face, handsome with a mixture of youthful smoothness belied by insolent eyes, a wide mouth, slightly open-jawed as he stared at her with startled interest, and a belligerent square chin that gave an impression of wilful stubbornness.

The man grimaced before heaving himself up beside her. He watched her carefully without speaking for several seconds. Then he grinned.

'Got away.' He busied himself brushing dirt and leaves out of his hair. 'I went after a snake.'

'I know. Jenny told me.' Erica looked around her nervously. He grinned again. 'It's all right. The snake went down that hole.'

'What is it, an old mine shaft?'

He shook his head. 'Bit of a cave-in. That's all. Just a plain old hollow in the ground.'

'Oh. Well, how did you get down there?'

He looked her over with his bold, challenging eyes.

'Would you believe, I fell down? So darn keen to catch the snake I forgot to look where I was going, and it opened up under me.'

'You could have been bitten.'

He shook his head contemptuously.

'Not me. I can handle 'em. I can handle most things.' He was assessing her speculatively, as if wondering how to deal with her. Erica resented that look, it held its share of impudence and she felt a surge of dislike, but she would not let Gregg see that. She must at all costs preserve her fragile link with Jenny.

She said hastily, 'I came to see why Jenny was alone in her wheelchair. I was checking supplies at the tennis court.'

He thought about that, all the time inspecting her boldly. Finally he pushed away some of the vines.

'We'd better get back.'

'Yes,' Erica agreed, 'But oughtn't you do something about that hole in the ground? It could be dangerous. You might have broken a leg.'

'Why? Nobody ever comes in here.'

'You came in, didn't you?'

'That I did.' He pursed his lips, picked up his hat, thrust it to the back of his head.

'Tell you what, ma'am. If it worries you I'll bring a shovel next time I'm near, and fill it in. Shouldn't take much filling, it's only a little hole.'

He walked behind her along the narrow track, and they were almost at the edge of the wilderness when Erica commented, 'It's kind of you to look after Jenny. I tried to make friends with her, but I don't think she has confidence in me.''

When she turned to look at him she found Gregg had jammed the hat down hard over his forehead again. All she saw was the jutting jaw.

'Aw, it's a kink I have, see? Stray dogs, lost kittens I'm always pickin' 'em up. Can't resist 'em. An' they go for me. I guess they get a feelin'. They know I'll take care of 'em.'

He tilted the hat suddenly, and his eyes were wide and hard and challenging. 'Can't be any other reason, can there?'

'I suppose not.'

He didn't look like a collector of stray kittens. His whole demeanour suggested brute strength and exceedingly strong will. Yet when they came out into the sun where Jenny waited, Erica noticed that his hands were careful as he turned the wheelchair towards the homestead.

'See you later, an' I'll do that little job for you.' He meant filling in the hole. He said it casually, but it was a dismissal nevertheless. He didn't want her tagging along while he walked with Jenny.

Erica finished at the tennis court, and on her way back to Vandellan homestead she found herself wondering whether she had imagined apprehension in Jenny's eyes as Gregg wheeled her away. She was certainly becoming imaginative lately, jumping to conclusions, reading hidden meanings into innocent situations. Probably it had been a trick of light making Jenny's eyes look even bigger, softer, more appealing than usual. Certainly there had been nothing menacing about the young stockman as he moved away.

Erica caught her lower lip between her teeth. She would have to take herself in hand, watch her behaviour, keep it sane and sensible. Even Jeremy realized that she was not herself.

It seemed another world, another life, when she had stood in the gipsy's caravan in the presence of the silent woman dressed in scarlet, yet the fleeting encounter had cast its shadow over her holiday. Nothing else could explain the way she was acting now, becoming so emotional in her reactions to people and happenings that she no longer understood herself.

Erica twisted the ring on her finger, the gipsy ring. Perhaps she should take it off and come down to earth. But there had been something wrong, her recollection insisted, about that look of appeal Jenny had thrown as the stockman wheeled her away. What a disaster it would prove if the handsome Gregg swept poor Jenny into heartbreak, instead of helping.

Erica found it difficult to accept that line about stray dogs and kittens. Gregg might be a lazy young man, an opportunist seizing the chance to get out of hard and dusty work out on the land among the sheep and the cattle.

As she entered the paved courtyard at the rear of the homestead Erica made herself a promise. If there was anything she could do to help Jenny, she would do it. Even at the risk of appearing intrusive or interfering, or worse still if it meant staying on at Vandellan longer than she had intended . . . and that, she acknowledged wearily, was the one thing she hoped would not happen.

CHAPTER EIGHT

As Erica opened Vandellan's back door Guy appeared from behind the raised trapdoor, arms full of bottles.

'It's on,' he announced cheerfully. 'Lots of Friday arrivals already. We can't have anybody thirsty.'

Erica glanced at her dusty clothes in dismay. 'I didn't think guests were due until tomorrow.'

Guy put down the bottles and closed the trapdoor. 'Special weekends begin on Fridays. And this one is very special.'

Erica hurried upstairs, freshened her make-up and changed. As she came down the staircase Matt emerged from one of the adjoining rooms. He watched every movement of her descent. Halfway down she paused.

The hall had been cleared, carpets taken up, pedestals removed. No ceramics, nor bowls of flowers, cluttered its spaces. The chandelier glittered, the polished wooden floor gleamed. Musicians were arranging their instruments on a makeshift dais. It didn't look the same place. The pale wraith of Waters had been completely exorcised. It was a different hallway.

With uncanny perception Matt asked bluntly, 'You'd prefer we did our dancing somewhere else?'

He waited as she walked slowly down the remaining stairs. 'Waters wouldn't, you know. She

129

had a very practical spirit, and she dearly loved Vandellan. A place of happy voices, she called it. It was so typical of her that she died with a flower in her hand. She was terminally ill, did you know?'

Erica raised startled eyes. 'No, I didn't.'

'I thought Nell might have mentioned it.'

'Do you think she jumped?'

'Never!' His voice was emphatic. 'Not in a million years. She was no coward, our Waters. No, I believe she over-reached and fell, while she tried to rearrange the flower vases, and things worked out for the best after all.' His graven mouth did not soften, but the cloudy eyes held more than a hint of sadness. 'She certainly had no time to suffer, and who knows what she might have gone through in the final stages of her illness?' He put out a hand and drew her into the hall. 'Waters wouldn't begrudge us our dancing. I should like to know that after I've gone myself there will still be laughter and music at Vandellan. Now, come and meet our guests.'

The stream of arrivals continued throughout the evening. Erica called to see Jenny, trying to coax her out to meet people, but Jenny resisted.

'I'm happier here in my own room. Thanks for coming to see me, but I don't want to meet anybody.'

Erica hung the rose-pink blouse outside Jenny's wardrobe. She said lightly, 'Just in case you fancy wearing it tomorrow night,' and Jenny set her lips tightly but said nothing.

She stayed in her room all day Saturday, while Vandellan overflowed with visitors.

As she dressed for dinner before dancing on

Vandellan's party night Erica took the gipsy ring
from her finger. She tucked it in a drawer, replacing
it with the pearl ring that matched her necklace. It
was her declaration of independence, the time for
shaking away fantasies.

The jade-green gown, so cleverly elegant with its
long slim skirt slit both sides, seemed to accent the
copper lights in her hair. The bodice, a frothy affair
of slanted pintucks and jade lace, was caught up by
the thinnest of shoestring straps, and Erica caught
her lower lip between her teeth, frowning doubtfully at the cleavage showing between firm breasts.
Did it look rather scandalous, she wondered,
judged against the background of Vandellan's conservative elegance?

Jeremy knocked and opened her door as she
clasped the pearl necklace around her neck. His
reaction restored her faith in the jade gown.

He whistled. 'A knock-out! My elusive lady.' His
grin became lopsided. 'You are being elusive,
aren't you, Ric?'

'Not intentionally.' That was an evasion, but it
would have to do for the moment.

As he closed her door behind them he murmured
softly, 'You know, Ric, some day I should like to
see you in the grip of consuming passion.'

'I've disappointed you, Jeremy.'

'No, you haven't. Not yet.' He led her into the
gallery. 'We're guests of honour. How does that
grab you?'

'Jenny told me. I'm flattered.'

He made a mock-gallant bow. 'Vandellan is
flattered. That is, as far as you are concerned. I'm
old stuff, but you must be the most beguiling guest

of honour this old homestead has entertained for a long while.'

Downstairs, Erica discovered with relief that she had no need to worry about her gown being too revealing. She could have stepped into a fashion parade. Nobody was going to notice her modest cleavage. Nobody but Matt, and even his reaction was guarded, a mere raising of one eyebrow.

In the dining-room Erica found herself separated from Jeremy. She sat between Guy and a friendly, tanned young man who entertained her pleasantly.

Lilyan played hostess expertly at one end of the extension table, and Matt presided at the head.

Tonight he was at his most dynamic, strangely impressive in dark blue velvet jacket, dark trousers, and crisp white ruffled shirt. Covertly Erica watched as he dominated the table. He was in full control, things would go as he intended, and he was there to make sure they did just that.

Several times he caught and held Erica's attention and once he smiled, a generous smile that lit his face from within, as if his thoughts smiled also, a warm and magic smile that curved his lips in the shape of good humour and something more, something magnetic that stirred her to instant distrust.

Just in time she remembered that Matt did nothing without good reason. Just in time, she scotched the answering gleam that leapt into life when he smiled at her. This is Matthew Crosswyn, remember, she warned herself silently, and because she had this unaccountable suspicion that he was playing with her she did not give him more than a stiff polite half-smile.

Perhaps to punish her for her lack of response, Matt did not dance with her that evening. The musicians were excellent, dancers crowded the hall and spilled out on to the verandah. Erica was dancing with Jeremy when Jenny appeared, and Jeremy said 'Ouch!' because she missed a beat and their feet tangled.

Jenny wore the pink blouse, which suited her, and she wheeled her chair beside the staircase and sat quietly observing, the fingers of one hand tapping faintly in time with the music.

Jeremy followed Erica's gaze and commented quietly, 'You must be making more progress than you think.'

'No.' Erica couldn't accept that. 'Jenny didn't respond to me. I think Nell must have wrought the miracle.'

Jeremy became faintly quizzical. 'Don't underestimate yourself, Ric. You are a lot more persuasive than you imagine.'

He went with her to talk to Jenny. Nell and Robert were already there. Jenny appeared faintly embarrassed at their attention, but to Erica's surprise Jeremy went out of his way to amuse her, and Jenny slowly relaxed.

She blushed faintly, looking at Erica. 'You look beautiful.'

'Doesn't she?' Jeremy slid an arm across Erica's shoulders. 'I'd like to tell you I chose that outfit, but honesty forbids me.'

Jenny's eyes rounded. 'Does he really choose your frocks?'

'He does not.' Erica removed Jeremy's arm firmly. 'He'd probably have me dressed permanently in something that clashed with my hair. I have to be careful what I wear.'

'I have excellent taste.' Jeremy gave Jenny a persuasive smile. 'I'd dress you forever in the colour you're wearing tonight.'

Jenny blushed even more deeply and Nell laughed. 'I agree. That shade definitely does something for Jenny. I wish I could discover a special colour that would light me up.'

'Try charcoal,' her husband chuckled, and Jenny joined in the laughter, hesitantly at first, glancing slyly at Nell to make sure she was not offended.

Guy claimed Erica for the next dance and Jeremy waved her away cheerfully. 'I want to talk to Jenny.' He sat casually on the bottom stair, beside her chair. 'They tell me you play guitar. Is this your kind of music?'

'N-not exactly.'

'If not, why not?'

Guy whirled Erica away, but not before she had seen the girl in the chair leaning towards Jeremy, with flushed face and bright eyes, explaining to him about 'her kind of music'. They were still deep in discussion when the band took a rest. Guy followed Erica's glance. 'Should we disturb them?'

'I don't think so.' They didn't look as if they would appreciate being disturbed, they were totally absorbed in each other.

As she went with Guy to find a cool drink, Erica admitted to herself there were facets of Jeremy she had obviously not understood. She had certainly not expected to find in him the ability to communicate so totally with a timid, confused girl like Jenny. But then tonight Jenny seemed different, more sure of herself, as if she might have made some decision to try and cope with what was happening to her.

How strange if Jeremy accomplished what she and Nell found almost impossible, and how would the young stockman react?

Erica decided it didn't matter. The important thing was that Jenny had come to join the party, and she was still there long after Erica expected her to slip away. Jeremy escorted her to supper and later, when Jenny signalled to Nell that she was ready to leave, her eyes sparkled and her face glowed with reflections of excitement.

She was a little overwhelmed when Matt came to say goodnight to her.

'Enjoy your night out, Jenny?'

She murmured 'Yes, thank you,' in a small breathless voice, but this time she was not too scared to look at him. Her amber eyes lingered on the crisp curly hair so black in contrast with the white frilled shirt. She licked her lips.

'You all look very handsome,' she announced with childlike politeness.

Matt's face remained grave. 'Thank you,' he said quite seriously, 'on behalf of everybody. Would you like someone to take you to your room?'

Jeremy put his hand on the chair. 'I'll see Jenny makes it safely.' Matt's eyes narrowed as he watched them go. 'So Jenny really enjoyed herself.'

Erica said honestly, 'Thanks to Jeremy.'

'Yes.' Matt showed no surprise, Perhaps he understood Jeremy better than she did, Erica thought humbly.

Somebody claimed her for a dance, and she did

not encounter Matt until much, much later, when the night had turned to early morning and Erica decided she could slip away to bed without offending.

She went to search for Jeremy, to thank him for his kindness to Jenny, and as she came out through the open front doors she found Matt standing on the top of the verandah steps, leaning lazily against a post.

He had seen her, so she collected her dignity and went up to him. 'I'm saying my goodnights. It's a wonderful party, but my stamina has run out.'

He laughed. 'You're not the only one. I'm propping myself up with the verandah post.'

He didn't look as though he needed propping up. Standing there so indolently, looking darker and more mysterious than ever in the muted light, Matthew would dominate his own world, without too much effort, and still not be depleted. It was all there in the way he stood, superbly confident, stronger than most men. For the first time that night Erica recalled the chill of foreboding she had felt on their first meeting.

He watched her calmly. She steeled herself to meet his inspection without flinching, and she must have done a good job because he drawled finally, 'All this excitement and the guest of honour remains unruffled and untouched.'

'That is not true,' she flashed, 'I've enjoyed every minute.'

'That's not what I meant.' He waved a casual hand towards the garden where figures flitted in and out of shadow and light, holding hands, disappearing into the inviting privacy of screening trees.

'Why aren't you out there?'

'Because I don't feel like it.' She eyed him coldly. 'Are you suggesting I should grab the first partner I can find and lead him out to an orgy among the roses?'

'No, I'm not. But I would like to show you something if I may. That is,' his eyes glinted, 'if you feel you can trust yourself with me.'

Erica said calmly, 'It depends. What did you want to show me?'

'Waters' garden.'

That startled her. She eyed him warily.

'I didn't know Waters had a garden. Where is it?'

'Not far away.'

Before she had time to make excuses he was leading her into the garden, across the lawn, around the poinciana tree. As they neared the widespread branches with their scarlet flowers Erica averted her face. She couldn't afford to have her imagination playing tricks in this situation.

As if he picked up her thinking Matt commented lightly, 'Not wearing your lucky charm tonight? Do you think that's wise?'

She stole a quick look at his face, mysterious in the shadow of the tree. How much did Matt guess about the ring? He was giving nothing away, and she wasn't going to tell him anything. They walked in silence through the rose garden, past an avenue of pepper trees, until they reached a small shade-house.

Matt opened the door and motioned Erica inside. The shadehouse was filled with tubs and flowerpots and hanging baskets of fuchsias, small and pale and dainty, bright and exotic, a vast range of colours and varieties.

'They were Waters' favourite flowers.' Matt leaned against the doorway, watching Erica's face. A trellis outside, vine-covered, sent heavy fragrance into the shadehouse. Erica sniffed appreciatively.

'Jasmine!'

'And honeysuckle. Because Waters loved sweet things. So you see she hasn't left us. She will always be part of Vandellan. I thought you might like to know, since you were so concerned.'

'It's beautiful. I wish I'd known Waters.'

'I'm not sure what she would have made of you.' That didn't sound like a compliment. 'Why not?' Erica demanded.

'You don't give much away, do you, Erica?' Exactly what she had been thinking about him . . . She was glad when he moved out of the doorway and she followed him, closing the door carefully.

'You must come and see it in the daylight. I have a feeling you and Waters might have something in common. I'm sure there was a side of Waters she didn't let everybody see. Come and look.'

He curved his hands over her shoulders and guided her to the rear of the shadehouse. Starlight outlined the glossy pointed leaves of another vine, almost covered with exotic white flowers.

'Passion flowers.' Matt's voice was enigmatic. 'They were her special delight.'

Erica stepped quickly away from the hands on her shoulders. This could be getting dangerous. It seemed a good time to start walking. She headed for the front of the shadehouse, out from under the screening trees, out from what might turn into a sticky situation.

'Of course Waters liked passion fruit,' she scoffed. 'There's nothing remarkable about that. So do lots of people.' She added daringly, 'You do like to find hidden meanings where there aren't any, don't you?'

Back there inside the shadehouse, he had fooled her. As he talked about Waters and the flowers she had left behind her he had seemed wistful, human, caring. But when he capped it with that bit about passion flowers Matt had shown himself in his true colours, and it was just as well. Because he had almost steered her into a trap.

Anxiously, Erica calculated in her mind the distance back to the homestead. It wasn't all that far, they should make it safely if she kept talking. She ought to be able to avert disaster.

She tried hurrying, but Matt slackened pace, deliberately she suspected. To dash away from him would make her look ridiculous, so Erica matched her steps with his, walking just a little in front, commenting on the perfume of the roses, pushing away the mounting feeling of unease by pretending not to notice it. Because if she were not mistaken, Matt was not going to let this night go by without making another pass at her. Erica blamed herself. She had been foolish. She should have read Matt's intentions before letting him coax her out into the garden.

As they reached the poinciana tree a boy and a girl, arms linked, vanished into shadows. Matt planted himself directly in front of Erica.

'Wouldn't you like to do what they are doing?'

'No, I wouldn't.'

He was perilously close. It felt as if they were touching, although their bodies made no contact. Yet her skin crawled in traitorous response to his nearness.

He would not move from her path, but stood like a dark figure propped between her and safety.

'I think you might be a liar. Shall we find out?' His teeth flashed in a smile of mockery, his bent head descended until his lips found hers and the touch, light and teasing though it was, set her alive and alight. He wasn't even holding her, this arrogant man, he was so sure that the touch of his lips would keep her there. He knew exactly what he was doing. Master of sensuality, he was breaking down her resistance without lifting a finger.

As his mouth moved restlessly against hers, Erica pushed her outspread fingers against his chest.

Slowly, reluctantly it seemed, Matt raised his head. 'No passion flowering?' His voice was husky, inviting.

She shook her head, and he lifted one hand and tangled his fingers in her hair.

'I still think you're lying. Let's find out, shall we, for sure?' He placed the other hand on the small of her back, pressing her towards him, accepting no denial, allowing no withholding. The lips that took hers were warm with seduction but they were adamant.

A surge of emotion held Erica helpless. As if some other person controlled her responses she felt her arms steal up to wind themselves around the strong column of Matt's neck, and as the pressure of his body increased she found herself behaving like a wanton, exchanging kissing for kissing, emotion for emotion, pressing herself ardently against the warmth of Matt's body.

He twisted her until she leaned against the poinciana, his hands caressing her body, tantalising, arousing sensations that set the whole world exploding.

The gardens dissolved into unreality, leaving a whirl of scents and shapes that could have been anything or nothing at all. Only Matt was real.

She found herself clinging, trembling, lifted high on an irresistible wave of sensation.

Somewhere in that mad, wild surge of emotion the kissing ended. She was enclosed by Matt's arms, her head against his shoulder, feeling the bemusing softness of the velvet jacket, listening to the beating of his heart. Their bodies trembled together. She heard him murmur incoherent words against her hair, and after a while the trembling ceased, the world shook itself out of its uncontrollable spin and rearranged itself into the shapes of reality.

Everything was as it had been before, yet somehow different. It had been a shattering experience.

On the homestead verandah a shaft of orange light appeared as someone opened a door.

When Erica moved in Matt's arms his grip slackened. She wet her lips, staring at him accusingly:

'How could you do that?'

'Why? Are you the property of my brother?' The leaves concealed his expression, but there was impatience in his tone.

'That's a rotten thing to say. I'm nobody's property.'

'Then why the protest? You can't ignore what's happened between us.'

'What happened between us is—is—despicable.'

'Is that so? Maybe you'd like to undo it, then.' Erica turned to run, but he was too fast for her. Panic set her struggling in his grasp and he dealt with it by pinning her arms to her sides, pressing his body hard against hers.

When she gave up the struggle he said in a withering voice, 'Have some sense, girl. How's it going to look if you rush headlong into the house at this hour of the morning as if you've a horde of bunyips after you? Calm yourself and I'll let you beat a dignified retreat. I don't take what isn't freely given.'

He made no attempt to hide the contempt in his voice. She quietened, giving him hard look for hard look as he slowly released her. He breathed heavily, but that could have been the effort of coping with her frantic struggles.

Erica smoothed the jade dress and rubbed her tender lips with one finger. Matt stood by, unmoved.

'You *are* rather ruffled, aren't you?' He sounded faintly malicious. 'Not quite so cool, my lady, as when you came out here.'

'But *you* aren't ruffled.' She would have said more but for the blast of anger that swept over his features.

He put out one hand and pushed her away from him. 'Go back to the house. Run inside and hug your pillow. Have a little think about how you'll enjoy being an iceberg for the rest of your life.'

He turned away abruptly, leaving her to walk alone through what remained of Vandellan's celebrations. A few couples still danced, a few more lingered in the gallery, looking at paintings, flirting among the flowers. Head held high, Erica managed to smile at them as she passed. But when she reached her room the smiling vanished.

'Go and hug your pillow,' Matt had jeered, his face taut with anger, and she could not honestly blame him. No doubt he believed that in going out into the garden with him she had led him on. Men like Matt usually took that attitude. She should have known. There would be plenty of lovers among the trees and shadows tonight.

Before she got into bed Erica crossed to her window and pulled the curtains firmly together. She shut out the stars and the moon and the scent of flowers, and that suited her very well.

Whatever was going on down there in the garden, she didn't want to know about it.

CHAPTER NINE

ERICA woke next morning to the sound of music. It sounded faint and far away, and she sat up in bed to listen. It must be downstairs, that sweet haunting sound of a plucked guitar. Surely not Jenny?

Erica looked at the clock. She had slept a good part of the morning away. She washed and dressed, then slowly, afraid to hope but still hoping, she followed the music to Jenny's room downstairs.

A flushed and elated Jenny was playing to Nell and Jeremy, but when she saw Erica she faltered, letting the music die.

'Oh, don't stop, please. I came to listen.' Jenny looked as if she might refuse until Jeremy urged, 'Go on, sing one for Erica,' then Jenny relented and began a simple folk-song. Her sweet plaintive voice pronounced every word with moving clarity.

As the song finished, a shrill whistle sounded from the verandah, and Jenny dropped the guitar on to her knees.

'It's Gregg! I'm late for my exercise. He'll be angry.'

Jeremy scowled. 'What right does he have to be angry?' and Jenny flinched at the harshness in his voice.

'Can't you see, he gives up his time for me—I shouldn't keep him waiting.'

'I'll take you.'

Jenny became really agitated. 'Oh no! I couldn't possibly hurt his feelings, he's been so good.'

Nell took the guitar and rested it on the bed, while Jenny smoothed her hair with shaking fingers. Scowling, Jeremy opened the doors to let Jenny push her chair outside. There was a thunderstorm in his face and Nell watched him anxiously. She didn't want Jenny upset.

The young stockman was waiting on the verandah. He must have heard the music but he gave no sign. He took Jenny away quickly, after a surly jerk of the head towards the three who watched.

'Odd sort of bloke.' Jeremy was not impressed. 'What's he doing around here, anyway?'

A faint frown pleated Nell's forehead. 'He's been wonderful to Jenny. I don't understand what's gotten into him this morning.'

Jeremy glared after the disappearing wheelchair. 'A man ought to go after them, and ask him what the hell he means, upsetting the poor girl like that.'

Nell and Erica exchanged hasty glances. Jeremy's interest in Jenny, however harmless, was not likely to be appreciated by the young stockman. Nell suggested diplomatically, 'Why don't you two have a swim before lunch?' and Erica flashed her a grateful smile.

'That's just what I need.'

'All right.' Jeremy backed into the room. 'I know when I'm being manoeuvred. Go and get your bikini, woman, and be quick.'

Erica hurried upstairs before he changed his mind. As she tied the laces on her black bikini she glanced down from her window to the pool. It was popular this morning. There was plenty of splashing and laughter, plenty of bodies, so why did her eyes cling to the sight of Matt standing in the sun, his gleaming figure reflecting the light as if he might have been carved from polished wood? He stood listening to Lilyan and two other young women, and there was no reason why Erica should have chosen him out of all the enticing landscape with its bright figures to stare at.

Furious with herself, Erica picked up her towel and hurried downstairs. Jeremy inspected her light skin doubtfully.

'Don't you want to go back and cover that scanty gear with a sundress?'

'I'm all right. I'll head for the shade.'

Nothing would induce her to go back into that room where she could look down and see Matt Crosswyn standing in the sun.

It was a foolish decision. Erica realized that as they came out into the sun's blaze. And worse was to follow.

They were passing the jacarandas when Matt strode towards them. He wasted no time on politeness.

'Don't you know better than to come outside without protection?' His steely glance slid over Erica's creamy skin in a blatant inspection that set her teeth on edge.

'Don't blame me,' Jeremy excused himself, 'I suggested a cover-up and nobody listened.'

Erica muttered 'Excuse me, I want a swim' and moved to a patch of shade, but Matt wasn't letting her escape so easily. Two strides and he was beside her, with Jeremy following.

'You'd better make it a quick swim and head for cover, my girl, until you're used to our climate.'

'That's what I intend to do.' She glared at him huffily. 'I know how to look after myself.'

'I'm surprised to hear it.' The hateful voice was bland, but Erica knew that somewhere in his comment was an echo of what had taken place last night. He was reminding her that she didn't always take care of herself, and that she could be lucky to have escaped unscathed from a situation that might have developed into something really explosive.

Matt wore a large towel of peacock blue over one shoulder. It changed the colour of his eyes, casting a blue veil across the grey. Erica looked away quickly. This was no time to be looking at anything so personal as Matt Crosswyn's eyes.

Jeremy moved restively. 'Why not come back and have a swim with us? I challenge you to four laps of the pool.'

'Sorry.' Matt's eyes narrowed as he stared towards the wilderness. 'I just saw young Gregg taking Jenny out. I'd better find out what he's up to, because he's carting a shovel around with him.'

'Oh heavens!' Erica flushed. 'I'm afraid that's my fault.'

'It is?'

'You see, there's a hole among the trees. Gregg fell into it the other morning and I—I did suggest it ought to be filled in.'

'First I've heard of it.' Matt sounded as if he might not appreciate her interference. She didn't seem to be able to do anything right. She explained defensively, 'I went in there because I saw Jenny alone and she said Gregg was after a snake. I'm sorry, I really am. I did mean to mention it to somebody, but when I got back to the homestead there were people arriving and everything was busy.' She faced him defiantly. 'I can't see that it matters all that much.'

His manner changed. 'You're probably right.' He shrugged carelessly. 'I couldn't help wondering about the shovel. It seemed an unusual accompaniment for a morning walk.'

Jeremy grinned. 'What were you thinking, brother? That your employee might be planning to clobber your—er—protégée with a shovel and dispose of the body?' He gave a mock shudder. 'Some people do have sinister minds.' He lost interest in Gregg and the shovel. 'Race you to the pool, Ric.'

Jeremy ran, without looking back, and Matt waited for Erica to follow. She said stiffly, 'I didn't mean to interfere with your administration.'

'Forget it.'

Unexpectedly, he whipped the bright blue towel from his shoulder. 'Here, you'd better take this. It might come in handy after your swim. Don't forget about the sun, or do you intend roasting to prove how independent you are?'

When Erica refused to take the towel Matt draped it around her shoulders, folding it on the nape of her neck and crossing it in front to shield her throat and breasts.

A faint smile softened his eyes, and his mouth curved as if he might have been mildly amused at her folly in venturing out into the heat. His fingers were not touching her skin, but they might as well have been. Erica stood spellbound while Matt arranged the towel. Before he turned to walk away he raised one arm in a lazy half-salute.

'Enjoy yourself. Another few hours and the party will be over.'

The words were double-edged. He was telling her something. The party will be over . . .

The ominous words carried a sense of irreparable loss. Another week and her visit to Vandellan would become history, an entry in the record book for her to look up when she felt nostalgic. Soberly Erica followed Jeremy to the pool. Afterwards she was to realize that the party had begun to wind down for her at that moment.

It seemed appropriate later that afternoon, when the last guest had departed, that Jeremy coaxed Jenny to play again and she sang slow haunting folk-songs. She had the voice for such music, a clear honeysweet soprano with undertones of heartache.

After dinner that evening, when Matt repeated his plans to arrange for another physiotherapist to care for Jenny, Jeremy became suddenly uncomfortable.

They were sipping after-dinner drinks in the drawing-room; Jeremy fiddled with his glass and shifted awkwardly in his chair, and Matthew became suddenly very interested in his brother. He asked softly, 'Well?' and Jeremy replied uncertainly, 'Matter of fact, I—I've been meaning to speak to you about that.'

It was the first time Erica had glimpsed Jeremy without his veneer of self-confidence.

'Actually, old chap, I've—I'm thinking seriously about taking Jenny with me when I leave. With your permission, of course.' He regained a little assurance. 'I believe what she needs now is treatment in a large city hospital.'

'Is that so?'

Matt was distantly polite, making Jeremy squirm and, Erica decided indignantly, enjoying it.

'There could be something in that,' she agreed sweetly, but Matt brushed away her comment as if she had not spoken. He took a long drink from his glass before he spoke.

'Have you discussed this impulsive plan with anybody else?'

'With Jenny, of course.'

'And she agrees?'

'Naturally. I wouldn't have spoken otherwise. She's with me all the way.' Jeremy's voice quickened. 'She needs the skill and attention of a medical team—'

'Jenny already has the attention of doctors, a skilled neurologist—'

'I know that.'

'And a psychologist,' Matt persisted relentlessly, 'And one physio who wasn't worth a damn. I grant you that.'

'You sacked her.'

'I had my reasons.'

Jeremy became passionate, pleading. 'I'm not criticising what you've done for the girl. Far from it.' He leaned forward tensely in his chair. 'But you must admit, old boy, it hasn't had the desired result.'

'Not yet.' Then, quite suddenly, Matt relented.

'All right. I see your point and Jenny's too, and since it seems important I don't suppose I can dissuade you. But see you make travelling arrangements with care. Guy and I will hold you responsible.'

'Yes. We both understand that and we're willing to take the chance. I'll talk to Guy. I'm sure he won't mind.'

Jeremy spoke as if he and Jenny had a long-standing relationship, yet they had only known each other a few days. So what is time, Erica quoted to herself wryly. A few meetings with an injured girl who sang like an angel, and Jeremy had forgotten her.

Not very flattering . . . she read the unspoken comment in Matt's eyes.

Jeremy disappeared, presumably to tell Jenny that the interview was over successfully. Matt said quietly, 'You don't look very downcast.'

'Should I be?'

'You just lost a lover, little Miss Redhead.'

'Don't wait for me to burst into tears.'

She knew it sounded flippant and uncaring, but she didn't want Matt probing into her private life. She added bitterly, 'You could turn into stone waiting, if you're expecting me to cry on your shoulder.' She produced an excessively sweet smile, tilting her chin at him in challenge. 'Or perhaps you're stone already.'

'You should know.'

So . . . she had asked for it. Now he was taunting her, reminding her again of last night, when neither of them had been made of stone.

Erica threw caution to the winds. 'I haven't seen anything,' she lied, 'that would persuade me to the contrary.'

That ought to quieten him . . . and it did, for a

couple of seconds. Then he put down his glass, stood up suddenly, and came towards her. Erica shrank back in her chair. What sort of a storm had she stirred up this time? She should have known he'd be touchy after Jeremy's bombshell. Now she'd really torn it, because Matt was not the man to suffer impertinence without taking revenge.

He halted, so close that she was sure he must hear the crazy leaping of her heart as he loomed over her. Then he stooped, his lips touching her ear, breath warm and feather-light on her skin.

'Some day soon I plan to answer that challenge. Unfortunately, I have something important to do just now. Lilyan will be here soon to keep you company. I'm sorry I must leave you.'

He paused long enough to place the curved palm of one hand lightly on her head.

'That's a ridiculous hair-style, all those silly little curls—' His voice held an amorous huskiness, a timbre that reminded her of that seduction scene in the garden. She dared not look at him.

Slowly he trailed one finger around her hairline, tracing the curve of soft jaw, the column of slender throat, as though he wished to remember every inch. Responses pricked her skin along the trail he made, as though somewhere a fuse had been lit, and Erica waited for it to crackle into wild sensation. Then he dropped his hand.

As he walked away Erica heard a faint sigh, as if Matt might have regretted the 'something important' that took him away.

Lilyan opened the door a few minutes later, complaining petulantly that Vandellan might as well be a morgue for all the life in it tonight. Erica crouched quietly in her chair, exactly as Matt had left her. She could not have moved, she knew, if an earthquake had shaken Vandellan; but she roused herself to answer Lilyan, in a voice so faint and faraway that Lilyan stared at her suspiciously.

'I'm sorry, I was daydreaming. Yes, it is quiet after the party.'

Lilyan pouted. 'I can't find Matt anywhere, or Guy. Even Jeremy has disappeared, although that child is playing her guitar again, so I suppose he's there.' She turned fretful eyes towards Erica. 'Don't you care? I'd be livid. I mean, he's supposed to be with you, and he's devoting all his time to that child.'

'Jenny isn't a child.'

'Doesn't that make the whole thing rather worse?'

'I don't mind.'

Erica sat quietly while Lilyan strolled restlessly around the room. She wondered whether Lilyan knew anything about Jeremy's plans to take Jenny with him. She sat up in her chair and said clearly, 'Jeremy is hoping to get Jenny into one of the big Sydney hospitals for special treatment. He's taking her with him when he leaves Vandellan.'

'Oh.' Lilyan digested that thoughtfully. 'And you don't object? I must say that's very generous of you. I'd certainly object if I were in your position. It looks like something more than brotherly interest if you know what I mean.'

'I know what you mean.'

Erica felt amazingly detached. She did know, and she didn't care. There was no pain at all. She found herself pleased for Jeremy, and for Jenny too.

Whatever happened in her life after she left Vandellan, it would not include Jeremy as more than a friend. Matthew had taught her that. There were depths of powerful feeling, intense emotions that could be stirred by the right man, and Jeremy had never touched them. She was certain, also, that she had never lit in Jeremy the fires that flared when Matt touched her.

How strange if Jeremy and Jenny discovered together something she and Jeremy had never dreamed of.

Lilyan was not disposed to waste her evening talking to Erica. It was male company she craved, that was clear. She picked up ornaments, put them down, at last admitting crossly, 'It looks as if we've been deserted. I wish I knew what Matt is up to.'

She shot Erica a sceptical glance. 'Are you certain you don't know where he went?'

'He told me he had something important to do. That's all.'

'I'll go and write some letters. Help yourself to anything you fancy. Music—there are plenty of records, or maybe you'd like a book from the library, or something to drink.'

She didn't say 'Help yourself to Matthew', and the sharp looks she sent Erica's way weren't exactly amiable. Perhaps that short episode with the powerful man had left its vibrations in the room, or it could have been the way she, Erica, sat there dazed as if fumbling her way out of confusion, but something in this room had aroused Lilyan's suspicions. She gave Erica another glittering look before she left.

Nobody came after that. The homestead quietened. Erica stayed hunched in the chair for a while. She didn't need music or a drink, and she was far too bemused to concentrate on a book.

When she finally stood up she stretched carefully, straightened her back and pushed her shoulders back, taking breath deep into her lungs as if to steady her whirling thoughts.

The click of the door shutting behind her made a sharp sound that emphasised the stillness.

The hall carpet had been replaced, flowers and precious antiques restored to their niches and pedestals. The unlit chandelier hovered palely overhead. Faint lights glowed in the gallery, others lit the stairs, but with the departure of all the vibrant people who had come to Vandellan to dance and laugh and enjoy themselves, a hush had come down over the homestead, as if Vandellan had gone to sleep.

Erica went up the stairs slowly, carefully, as if it were essential that she did not disturb the silence.

Whatever the important task Matthew had found to do, it was taking a long time. Jeremy must have retired, also. No guitar sounded, Vandellan seemed to have turned into the sleeping palace of old fairy tales.

It was only as Erica began undoing the ties of her dress that a long low rustling, like a vibrant sigh, shook itself out of the trees in the wilderness and floated across the jacarandas before it brushed against the homestead, setting a thousand small voices whispering.

Erica imagined the branches of the poinciana, scarlet flowers swinging in the wind, and Waters' passion flowers swaying while the roses bobbed and danced and dropped their petals, and as she listened another breath of wind came, stronger than the first, and all the whisperings began again.

She had been wrong. Vandellan was not asleep. It was waiting for a happening . . .

CHAPTER TEN

AFTER breakfast next morning Jeremy took Erica driving over Vandellan, and she marvelled at the size of the kingdom Matthew Crosswyn ruled. No wonder he had that autocratic manner, that devastating air of strength proven and unassailable.

She had been wise to feel that recoil at their first meeting, and she would have been even wiser had she not allowed herself to forget the difference between their two worlds even for one moment. Matt was strong medicine, and he was not for her. She had considered Jeremy a complex man, but he was an open book compared with his brother.

Jeremy was taking a lot of trouble to entertain her this morning. He showed her emus and kangaroos, cockatoos and parrots and budgerigars in great flocks, and her excitement amused him.

'Very naive, you city girls.' He spoke as if he had never left Vandellan. 'Anyone would think you'd never sighted a bird before.'

'Not like this, not so many, nor in such bright colours.' Later, when he pulled up to show her a scrub turkey scratching among undergrowth she asked him, 'Don't you miss all this in the city?'

'There are compensations.' He smiled wryly, then as if taking courage in both hands he said, 'Ric, I've been meaning to talk to you, but there hasn't been much chance. I feel a right heel, bringing you here—'

157

'Don't give it a thought.'

His smile twisted. 'You mean, you aren't exactly heartbroken?'

Erica touched his cheek with her hand.

'What I'm saying is, if you've found a new interest in Jenny, as I think you have, you'd be foolish to let our—our friendship—keep you from something deeper.'

'Ridiculous, isn't it?' The boyish veneer he cultivated so carefully had become real now, his own emotions and reactions had taken him by surprise, but he was sure of what he wanted.

'I can't explain what's got into me, I only know that Jenny and what happens to Jenny is so important to me I can't cut myself off.' He turned to her, almost desperately. 'She has to walk again, Ric. She will, won't she?'

'The doctors say Yes, and they know. They don't practise holding out false hopes.'

He grinned, relieved that she had taken it so well. 'Jenny and Jeremy. Sounds like something cooked up for a pantomime, doesn't it?' Then the grin vanished. 'So long as you don't mind.'

Erica reassured him. 'I think I realised we could be making a mistake about the same time you did. Good luck with Project Jenny. I'll do everything I can to help.'

'I knew I could rely on you.'

He turned the key in the ignition, and headed towards home. Erica thought perhaps she loved him—really loved him with a deep affection—more at this moment than she ever had before. Jeremy was far more endearing with this new humility than the shrewd operator she had known. Before they started off she whispered softly, 'Jenny is a lucky girl', and he took one hand from the steering wheel and squeezed her fingers, offering her a crooked sideways smile, full of warmth.

It was midday when they returned to the homestead, just in time to see Gregg wheeling Jenny to the paved courtyard. Jeremy parked the station wagon in the shade and got out quickly. Erica saw Jenny's face alight as Jeremy approached, but Gregg's expression was black. He offered no greetings. Indeed, he made a movement as if he might have whisked Jenny away, but she called, 'Wait, Gregg, oh please wait,' and he had no option but to stand and wait for Jeremy.

The look that flashed in his eyes made Erica shiver. It was pure hatred. Then he tugged his hat down low over his forehead and walked away, leaving Jenny with her face upturned to Jeremy, her expression radiant. Erica said 'Hello' and went inside, leaving the two of them alone. There was no place for an extra person in the strong feeling that pulled those two people together.

Jeremy came to lunch with a look of aliveness that set Lilyan eyeing him speculatively. She did not know about his meeting with Jenny, she was only aware that he and Erica had spent the morning together, and she watched shrewdly for a glimpse of betraying emotion between them. She was unusually gracious today, as if something very pleasant might have happened at the homestead while Erica and Jeremy were away.

They were finishing lunch when Matt announced, 'You girls have an invitation to visit Robert and Nell in the manager's house this afternoon.' He tilted an eyebrow at Ric. 'Can you manage to walk that far or do you require transport?'

'I can walk that far—just,' Erica answered pertly, and he gave her a tight-lipped smile that was hardly a smile at all.

'Good.' He accepted a second cup of coffee from Lilyan before he added casually, 'I have something for Jeremy to do this afternoon.'

So they were to be fobbed off on Nell, so that Matt and Jeremy could get on with whatever they had to do. Erica said tartly, 'I wonder what you're up to, that you're so anxious to get rid of us for the afternoon.'

Matt's hand, holding his coffee cup, froze halfway to his lips. He shot Erica one sharp piercing look, staring at her intently, as if she might have said something dangerous, before he resumed drinking. What a merciless adversary he would make, this harsh-featured man who sat there despatching people in all directions to suit his own dark purposes. And he hadn't finished yet . . .

Jeremy asked, 'Where's Guy, isn't he having lunch today?' and Matt took his time about replying.

'Guy had a quick snack in the kitchen. I've asked him to drive Jenny into town for a final medical check. I won't take the responsibility of allowing her to travel if it can do any harm.'

'I could have taken her.'

'Jenny is our responsibility, Guy's and mine, while she remains at Vandellan. After that, it's up to you.' He added more reasonably, 'It won't hurt Guy to handle a little responsibility for a change.'

'I suppose not.'

So now they were all dancing to the tune of this taciturn man! Erica protested, 'I don't think I want to go to Nell's this afternoon', and Lilyan almost spilled the coffee she was pouring. 'Of course you do. Don't be so obstructive, Erica.' She added silkily, 'I'm sure it will do us both good to get away from the homestead for the afternoon, and no doubt the men will appreciate a little relief from feminine company.'

Erica gave up. It almost sounded like a conspiracy. There seemed some kind of new understanding between Matt and Lilyan. She sensed it in Lilyan, who was looking extremely pleased with herself.

Yet as she went upstairs to change into a long skirt of green and gold, with a crisp apple-green blouse and a pair of golden earrings, Erica knew that she definitely did not want to leave the homestead this afternoon.

The sun was throwing gold lights everywhere, turning Vandellan into a paradise-picture. It was a day made for being carefree, but Erica's unease grew with every step she took away from the homestead.

They had reached the citrus grove, the scent of oranges and orange blossoms drifting beautifully around them, when Erica suddenly stopped walking, her feet coming to a halt as if somebody, somewhere, had pressed a button, turning off power.

'Whatever is the matter?' Lilyan's impatient voice brought her back to reality.

'I think I'll go back to my room and lie down.'

'No, you don't.' Lilyan's fingers dug into her arm. 'I promised to take you to Nell's this afternoon. I especially promised Matt—'

Erica's eyes widened. 'You can't force me.'

'I'm not forcing you.' Lilyan became sweetly reasonable. 'You must admit you and Jeremy have been far from perfect guests. After all we—he—has done for Jenny, the whole matter is taken out of Matt's hands. Later, he may have to pay damages on Guy's behalf, or didn't you understand that? If you took the trouble to appreciate Matt better, maybe you and Jeremy might not be making things so difficult for him.'

You couldn't demolish that argument, Erica admitted. Whatever had caused that sudden desperate urge to return to the homestead she had better forget it, and go with Lilyan. Obediently, she continued walking.

Lilyan said waspishly, 'You really like being difficult, don't you? If I were Matt I'd send you packing.'

'But you aren't Matt, are you?'

'A flash of triumph lit Lilyan's eyes. 'I suppose I should have told you, Matt and I had a talk this morning, and very soon,' she pronounced each word as though it gave her great pleasure, 'very soon I shall be the permanent mistress of Vandellan.' She gave an artificial laugh. 'I shall have to warn all those ambitious females who keep throwing themselves at Matt that he is no longer available. I'm afraid there will be quite a few disappointments—'

Erica screened her reaction from those bright, calculating eyes. 'I must congratulate you.'

'I knew you'd understand. Next time Jeremy comes to Vandellan, if he ever does come back after his peculiar affair with that dubious girl, Matthew and I will be—shall we say—we will have a much closer alliance.'

So they were to be married, Matthew and Lilyan. Erica told herself fiercely that they deserved each other. Her feet felt lead-heavy as she followed to where the green tin roof of Nell's house showed behind a windbreak of cypress, and Nell waved a welcome.

Robert was wielding a garden fork among a border of golden cassias, and as Lilyan led Erica onto the pathway he put down his tool and shook the earth from his fingers.

'I shan't offer to shake hands, but you're very welcome.'

Here in his own surroundings Robert looked taller than Erica remembered, a lithe lean man with the same outgoing friendliness that made Nell so easy to warm to. His twinkling eyes noted Erica's flyaway curls, her bright appearance with the golden earrings, and lingered appreciatively on Lilyan's elegance. He grinned, 'My flowers have never had such competition,' and Erica said 'Thanks', but Lilyan scarcely paused before she continued on to where Nell waited.

Compliments from Robert were obviously not going to make Lilyan's day. Erica pointed to the fork in Robert's hands. 'Don't stop for us. We didn't come to interrupt.'

But Robert pushed the fork into the ground beside one of the cassias and left it there. A pleasant uncomplicated man with honest eyes, he remarked happily, 'I'll finish later. I'm only idling, as Nell will tell you.' He joined Erica on the pathway, walking towards the verandah.

'I offered Matt my services this afternoon but they were declined. So here I am, having a lazy day. Whatever he has lined up, he seemed determined to manage it without me, but I wish he wouldn't be so independent. After all, I'm manager. I should be doing the work, not Matt. I wish he'd share it.'

There it was again, the niggling alarm sounding with quiet insistence in the back of her mind. Erica said softly, 'Matt asked Jeremy to do something for him this afternoon. Perhaps it only required one extra pair of hands,' and Robert nodded.

'Maybe that's why he said I'd be in the way.' His face sobered. 'I must say I feel guilty about it. Matt always takes too much on his own shoulders, he always has, since his mother's death. Leonie Crosswyn died suddenly in an accident and her husband, Jason, never really recovered from her death. He was shattered. So the burden of running Vandellan, and a couple of other properties, fell mostly on Matt. Jason tried, but he just wasn't up to it, so young Matt—and he was young then—found himself taking over more and more of the workload until almost all of it became his responsibility.'

Erica's eyes widened. 'I didn't realise—'

Robert smiled at her with complete understanding. 'Of course you didn't. Not many people do. It was only in the last twelve months of his life that poor old Jason met Lilyan and brought her home to Vandellan with the intention of marrying her. We all hoped it would make a new man of him, but it was not to be.'

He paused to brush a drooping branch of golden cassia away from the path.

'It's difficult to know who to be sorriest for, Jason with his grief that he couldn't throw off, or Matthew who had to accept not only the loss of his mother, but the loss of his youth as well. When he should have been playing about, discovering all the fun young lads get up to, and getting the high spirits out of his system, Matt found himself poring over ledgers, making decisions, taking a command he wasn't ready for. Not much fun in that.'

'No.' Erica could understand that. She wondered whether Robert was telling her all this for a reason, but his honest friendly face dispelled her doubts. He was a discerning man, a good friend and a caring person who had ached to see a young boy grow up too soon, without his share of laughter.

And it seemed to her that she had a fleeting memory of Matt's face, sombre, secretive, and for the first time she experienced a feeling of deep sympathy. Most of his laughter must be buried deep under the burden of responsibility.

Nell called gaily, 'Why so serious?' and Robert's face lightened. 'We were wondering whether that smell means you've burnt the scones,' he teased, and Nell pulled a face at him. 'Don't be too cheeky, or you won't get any.'

Robert showed them around his garden and afterwards they sat on the verandah in deckchairs, talking cheerfully.

'When does the new housekeeper arrive?' Nell asked, and Lilyan said promptly, 'Matt picks her up tomorrow. I suppose I'd better go with him, because if I don't fancy the woman it won't be any use bringing her out. I certainly don't intend working with someone I can't get along with.'

Her sharp eyes caught a quick exchange of glances between Robert and Nell. She added clearly, 'I told Erica on the way over, Matt and I had a long intimate discussion this morning. We are making new arrangements for the running of Vandellan.' She turned to Nell. 'There won't be any need for us to call on your services in future.'

Robert said bluntly, 'There will, if you go about discharging housekeepers before they set foot in the kitchen,' and Nell made a shushing sound.

'Does that mean you and Matt have set a wedding date, or anything exciting like that?'

Lilyan shrugged elegant shoulders. 'We haven't exactly set the date. You might say, we're reserving our decision for another few weeks.'

Robert had a marvelling expression as if he did not like very much what he was hearing. He said very little after that, until Nell announced it was time for afternoon tea. She looked at Erica.

'Don't get up if you don't feel like it,' she murmured, and Erica knew this was an invitation. She followed Nell into the kitchen. Nell was bursting with curiosity. 'Has Matt made any official announcement?'

Erica shook her head. 'He wasn't communicating at lunch. Just gave us our orders and sent us down to see you. Not that we didn't appreciate the invitation,' she added hastily.

'I never thought it would happen, you know, that Lilyan would get her own way with Matt.'

Erica raised her eyebrows. 'You think Lilyan made the running?'

Nell twinkled. 'Oh, undoubtedly. And I don't care if that does sound a bit scratchy. There were rumours soon after Lilyan came to Vandellan that it was Matthew she really wanted. Poor old Waters got upset on a few occasions because there were arguments, not enough to cause Jason distress, but Lilyan seemed to expect him to do the things Matt did, and Jason was such a vulnerable man.'

Erica collected the scones from the bench. 'Well, maybe Matt will prove not so vulnerable. He ought to be able to deal with her haughty highness.'

'I don't know about that.' Nell pushed jam and cream towards Erica. 'A lot of people misunderstand Matt,' she murmured softly. 'Because he doesn't show his feelings easily they're inclined to believe he doesn't feel deeply, but it isn't true. I often think they are the most vulnerable of all, don't you—the ones who clamp down on their feelings so nobody will know what they're going through.'

'Perhaps.'

The kettle boiled and Nell turned it off. 'So long as you're not downcast.'

'Why should I be downcast?'

Nell laughed. 'Because I am a conspiring woman and I decided you and Matthew were made for each other, and wasn't that foolish?'

'You decided?'

Nell's mouth smiled but her eyes were serious. 'Imaginative of me. I always wanted something extra special for Matt by way of compensation, I suppose, for everything he's missed. And when you came to Vandellan, although you arrived with Jeremy, it seemed all the ingredients for my plans

were put together.' She pulled a wry face. 'You
were supposed to look at Matt and fall head over
heels.' She began pouring tea. 'That'll teach me to
go around getting wrong answers.' She looked at
Erica, suddenly even more serious. 'So long as
you're not hurt.'

'No, I'm not hurt. I don't care if Matt marries
Lilyan tomorrow.'

Erica had spoken those words with conviction.
How could it be, then, that they turned suddenly
into the greatest lie she had ever told? She did care,
she cared desperately . . . A deep raw hurt spread
until she felt tears stinging behind her eyes.

Matt Crosswyn was the last man she would have
chosen to fall in love with, but after the day Matt
married Lilyan there wouldn't be a day, an hour, a
minute of her life not shadowed by the event.

Nell said, 'Do you mind taking the tray?' and
Erica carried it out to the verandah and smiled
sweetly at Lilyan. 'Try one of Nell's wonderful
scones,' she invited, and registered calmly, without
any outward show of emotion at all, that Lilyan
took the largest, creamiest scone from the plate and
clamped her white teeth on it.

When five o'clock came Nell said restlessly, 'I
wonder whether Guy has brought Jenny back yet.
She really shouldn't be left alone. Those examin-
ations can be a bit of an ordeal.'

'I'll go and see.' The words were out before Erica
even knew she was going to say them. She hurried
through the citrus orchard. Vandellan lay in late
afternoon peace, a picture of serenity. Her footsteps slowed, but she listened . . .

In the hospital Erica had learned to trust her

intuition. She knew it was composed partly of experience, a dash of caution and some awareness, plus an extra dose of protective feeling towards those she cared for.

But there was another ingredient, an instinct that sometimes sent her hurrying to a bedside to check some patient who had developed a sudden need. It had happened several times. Not often, but enough to teach Erica not to ignore the warning.

Yet nothing could have been more peaceful than Vandellan as she opened the carved front doors and went inside. There was no car outside to signal Guy's return. She opened Jenny's door to an empty room, as she expected. So she had behaved like an idiot, carried away by galloping imagination. Yet surely there ought to be somebody moving, somewhere, in the wide land that stretched around Vandellan.

She wandered into the kitchen. Nobody there. Then as she turned to leave the empty room, Erica heard a distant sound, as though far away somebody was hammering in a limping rhythm that faded, resumed, then faded again.

As if by intuition her feet carried her out through the rear door of the kitchen. She knew what she was going to find, as clearly as if someone had spoken it aloud. The muffled thumping came from beneath the trapdoor.

Someone had secured the heavy bolts, and although the thick timber jerked with each impact, whoever was trapped below had a hopeless task.

Desperately, Erica searched around her. She could call for help but there didn't seem any point in it, since there was no one to answer. She opened a nearby cupboard and seized a broom, banging hard on the trapdoor. At least the person below would know there was somebody listening. After a few seconds, a man's voice called,

'Open this thing, for heaven's sake!' It was Jeremy. She used the broomstick to prise open the first bolt, then the second, then rubbed the palms of her hands together to ease the soreness before she pulled the metal ring from its groove, curling her fingers around it, shouting, 'You'll have to push. Can you help?'

Jeremy heard her. From below she felt a steady assisting pressure, then the trapdoor lifted several inches. Jeremy's voice came through the aperture.

'Good girl. One more shove should do it, Ric. Can you manage another?'

Together they exerted all their strength and the trapdoor lifted, hovered, then fell with a clatter, leaving the entrance clear. Jeremy scrambled out, face and clothing streaked with dust.

He stared around him, as if he expected somebody to emerge from one of the doorways, as if he could not believe there were just the two of them.

'Matt sent me down to check on a passage.'

He kicked at the trapdoor. 'Nasty bit of work, that. First time I've ever tried to lift it from below. It sure as hell ought to be easier than that.'

Erica closed her eyes to shut away the bitterness, but her voice was quite steady. 'It was bolted.'

His jaw dropped. 'You mean, somebody meant me to stay down there? What the hell for?'

Erica shook her head. Her throat ached, her eyes stung. She set herself to calm down, regular deep breaths, deliberately relaxing. Her back ached, perhaps she'd strained it. Vandellan loomed around them, so still and quiet it was like foreboding.

Jeremy was inclined to be annoyed, as if he suspected somebody had played a joke on him, then he began to doubt, and the doubting turned to slow realisation that it might not have been a prank at all. It could have been deadly earnest.

He said suddenly, 'Jenny! What's happened to Jenny?' and Erica answered through stiff lips, 'Jenny isn't back yet. Nor Guy.'

Now Jeremy was fully alert, functioning with all his energy.

'If I was locked down there deliberately it has to be something to do with Jenny. I know it.'

As if the words were dragged out of her Erica asked, 'You think Matt planned to take her away—?'

'—While I was down there and couldn't stop him.'

'No!' It was her heart that cried denial, and Jeremy looked at her quickly.

'Well, whatever is going on, we've got to protect Jenny.'

'How?'

'I'll meet Jenny and Guy when they arrive.' Jeremy's face was grim as he levered the trapdoor back into place. 'To think I let him decoy me down there like an innocent babe.'

'It might have been somebody else who shut you down there.'

To her astonishment Jeremy looked at her with a world of pity in his eyes, as if her grief were showing, her pain transparent.

He said softly, 'If that's so, where's Matt?' and Erica could find no answer. She ached with caring. Oh, let it not be Matt! Whether he is Lilyan's, or mine, just let him not be guilty . . . . It was worse than physical pain. Jeremy shook her arm.

'Snap out of it, Ric. Have a look outside, see if you can find Matt. Whoever locked me down there won't hurt you. It's me he's after, because I'm taking Jenny away. So if you want to help, find Matt.'

'All right.'

The afternoon was fading, and as Erica wove her way among Vandellan's trees she heard the first stirring of the afternoon breeze. Matt was not among the flower gardens, she hadn't expected him to be.

She passed the shadehouse where Waters' passion flowers floated like a snowdrift, and without knowing why Erica found tears pouring over her cheeks.

Once, she thought she heard soft footsteps behind her, but when she peered through her tears the trees swam like a green sea with no dark shadow moving among them.

She looked at the wilderness doubtfully. Matt could be in there, but it wasn't likely. She took a few hesitant steps along the overgrown track where she had found Gregg a few days ago. The green closed around her. She wanted to call Matt, to fling his name among the trees in the hope that he would answer, but she didn't trust her voice now.

She had reached the fallen tree-trunk when somewhere behind her a twig snapped. Without stopping to reason she plunged off the path, brushing aside vines, fumbling her way around the tree with its splayed roots.

She was pressed against a drift of overhanging creepers when an arm clamped around her shoulder and outspread fingers covered her mouth. She twisted and the arm around her tightened and held her still, but not before she glimpsed Matt's harsh face staring down at her. As she sagged against him he put his lips close to her ear.

'Quiet, for God's sake. You're being followed.' Over Matt's silencing fingers she peered through the tangled greenery. It shook and parted, and the surly face of Gregg, the young stockman, peered through.

Despite the reassurance of Matt's strength pressed against her, Erica's heart lurched with panic. Then she was thrust firmly into the protecting creepers and the crackling of branches told her Matt had dived after the stockman. She heard Gregg's grunt of surprise, then the wild brushing of undergrowth as both men scrambled through the trees.

She waited. The green world of the rain forest quietened. She fumbled her way out onto the track, and at the edge of the wilderness Matthew stood alongside Jeremy, who was sprawled on the ground.

As Erica appeared Jeremy scrambled to his feet. 'You all right, Ric?'

'Yes. I'm better than you look.'

He grinned ruefully. 'I just botched up a citizen's arrest.' The face he turned to Matt was flushed and apologetic. 'Sorry, old man.'

Strands of grass clung to his shirt, and Erica

pulled them off without knowing exactly what she did. 'I thought you were looking after Jenny,' she queried.

'Guy and Jenny arrived just as you left. I told them what had happened—at least, what I thought had happened'—he shot another apologetic look towards his brother—'and Jenny said, "Find Gregg. It's Gregg you have to worry about".' Jeremy went on:

'We saw you in the garden dodging among the trees and Guy thought he saw Gregg following, so', he shrugged, 'I set out to rescue you and succeeded in getting in the way.' His grin became half ashamed. 'That young bloke picked me up like a bale of hay and pitched me at Matt, and while we picked ourselves up he got away.' He grinned cheerfully. 'Never mind. We'll get him.'

'I doubt it.' Matt's voice was grim. 'My guess is he'll stay under cover until dark and then be on his way. I doubt we'll ever see him again.'

'But why did he do it?' Erica wondered aloud.

Matt's jaw tightened. 'That I expect is a very long and complicated story, and when we get back we'll sit down and have a talk with Jenny. It's time we had a few answers.'

Jeremy responded quickly. 'Jenny can't stand up to much tension, old man. You'll have to go carefully.'

'Telling the truth shouldn't be difficult,' Matt retorted, and nothing more was said until they reached the house.

Erica shivered. She didn't fancy being Jenny when question-time began, not with Matt wearing this daunting expression. Brushing through the undergrowth had torn open his checked shirt, and there were scraps of dry leaves twisted among his black curls. She had brushed the grass from Jeremy's clothing without hesitation, but she dared not reach out and untangle the wisps from Matt's hair, although her fingers tingled with the urge to do just that.

The open shirt revealed a cluster of similar dark curls on his chest, and the torso muscles moved with fascinating rhythm as he strode. Erica's lips quirked as she told herself, 'You've seen muscles before. What's so marvellous?' but she knew she could not hope to control the inexplicable reactions she was experiencing just because a man she hardly knew strode beside her with his shirt flapping in the afternoon breeze.

CHAPTER ELEVEN

As they entered Vandellan's hallway Matthew gave Erica a gentle push towards the stairs. 'Go and have a rest. Give yourself a chance to relax and get yourself together, then come downstairs and join us for a drink. Are you all right?'

Those penetrating eyes searched her face, seeking for signs of inner reaction. If he ever discovered the monstrous suspicions she had conjured up in her terrified imagination this afternoon, he would never forgive her. For some obscure reason, it seemed important that he should not hate her.

She asked humbly, 'Why did Gregg follow me? Was I in danger or did I just panic like an idiot?'

'Probably he just wanted to frighten you away.' He dropped a comforting hand on to her shoulder, and she might have disgraced herself then, by bursting into tears, had not Lilyan and Nell appeared, full of questions.

'Whatever happened? We just met Jeremy and he demanded to know if we'd seen Gregg, and somebody ought to shoot the so-and-so—'

Lilyan twined her fingers around Matt's elbow. 'You should take more care,' she crooned, 'Vandellan can't afford to have you getting involved in other people's messy problems. You're too important.'

The glance she gave Erica was slightly vindictive

as if she might be including her in the 'other people'
who dared endanger Matthew.

Erica drew back. But of course, Matt was Lilyan's now. The chill came down, and she turned
away from them all, even Nell, dragging her tired
feet upstairs. Lilyan and Matthew had their new
understanding to hold them together.

'See you later, everybody. I shan't be long. At
the moment, I'm—' her lips quivered—'I'm rather
tired and confused.'

As if she might have sent him a signal, Matt
untangled himself from Lilyan's possessive grasp
and took the intervening stairs two at a time. He
smiled at her averted head before he reached out an
arm and touched her red curls gently.

'Not so cool as you look, my lovely redhead, are
you?'

Before she had time to reply he moved away
down the stairs, turning sharply towards Jenny's
room. Erica was glad not to be in that room.
Whatever the explanations were, they must be
devastating to Jenny, and Matt would leave no part
of the truth untold.

Erica took her time about freshening up,
brushing her hair, adding a golden band to brighten
it. If there were any more pressures to be faced
today, she would be ready for them.

As Erica came downstairs Nell waited, nodding
approval at her refreshed appearance.

'I'm on my way home to prepare dinner for all.
I'll whip up a couple of casseroles, so come as late
as you like. Meanwhile,' she pointed to the drawing-room, 'they're all in there, except Jenny. She's
resting in her own room, glad to have it all off her

chest, I expect.' She gave Erica a small push. 'Go and ask all the questions you want.'

Slowly Erica turned the door-handle and went in. Matt handed her a drink, and she offered him her brightest, most confident smile, which made him lift his eyebrows and let his lips curve in the faintest of smiles. Jeremy and Guy sat on the leather armchairs and Lilyan on the divan. She commanded pettishly, 'Tell us, darling. I can't understand a thing with everybody talking at once.'

Matt reached for his glass and took a deep drink before he began.

'It's all quite simple, really. I suppose we should have guessed. A young bloke like Gregg, so full of himself and his own ambitions, doesn't get carried away with sympathy for anybody. Certainly not to the extent of giving up his work with the men to do boring jobs around the yards. Then I became suspicious, thanks to Erica—'

He quirked one eyebrow in her direction. 'Erica asked me how much did I know about Gregg, and I realised I knew precious little. I don't delve too deeply into the outside backgrounds of my employees, nor does Robert, so neither of us knew that while Gregg was away trying his luck with the rodeo he had already met Jenny. He found her singing at one of the hotels, and persuaded her to follow him back to Vandellan when her contract finished. She was on her way to meet him that day when Guy picked her up.'

'When they had that unfortunate accident', he turned his attention to his youngest brother and Guy reddened, 'both Jenny and Guy were swept off the horse by the overhanging branch, but Guy took the worst of it. Jenny was scarcely hurt at all, only a few scratches.'

Guy's face whitened. He leaned forward in his chair, hanging on every word. Matthew's face sobered.

'We—I—should have paid more attention when Guy said he saw Jenny walking before he collapsed. I imagined him to be hallucinating because of the concussion. I was wrong. Jenny walked.'

They were all attention now, forgetting their drinks, watching Matt's face as he spoke.

'In her distress at finding Guy unconscious, Jenny dashed out on to the road to get help when she heard another horseman coming. It was Gregg, riding flat out because he was late for his meeting with Jenny. Jenny ran out of the trees so fast Gregg wasn't able to pull his horse up in time to avoid her.'

Guy whispered, 'That's when she got hurt?'

'Yes. That's it.'

Guy sagged back in his chair, and Matt said tersely, 'We owe you an apology,' and his voice shook a little as if he might have blamed himself, but Guy's face was flooded with joy.

'Don't give it a thought. I'm damned grateful—'

Jeremy cut in, guessing ahead, 'So Gregg cooked up this story about Guy being responsible because he knew head injuries would have him so confused he wouldn't know exactly what happened.' He directed a question at Matthew. 'What did he have in mind? Was he planning to marry Jenny and make a packet suing Guy for compensation?'

'Probably.'

Jeremy swore. 'The cunning devil. But why lock me underground today?'

Matt became suddenly grave. 'You blasted his plans from under him when you decided to take Jenny away. I don't suppose we'll ever know exactly what he planned. Perhaps he hoped to gain time to grab Jenny when Guy brought her back, and take her away from your influence. At the worst,' the gravity on his face deepened, etching lines around his tight mouth, 'he might have intended doing you some—ah—grievous bodily harm, down there in the cellars.'

'How could he do that, with the trapdoor bolted?'

'By using another entrance.'

'What other entrance, may I ask, dear brother?'

Matt stared at their bewildered faces. 'The shaft in the Wilderness, of course. I should have realised it immediately. That shovel he carried'—his eyes gleamed at Erica '—was not for the purpose of filling in the hole. It was to dig deeper, to find and clear the access. Gregg guessed immediately it led to one of the tunnels under the homestead, probably the reason great-grandmother Marion preserved the rain forest. In case of prolonged attack, women and children could crawl out and hide among the trees, if they had to, until the men of the household came back to rescue them.'

Jeremy's face lightened. 'You set it all up, didn't you? Sent me into the cellars looking at tunnels, Guy and Jenny to the doctor's, Lilyan and Erica to Nell's.' His grin twisted. 'Clearing the stage, so to speak.'

'That's right,' Matt agreed calmly. 'I have a theory that if you have an adversary it's better to bring him into the open where you can see what he's up to, rather than wait for him to surprise you. I took care to allot Gregg some work close to the homestead, after letting him know Jeremy would be down in the cellars and everyone else away. So if he was going to do something, it had to be done this afternoon.'

Jeremy said slowly, 'But he already had that other entrance prepared. What for?'

'Perhaps in the beginning he planned a night visit, with robbery the motive. We'll never know. But of course once he learned you were interfering with his set-up with Jenny he concentrated on you instead.'

Now Jeremy's face tightened. 'You're saying he bolted me down there and he planned—Well, thank you very much. I suppose you know exactly what he had in mind?'

Matt hesitated, giving Jeremy a sideways look. 'I suppose he might have planned another accident. He was a good hater, that lad. He might have planned to put you out of the way permanently.'

Guy added eagerly, 'Then he would come back and unbolt the trapdoor, to make it look like an accident!'

Matt nodded. 'That could be the way of it.'

Jeremy took a good strong drink from his glass. 'Clever!' he drawled slowly, trying to make it look as if he were not shaken, and Matt said, 'Don't worry. I was waiting at the other entrance, you weren't really set up as a sacrifice.'

'Thanks, old chap.' Jeremy's grin was crooked but appreciative. 'I must say I don't relish the idea of being locked down there while he arranged for something to fall on me.'

Matt offered him a strangely youthful grin. 'Fortunately you were too smart for him. You hammered away, yelling for help, until Erica came back and released you. Incidentally,' the eyes he turned on Erica were warm, 'that must have been a hefty pull. You'll have sore shoulders tonight.'

'Jeremy helped from below.' She brushed away Matthew's praise. For some reason, it embarrassed her.

Jeremy stood up to refill his glass. 'Best story I've had my nose into for years, and I can't print a word of it.'

'No, you can't.' Matt sounded adamant and Jeremy flushed. 'I didn't intend to. There's no way I'd crucify Jenny. You should know that.'

Matt sat back on the divan with a sigh. 'Any more questions?'

'Thousands,' Guy replied cheerfully, 'but I can't think of them now. I must say,' he flushed, looking awkwardly at Matt, 'thanks a lot. I don't know when I've felt so good. I've caused you a lot of trouble.'

'You're young. You'll learn. Thank heaven it's over.'

'Yes,' Jeremy agreed cheerfully, 'and we've all survived. They don't call us the tough Crosswyns for nothing.' His look at his older brother was clear and direct. 'I'm sorry about Jenny, but I still want to take her away when Ric and I finish our visit.'

'I shan't argue.'

Jeremy glowed with confidence. He would be just what Jenny needed to take her over the rough days before she was able to take up her life as it had been before the accident, just the partner to walk with her into the future.

Erica put down her glass and stood up, averting her eyes from the divan where Matt and Lilyan sat together.

'If nobody minds, I'd like to go and talk to Jenny?' She made it a question, and Jeremy nodded agreement.

Jenny sat in her wheelchair, the silent guitar resting on her knees. 'I've tried to play but I can't. I don't deserve to ever sing again.'

'You will.'

'Don't you—don't you hate me? I thought everybody would.' Her eyes filled with tears. 'I feel so ashamed. Everybody so kind, and I cheated—'

'Not you. It was Gregg.'

'I should have resisted.' Her lips quivered. 'I tried to. I kept telling myself that if I hadn't been so confused, so scared, I wouldn't have let him persuade me. I felt so hopeless—'

'And shocked.'

Jenny lifted velvet eyes to Erica's gratefully.

'Thanks for the vote of confidence. I hope I was shocked. I just had this voice in my head saying What else could I do? I might never walk again. Then Waters died—'

'Don't think about Waters. Brooding over her won't help.'

Jenny reached out and clutched Erica's wrist. 'How did Waters die, Ric? Was it an accident? What does Matthew really believe?'

'He believes it was an accident, so does everybody else.' Erica patted the nervous, clutching fingers. 'Did you wonder whether Gregg might have pushed her?'

Jenny said wildly, 'I didn't know what to think. He went in first, you know, the day we found her.'

She wanted so much to say that, to spill out the suspicion that must have eaten into her ever since that tragic day. 'He—he didn't come out right away.'

'Of course not. He had to get help for Waters, in case she wasn't dead.'

Jenny's fingers moved in Erica's hand in a slow relaxing. She bit her lip.

'I've been very foolish. It's so difficult once you start doubting a person. At least it was for me.'

For me, too. Erica made the admission silently. Once she had begun to doubt, her suspicions of Matt had carried her beyond reason. She wondered how far he had sensed her distrust in that moment when he held her helpless in the wilderness. Surely he must have felt the wild, uncontrollable beating of her heart. He would probably never forgive her.

Jeremy was waiting outside Jenny's door. He went in swiftly as Erica came out. Erica saw him bend and take the guitar. Then he softly closed the door.

So that was that. A new chapter for Jeremy and Jenny. A dark new chapter for Gregg, who would spend the rest of his life looking back over his shoulder, wondering whether his guilt would catch up with him. A new beginning for Lilyan and Matt also.

Even Guy had been granted a new outlook to-day, freed of guilt and the burden of responsibility

for a careless action that had born such bitter fruit.
The only loser appeared to be herself.

Disconsolately, Erica wandered across the deserted hall on to the verandah, and there, leaning
nonchalantly against the railing, Matt waited.

'Care for a walk?'

Erica searched desperately along the verandah.
'Where's Lilyan?'

His eyebrows rose. 'I really don't know. Should
I?' That confused her. He didn't sound the devoted
lover. Obediently, she let him lead her down the
steps. A desperate memory of what had happened
last time she walked in the garden with Matt checked her, and he gave a small tug at her arm, pulling
her after him.

'Why that question about Lilyan? Are her
whereabouts supposed to be of special interest to
me?'

She floundered, then decided truth was better
than trying to deceive those penetrating eyes.

'I understand you and Lilyan are—are—' she
searched for the right expression, and he wasn't
helping at all, watching her attentively, carefully,
while she fumbled for words. She said furiously,
'Lilyan says you've come to a new arrangement and
she is now permanently hostess of Vandellan.'

'So she is.' His voice was mild. 'That is what my
father would have wished. I didn't do anything
about it before this, because Lilyan was thinking
about marrying somebody else. Now I understand
those plans have been changed, so,' his lips curved
teasingly, 'until she wants to live somewhere else,
or decides to marry some other man, Lilyan will
regard Vandellan as her home.'

Marry another man? Erica's mind repeated the words numbly.

He added smoothly, 'The woman I marry will become mistress of two other properties, one of them even lovelier than Vandellan.'

'Oh.'

They were walking through the rose garden, and the setting sun threw pink light over the petals, making them lovelier than ever, but Matthew did not stop. They passed the jacaranda trees before he spoke again. 'Could it be that Lilyan gave you a false impression this afternoon?'

'Of course not.'

'I'm pleased to hear that.'

Erica peeped at him from under lowered lashes, but he wasn't giving anything away. She dared not let him see her face in case the joy was showing. She struggled for indifference.

'Shouldn't we be on our way to Nell's for dinner?'

'Not yet.' A gleam of amusement sparkled in those clear grey eyes. The sun was disappearing below the horizon, but the afterglow would keep the air light and bright for a while longer. When they reached the swimming pool Matt paused suddenly, stepping in front of her, turning her slowly to face him.

'Is this the appropriate place for a man to make advances to a volatile redhead, or would she be likely to throw him in the pool?'

How could she ever have imagined his features harsh, his face secretive? A laughing youth smiled down at her. She said shakily, 'What kind of advances do you have in mind?'

Don't leap ahead, she warned herself. You could be wrong. That wonderful way he's looking might not mean what you hope it does.

He rested his cheek against her hair.

'The most incriminating kind. I was thinking about proposing—'

'No, you weren't. You're thinking about amusing yourself.'

He pulled her against his body, framing her heart-shaped face with the lean fingers of the other hand.

'This may surprise you. It certainly surprised me. But I think my days of amusing myself are ended. They've been over,' he confessed, 'ever since the night I met a saucy-looking nurse with red hair and the most enchanting face I have ever seen.'

'You didn't even want me at Vandellan,' she accused. 'You tried to put me off.'

'I didn't want you coming to Vandellan as Jeremy's companion. I knew what he had in mind for you, he'd already put in his order. Adjoining rooms, he said, so I won't have to walk so far in the night. Those were his exact words.' He groaned. 'I wanted to strangle him with my bare hands.'

She leaned against his shoulder. Dear strong Matt, how could she ever have doubted him? He let her rest there, as if he sensed her need to feel the reassurance of his strength. His lips moved softly against her ear, 'I love you, want you, covet you. I will take care of you—'

She threw back her head.

'And intimidate me!'

'Never.' He stroked her face, outlining the shape of her lips with a warm fingertip.

'Do you mind not living at Vandellan?'

'No. I'm glad, really. Too much has happened here.'

He teased her lightly, with soft kisses. 'Some of it good?'

'Some of it heavenly.'

'You haven't answered my proposal.' He asked it lightly, but she knew by the trembling of the arms around her that it was desperately important to him. Her clear green eyes looked into his with complete honesty.

'You always disturbed me. I thought you threatened—'

He traced the shape of her eyebrows, her hairline. 'Only your independence, my dear, and not much of that. Just enough to hope you want me the way I want and need you.' His mouth curved in a beguiling smile. 'Shall we call it a sort of interdependence?'

'That sounds interesting. It was the first time she had ever dared tease Matt, and it brought a flash of joy to his eyes.

'Does that mean yes?'

She said demurely, 'They tell me that what Matt Crosswyn wants, he gets.'

'Not always. Lord knows, this is the one thing I want most of all.'

'Then I think you should have it.' He hesitated, and she threw her arms around his neck and pressed her slender body against his. 'Yes, yes! Can't you see I'm saying Yes . . . if you'll have me Because I love you.'

Half-laughing, half-crying, she lifted her face so that he could see the tears spilling from her eyes and his beautiful seductive mouth came down to claim hers, as he demonstrated the power and persuasion of his love.

Passion and pleasure might have overwhelmed them, except that Matthew finished the kissing slowly, reluctantly, holding her gently away from him, and the shining in his own eyes told her that he too had felt the springing of tears that is part of all true happiness.

He curved his hand around his fingers. 'We'd better save something for our wedding night,' he suggested ruefully, 'if you can wait another few days.'

'A few days!'

'As few as possible. I can't wait too long.' Lightly, he played with the band of gold and diamond crystal on her right hand. 'I'll buy you a ring for the other hand tomorrow, then you'll have rings on your fingers just like the gipsies,' he quoted quizzically. Dear Matt, how much had he guessed about the ring? Some day she must tell him about the gipsy in the hospital and her farseeing prophecy, and they would marvel over it together. But today and tomorrow were for their loving.

He said, 'Will you care for my ring as you care for that one?'

'Even more.'

The clouds were crimson smudges, there were flame colours glowing behind the trees, and the last bright rim of the setting sun flung its red reflection across the water in the pool. From the security of Matt's arms Erica watched the glinting pattern spread across the water.

It could have been a bright red fan, fluttering as

the ripples moved beneath it. It might have been an image of the poinciana tree waving outspread arms laden with vivid flowers; or it might have been the blurred reflection of a woman in a scarlet gown.

Take 4
Exciting Books
Absolutely
FREE

Love, romance, intrigue... all are captured for you by Mills & Boon's top-selling authors. By becoming a regular reader of Mills & Boon's Romances you can enjoy 6 superb new titles every month plus a whole range of special benefits: your very own personal membership card, a free monthly newsletter packed with recipes, competitions, exclusive book offers and a monthly guide to the stars, plus extra bargain offers and big cash savings.

**AND an Introductory FREE GIFT for YOU.
Turn over the page for details.**

As a special introduction we will send you four exciting Mills & Boon Romances Free and without obligation when you complete and return this coupon.

At the same time we will reserve a subscription to Mills & Boon Reader Service for you. Every month, you will receive 6 of the very latest novels by leading Romantic Fiction authors, delivered direct to your door. You don't pay extra for delivery — postage and packing is always completely Free. There is no obligation or commitment — you can cancel your subscription at any time.

You have nothing to lose and a whole world of romance to gain.

Just fill in and post the coupon today to MILLS & BOON READER SERVICE, FREEPOST, P.O. BOX 236, CROYDON, SURREY CR9 9EL.

Please Note:- READERS IN SOUTH AFRICA write to Mills & Boon, Postbag X3010, Randburg 2125, S. Africa.